PRAISE FOR *RUN*

"ASICS was on to something when it cho. ⸺ ⸺ tion for 'a sound mind in a sound body.' This philosophy is the key to unlocking all the potential we hold. From my first race in junior high gym class to competing in the 2008 Olympic Marathon, I have found that the stronger my mind and spirit are, the further I am able to push myself. Any runners interested in maximizing potential must study the mind-body connection or their journey will not be complete."

> —**RYAN HALL,** 2008 Olympian and two-time American record holder

"The elements and philosophy laid out in *Run* were fundamental and played an essential role in my overall success throughout my career as a self-coached athlete. The ability to run by feel is a learned skill, and without the capacity to self-assess and adjust your training intuitively, you will inevitably fall short of your potential."

> —**ALAN CULPEPPER,** 2000 and 2004 U.S. Olympian,
> sub-4-minute miler, and sub-2:10 marathoner

"The coach knows what to do; the scientist tells us why. Fitzgerald's *Run* artfully and responsibly blends scientifically grounded, supportive research and convincing anecdotal evidence into a message that those of us who take running seriously must heed. Now U.S. athletes can learn the true secrets of the great African runners: That voice in your head that says, 'Too much, too little, too hard, too easy,' despite what the device on your wrist says, is probably right!"

> —**BOBBY McGEE,** renowned running coach and author of
> *Magical Running* and *Run Workouts for Runners and Triathletes*

"In his latest book, Matt Fitzgerald successfully explains the mind-body method of running. While this concept can be difficult to understand, Fitzgerald describes it in a way that will speak to beginners and elite runners alike. Anyone trying to improve and realize their true running potential should read *Run*."

> —**KARA GOUCHER,** 2008 Olympian and World Championship medalist

"After years of searching science journals for secret workouts and fitness techniques, Matt Fitzgerald has decided that the brain is the ultimate training tool. In this insightful and evidence-based book, he challenges us to achieve our potential by enjoying every run and race, even as we accept the pain."

—**AMBY BURFOOT,** *Runner's World* editor-at-large
and 1968 Boston Marathon winner

"As a longtime proponent of effort-based training, I highly recommend *Run*. The reader will learn the most important concept in all of training—how to connect effort with pace. Using the techniques and ideas in this book, runners can expect more consistent training and racing results without the worry of external feedback from devices like GPS and heart rate monitors. I use effort-based training with the beginning runners, middle-of-the-packers, and Olympians I coach, and I recommend that all runners learn this valuable technique."

—**GREG MCMILLAN,** MS, McMillanRunning.com online coach

RUN

RUN

THE MIND-BODY METHOD OF
RUNNING BY FEEL

MATT FITZGERALD

VELO press

BOULDER, COLORADO

▼velopress®

1830 55th Street
Boulder, Colorado 80301-2700 USA
(303) 440-0601 · Fax (303) 444-6788 · E-mail velopress@competitorgroup.com

Distributed in the United States and Canada by Ingram Publisher Services

Library of Congress Cataloging-in-Publication Data
Fitzgerald, Matt.
Run: the mind-body method of running by feel / Matt Fitzgerald
    p. cm.
ISBN 978-1-934030-57-8 (pbk.: alk. paper)
1. Running—Training. 2. Running—Physiological aspects. I. Title.
GV1061.5.F573 2010
612'.044—dc22

                                        2010008956

For information on purchasing VeloPress books, please call (800) 811-4210, ext. 169, or visit www.velopress.com.

This book is printed on 100 percent recovered/
recycled fiber, 30 percent postconsumer waste,
elemental chlorine free, using soy-based inks.

Cover design by Erin Johnson
Cover photograph of Alan Culpepper by Brad Kaminski
Interior design by Jane Raese
Illustrations in Chapter 11 by Chris Gallevo

10   11   12 / 10   9   8   7   6   5   4   3   2   1

My muscles are the type that need a long time to warm up.... And I feel that this type of muscle is connected to the way my mind works. What I mean is, a person's mind is controlled by his body, right? Or is it the opposite—the way your mind works influences the structure of the body? Or do the body and the mind closely influence each other and act on each other?

—Haruki Murakami, *What I Talk About When I Talk About Running*

CONTENTS

FOREWORD

SOMETIMES THE SIMPLEST ANSWER IS THE RIGHT ONE. I have spent many years trying to outthink my competitors and have always looked for the cutting edge. In *Run: The Mind-Body Method of Running by Feel*, Matt Fitzgerald has identified the scientific reasons for the obvious: We know our bodies best; we just need to know what our bodies are telling us.

There are many "industry standards" for the components needed to perform at our best, but sometimes applying those pieces to our training can be difficult. Too often we become dependent on literature and specific training models, and we forget common sense. Matt tries to bring us back to that common sense, encouraging us to listen to our bodies and use their signals to adapt our training programs to help us get the most out of them.

Those signals are not just vague, unimportant feelings that have no bearing on how we feel. They are valuable information about what is the best course of action. Matt brings together the most recent research explaining why we might be feeling a certain way at a specific time and what that feeling might be trying to tell us about our training.

Thinking back to my best races and my most consistent training blocks, I can honestly say that I have thrown out the book, so to speak. There were times when I was completely dependent upon measuring everything. I lived by a heart rate monitor. I measured every course I ran, and I never backed off when my body told me I was tired. As Matt acknowledges, all of those tools can be very useful, and at times they are essential to knowing exactly where you are in training. But when they take priority over what your body is telling you, injury and overtraining are just around the corner.

If I had always followed the signals my body was giving me the way Matt instructs, I believe I could have avoided most of the injuries and bouts of overtraining I have had in my career. The signs were obvious before I broke the 5,000 m American record and before I won a bronze medal at the World Half-Marathon Championships: I was listening to my body and following my intuition in training on a daily basis, and when I got to the start line, my confidence was unmatched.

The culture of distance running, especially in the United States, is one of "push through the pain" and "the harder you work, the better." What Matt shows in this book is that there are reasons we feel the way we do, and those indicators can tell us if we are ready for a huge breakthrough or if we are on the cusp of breaking down. Highlighting the experiences of some of the best distance runners in the world, Matt shows what is possible for even the most modest runner. One of the greatest things about distance running is that you can learn the same lessons from your body and mind as can a sub-13-minute 5,000 m runner—you just have to pay attention!

Dathan Ritzenhein
Two-time Olympian,
World Championships medalist,
and U.S. record holder

PREFACE

RUNNING IS AN ENDLESS SOURCE OF LEARNING, especially if you pay attention. It teaches you about your body, about your self, and, of course, about running itself. Most runners apply the knowledge and wisdom they gain from running to their own running, toward the goal of running faster or more enjoyably or with fewer injuries, and to a lesser but not insignificant extent to their lives apart from running.

I'm a little different from most runners in having made a career out of learning from and about running. For many years I have been an ardent student of the sport. I actively seek out knowledge and wisdom not only for my own use but also—even primarily—to share with other runners. I consider it my job to help other runners run faster, more enjoyably, and with fewer injuries.

I have learned that no runner, writer, or coach can ever know all there is to know about running. As long as I keep paying attention, I will never stop learning. If I could continue running (and thinking about running) for another 200 years, I know I would continue learning.

As a prolific author of books on running, the only downside to this unending learning curve is that now and again I discover errors in my previous beliefs or I simply change my mind about past ideas. Sometimes I go so far as to wish I had never written some of the articles and books I've written.

Fortunately, I have never changed my mind about anything really important (my previous books are still worth reading!), but I have discovered lots of small errors and have shifted my perspective on many small matters.

In an interview, the late, great French philosopher Michel Foucault was confronted with the fact that something he had written in his latest book contradicted something he had written in a previous book. Foucault answered that the contradiction did not bother him in the least because the very point of writing books, in his mind, was to transform himself. He would never want to write a book that left him unchanged, he said, and if that preference was exercised at the cost of contradicting his past writings occasionally, then so be it.

I comfort myself by remembering this exchange whenever I generate my own contradictions. I really do feel exactly as Foucault did, yet I can't help but also dream of writing something that I will never change my mind about on any important level.

I believe this book marks a culmination. It certainly contradicts things I have written in the past, not least in *Brain Training for Runners*, which I now view as a sort of rough draft of the present volume. But I have a good feeling that the philosophy that is manifest here is one I will hold on to as I continue my pursuit as a student of the sport of running.

The core of this philosophy, unchanged from *Brain Training*, is that the brain is the seat of all our possibilities and limitations as runners. The brain governs how fast and how far we can run. If we become faster and more enduring, it is mostly because we have changed our brains or better harnessed their power. And, of course, our brains do all the learning that we use to improve our future running. The governing role of the brain in relation to running performance has been proven by recent research in exercise science, which has taken advantage of our lately acquired ability to look inside our minds in ways that were previously impossible. Yet this new research suggests that we don't exactly have to be brain scientists to harness this power and become better runners. In fact, it suggests that the best possible way to improve over the long term is to run almost completely by feel because our perceptions, intuitions, and feelings—delivered to our conscious minds from our bodies through our unconscious brains—tell us everything we need to know about how to run faster and farther, provided we know how to interpret these messages.

For example, a 2010 study by Samuele Marcora, an exercise physiologist at England's Bangor University, provides compelling evidence that perception of effort—basically, feeling miserable—is the true cause of fatigue in endurance events, not physiological limitations, as previously believed. Other recent studies have shown that not only does feeling lousy cause fatigue but that athletes' tolerance for suffering is trainable. Thus, increasing our tolerance for suffering should be a primary objective in the pursuit of better performance through training, not a secondary consideration as it is for many runners.

This notion that running by feel is the best way to shape our running escaped me in my first attempt to work out the practical implications of the new science of the running brain. I mistakenly assumed that the best runners were not already "brain training" in the best possible way. I've since realized that the new science of the running brain makes it possible for us to better understand what the best runners are doing and why it works so we can emulate it.

In my work I am fortunate to spend a lot of time observing and talking to the most accomplished runners and running coaches in the world, and learning from them. Over the past several years I have naturally interpreted their training methods from the perspective of the new science of the running brain. Through this process I realized that most of the world's best runners run by feel, and that running by feel is in fact what the new science of the running brain implicitly advocates more than anything else. Previously, I tried to identify a universal "best way to train" to harness the full power of the brain. But the most common feature in the training of the most successful runners is not a particular method but a reliance on mind-body communication to learn which methods work best for the individual, to choose the right workout to do each day, to pace optimally through hard workouts and races, to push through performance barriers, and so forth. The best runners listen and talk to their bodies more effectively than the rest of us, and that is one of the secrets to their success.

Practice is always two steps ahead of theory in running. Science never reveals the best way to train. The best runners do. Science is valuable because it helps us understand why the best practices are so effective, which in turn helps us emulate these practices more successfully than we might if we did so blindly. If not for my understanding of the new science of the running brain, I don't know if I ever would have realized what was really most worth emulating in the practices of the best runners: not their workouts but rather their remarkable capacity to run by feel.

Here's a specific example. In a recent conversation, Adam Goucher, a former NCAA champion and Olympian, told me, "At this level, you've got to work your ass off, but you've got to love it; it's got to be fun." I hear this all the time from elite runners, and I see that many of them make every effort to maximize the enjoyment they derive from their training. Indeed, they are much more serious about enjoyment than the typical non-elite competitive runner. The latest research in the psychology and neurobiology of exercise reveals why: The more we enjoy training, the better we perform. The best runners instinctively try to keep their training as fun as possible because doing so helps them win races.

In this book I will show you how the world's best runners run better by running by feel, in specific ways that range from maximizing their enjoyment of training to maximizing their tolerance for suffering (hence their resistance to fatigue). I will also describe the fascinating science that explains why these methods work. This combination of elite role modeling and scientific deciphering will give you the tools to improve your own capacity to run by feel and, through that, to improve your running performance.

The human brain is fundamentally a learning machine. The best runners learn the most from their running because the mind-body connection is especially strong. You will become a better runner by recognizing the importance of the mind-body connection and using yours to run by feel, as the most accomplished runners do. However, you cannot simply borrow the things that other runners have learned through running by feel because, like them, you are unique. Ultimately, you are on your own. The process of discovering your own optimal training formula and defining your unique motivations and limits will come only through ongoing communication between your mind and your body.

So please don't expect to finish the book and have it all figured out. If it were that easy, the world would have more successful runners. But as long as you keep paying attention, you will continue to learn new things. You might even find yourself thinking, "If only I'd figured this out sooner!" Believe me, I know the feeling.

RUNNING BY FEEL

I can run faster.

—Haile Gebrselassie

I DO NOT HAVE MANY HEROES IN SPORTS. One of the few athletes I venerate is the great Ethiopian distance runner Haile Gebrselassie. I love Geb for more or less the same reasons I love Muhammad Ali, another of my sporting heroes. Geb is not quite the deific figure that Ali is, but he creates a similar type of excitement by combining once-in-a-generation athletic performance with infectious charisma. Such people are very rare. More common are the likes of Michael Jordan, who manifest once-in-a-generation performance and just a regular personality. Ali and Geb are special because their athletic performance seems to be fed by the same source as their towering personalities, and that source is an overflowing lust for life, which to me is perhaps the most attractive of all personality characteristics.

I met Haile Gebrselassie in March 2009, in Los Angeles, at a media event hosted by his shoe sponsor, adidas. Geb made his first appearance at the event with no entourage. He had come all the way from Ethiopia alone. The photographers and video crews present showered him with digital attention as he walked outside surrounded by a mob of starstruck writers, including me. Geb then led us on a short, slow jog along the beach, which he interrupted to guide us through a brief session of those crazy calisthenics that Ethiopian runners like to do before workouts. Of the scores of people

1

we passed on our little jaunt, only two recognized Geb: a German tourist, who behaved like a 12-year-old girl at a Jonas Brothers concert, and an Ethiopian American cab driver who shouted delightedly, "Haile!" from the window of his passing vehicle.

Geb is known as the runner who always smiles, and indeed he wore a childlike grin throughout our run. I think he smiles all the time partly because he is an innately positive person and partly because he is thrilled by how his life has turned out. Much as Muhammad Ali loves being Muhammad Ali, Haile Gebrselassie loves being Haile Gebrselassie. His passion for running is unmatched, and he can scarcely believe his good fortune at being the second-fastest distance runner in history (after his younger countryman Kenenisa Bekele).

His will for speed is insatiable. After he set his second marathon world record in the 2008 Berlin Marathon, the first words out of his mouth were, "I can run faster." That is all the proof anyone could need that being a happy runner is compatible with being a runner who is never satisfied. In fact, the spirit of discontent does not stand in the way of Gebrselassie's enjoyment of running; it is the very manner in which he enjoys running. He just can't get enough speed in the same way new lovers can't get enough time together and some musicians can't get enough performing. In interviews, Geb refuses to talk of retiring, but promises instead to keep training, racing, and striving until he is effectively dragged out of the sport by the corporeal disintegration of aging.

On the morning after our beach run, we journalists took a bus to the Home Depot Center in Carson and gathered at the track. Geb was now joined by the other big adidas track-and-field stars: world champion sprinters Allyson Felix, Tyson Gay, and Veronica Campbell-Brown; world and Olympic champion 400 m runner Jeremy Wariner; Olympic medalist sprinter Christine Ohuruogu; and Olympic champion high jumper Blanka Vlasic. One by one these winners were paraded before our seated journalistic assembly until they stood in a line of self-consciousness like so many beauty pageant contestants. After joining the lineup next to the 6-foot-4 Vlasic, Gebrselassie, all of 5 foot 3, made a show of standing on his tiptoes and drawing up his shoulders as he stole a glance upward at her head. We laughed heartily as the other star athletes stood stone-faced.

Throughout the morning, the champions took turns demonstrating for us various training drills and exercises and describing how their adidas footwear and apparel helped their performances. Each did so with the posture and attitude of a person fulfilling a contractual obligation—with one exception.

A treadmill had been set up at the edge of the track some distance away from the high-jump area. As Vlasic entertained us with a demonstration of her practice run-ups, Geb began warming up on the treadmill, gradually increasing his pace. By the time we were shepherded over to him, he was running at his world record marathon pace of 4:43 per mile. It was an awesome spectacle to behold. What struck me most was that I could not hear his feet landing on the treadmill, although I stood six feet from him. There was just a slight change in the pitch of the machine's whirring motor when his foot struck the belt, but the actual impact of the shoe on the belt was totally inaudible. The man was light on his feet.

Something called a heat camera was trained on Geb as he ran. A video screen displayed an image of him with coloring effects that showed how much heat was coming off various parts of his body. The ostensible point of this demonstration was to show off the thermoregulation properties of Geb's adidas apparel. As an adidas rep blathered on and on about this stuff, Geb just kept running. Eventually, he started jabbing at the treadmill's control panel. Is he going to slow down? I wondered. No, he was speeding up. Geb's thighs were now coming up nearly to 90 degrees on each swing-through.

"How fast are you going now?" someone asked. Geb used a hand to create shade over the machine's display console (a bright morning sun stood smack behind him) and positioned his nose just inches away from it, squinting. "Four thirty-six per mile!" he announced with boyish enthusiasm. There were murmurs and whistles.

The adidas rep wrapped up his song and dance and asked Geb if he would like to slow down and step off the treadmill so that he could talk about his shoes, shorts, and singlet. Geb politely refused, saying he could talk as he ran. Moments later he was jabbing at the control panel again, and his pace accelerated further. He knew what we were really there for, and he was happy—beyond happy—to put on a show.

"How fast now?" someone shouted.

"Four twenty-six!" Geb beamed. His next move was now inevitable. He jabbed his right index finger into the panel repeatedly, and his stride opened up wider and wider.

"Four minutes per mile!" he shouted with the pride of a motorcycle daredevil taking a bow after leaping over a bunch of school buses. He held the pace for maybe half a minute, throwing his arms overhead and pumping his fists in celebration before quitting at last. When he stepped off the treadmill, he was given a rapturous ovation.

I guess you could say he won the beauty pageant.

As a final encore, Geb talked very sincerely about how much he liked his adidas racing flats. Whatever adidas paid this peerless ambassador, the company was getting its money's worth.

After lunch I sat down with Geb one-on-one for a 15-minute interview. I was a bit apprehensive because I had never read or seen an interview with him that was particularly revealing. He always spoke in generalities and platitudes, such as "One must train very hard." At dinner the previous night, I had asked *Track & Field News* managing editor Sieg Lindstrom, who has known Geb since he burst onto the international athletics scene in the early 1990s, for some tips on interviewing the great man. Lindstrom was not terribly encouraging.

"Is it a language barrier?" I asked him.

"That's part of it," he said. "English is his second language, so he puts things in simpler terms when he's speaking it. But the other part is that the Africans think about running in simpler terms anyway. I think they feel we overanalyze it and make it more complicated than it needs to be."

This advice did not help me coax any more from Gebrselassie than I had heard and read before, but it did help me understand his answers a little better. I asked how he plans his training, and he answered, "It comes from what kind of competition. Is it marathon, half marathon? What level I am. What I have to do. Stuff like that, you know? You just put it together, just like that."

Yes, just like that. I guess.

Only later, through conversations with English sports nutrition researcher Asker Jeukendrup, Geb's onetime nutrition adviser, and other native English speakers familiar with the details of Geb's training, did I learn that he really does not plan his training in the way that most Western runners do. There are no fancy multiphase periodization schedules. Instead, he trains the same way pretty much all the time, going a little lighter when he has just come off a big race and a little heavier when the next big race is close, and going a little faster when the next big race is shorter and a little slower when the next big race is longer.

I got a hint of the repetitiveness in Geb's training formula when I asked him, "Do you have certain test workouts that you do to measure your progress in training?"

He replied, "Because I am training for a marathon now, once a week there is a route in training—20 km, 30 km—I will run that and compare it to just a week ago, a few weeks ago, last year."

Again, through later research I was able to determine that this 20 km or 30 km run was in fact a time trial. He runs a 20 km or 30 km time trial every week in marathon training, which shows not only how repetitive his training is, but also how hard.

I asked Gebrselassie to name his favorite workout. If I had known him better, I would not have been so surprised to learn that his favorite session was also his toughest. "Hill training is my favorite," he said. "Because that's the one that gives you a lot of problems. Pain. Breathing too much. Struggling too much. Of course, you don't enjoy it during training, but after training, after you reach the top and you look down, and say, 'That is what I did,' it gives you confidence."

Let me just repeat that, with emphasis. Hill training (by which, I later learned, he means 90 minutes hard straight up Entoto Mountain outside of Ethiopia's capital city, Addis Ababa) is Gebrselassie's favorite workout, he says, "*because* that's the one that gives you a lot of problems. *Pain*." Now that's interesting.

I asked Geb if he still worked with a coach. He answered: "I have a coach, but he just tells me the things I know. I don't do it if he tells me to do just 200, 400 m [intervals] today. No use. I know already this kind of program is going to kill me. I need a coach, but when you talk about a coach, a coach's job is not only to arrange a program or to take a time."

I took this answer to mean that Geb knew what worked for him as a runner, and he therefore did not need a coach to prescribe workouts. While he did not spell out what he needs a coach for, I guessed it is to hold him back when he needs to be held back, help him troubleshoot when problems arise, and perform other counseling and advisory services, as many coaches of experienced elite runners limit themselves, or are limited, to doing.

Being one year older than Geb, who was 36 at the time of our interview, I did not allow our little sit-down to conclude before I had asked him a few questions about age. While he did confess to having altered his training for fear of injuries—avoiding those 200 m and 400 m repeats, lifting weights, riding a bike, and (if we can call it training) getting daily postworkout massages—he also said regarding his age: "That's why I keep winning. One of my advantages now is longtime experience. I know what I have to do to win the race, before the race, after the race, with recovery. That's one of the advantages for old runners. That's why I keep running well. The young runners have enough power just to do whatever they want. But if you think with strategy, you have a kind of advantage."

HAILE GEBRSELASSIE, NEUROSCIENTIST

I thought about my experiences with Haile Gebrselassie while driving home to San Diego. There was a certain pattern in his behaviors and words. They expressed a man who very much runs by feel—whose choices and actions as a runner are determined by what his body, and in particular his gut and his heart, tell him to do, rather than by theory or convention with some assistance from technology. His happiness is not incidental to his success in running; it is the secret to his success. He not only runs because it makes him happy, but he also runs in the way that makes him happiest. If it feels good, he does it. Although living by such a principle might lead a runner to avoid pain, Geb derives so much enjoyment from his never-ending quest to run faster than he has ever run before (and often faster than any human has ever run before) that he has learned to enjoy the pain that comes with it, such as the pain of those mountain climbs.

He does not perform specific workouts in a particular sequence to stimulate a precise set of physiological adaptations calculated to increase his performance; he trains to build confidence. If a workout makes him feel ready to break a world record, he's ready to break a world record. He can just feel it. His coach's job is mainly to help him develop confidence in his ability to achieve goals.

His training is a familiar, trusted routine. It is not exactly the way he was taught to train as a young runner. That is the foundation, but he has customized the details based on an ever-improving sense of which methods work for him individually and which ones do not. He not only was born with near-perfect running genes, but he also learns from experience in running better than others learn. No wonder he rates his experience as an advantage against the greater power of younger runners.

What interested me particularly about this notion of history's second-greatest distance runner also being the ultimate run-by-feel runner was how it validated new scientific ideas about the functioning of the brain and the singular importance of the brain—not merely the mind, but that wet, three-pound, electrified physical organ the brain—in relation to endurance performance. Recent discoveries in the neurophysiology and neuropsychology of exercise have inspired the development of a new model of endurance performance that views the brain as a central hub regulating every facet from pacing and fatigue to adaptation and recovery. This new model has important practical implications for how runners approach the sport, and I believe that it calls for a train-by-feel approach specifically. Consider these selected findings:

- Research out of the University of Cape Town, South Africa, has shown that subjective perception of effort (how hard exercise *feels*) predicts fatigue in exercise better than heart rate, blood lactate level, oxygen consumption, muscle fuel depletion, or any other physiological factor.[1] As the great Dr. Timothy Noakes likes to say, "The feeling of fatigue *is* fatigue."
- Research by exercise psychologists has demonstrated strong correlations among exercise enjoyment, exercise adherence, self-efficacy, and endurance fitness.[2] Specifically, the fitter people are, the more competent they feel in exercise, and the more competent they *feel*, the more they enjoy exercise, and the more they enjoy exercise, the more likely they are to stick with it, and so forth. But there's

real-world evidence that the converse is also true: The more people enjoy exercise, the fitter it makes them.

- In a study performed at the University of Exeter, England, subjects were given four chances to complete a 4 km cycling time trial as fast as possible. However, they were not told the distance of the time trials before starting the first; they were told only that whatever it was, the distance was the same in all four. Nor were they given any distance or duration feedback during the cycling time trials. Yet despite this blindness, the subjects completed the last time trial in exactly the same amount of averaged time as another group given time and distance information. The subjects in the first group naturally and cautiously went much slower in the first time trial, became a little more aggressive in the next, and so forth. They gradually *felt* their way toward optimal pacing.[3]
- Research by biomechanics expert Benno Nigg has shown that runners are less likely to suffer injuries when they choose running shoes that *feel* most comfortable.[4]
- A team of scientists at the University of Birmingham, England, discovered that subjects performed better in a cycling time trial when they rinsed their mouths out but did not swallow a sports drink, because the carbohydrates in the drink activated a reward center in the brain that made the effort *feel* easier.[5]

Such studies hint at an overarching truth: Through our brains, our bodies tell us almost everything we need to know to maximize our performance as runners. Tuning in to how we feel—and manipulating how we feel where possible—is a more powerful way to monitor and delay fatigue, control pace, prevent injuries, enjoy running, and simply run faster than guiding ourselves strictly by conventional training methods, science, and technology.

MIND-BODY RUNNING

"Mind-body running" is the term I use to refer to the practice of feeling our way toward better running performance and a better running experience. It is something that we all do to some degree. For example, every time we step outside and run at our natural running pace, which research has shown to be determined by feel (that is, by perceived exertion), not physiology, we are practicing mind-body running as I define it.[6] But while running by feel is automatic to an extent, some runners do it better than others—for example, Haile Gebrselassie has elevated mind-body running to the level of genius—and virtually all runners in the Western world are actively discouraged from running by feel beyond a certain point. Just about any running book or magazine will show this to be the case.

Since learning about the run-by-feel implications of the new brain-centered model of running performance, I have noticed that many of the world's most successful runners rely on a mind-body approach to training. Haile Gebrselassie is not unique. For example, listening to his body instead of doing what other elite runners of his era did led Steve Jones to run much less and much faster in training than was normal and also led the Welshman to run a 2:07:13 marathon in 1985. Now an elite coach based in Boulder, Colorado, Jones shows his athletes how to trust their guts and hearts in their training, saying he would rather inspire them than know what the hell he is doing. Members of the Nike Oregon Project, including Galen Rupp and Amy Yoder-Begley, have discarded the practice of following training plans and instead, under the guidance of their coach, Alberto Salazar, they decide on the format of each run only hours before doing it.

Over the past few years, I have studied the run-by-feel methods of the world's best runners through the prism of the new brain-centered model of exercise performance and applied them in my own running. Following the examples of Salazar's runners, and mindful of research suggesting that intuitive decisions are often better than deliberative ones, I abandoned the use of scripted training plans and began winging it. Then following the example of Haile Gebrselassie, and aware of studies showing that exercise is more effective when it is more fun, I began to rely on enjoyment as much as objective performance data in steering the course of my training. And so forth. This mind-body approach lifted my running to a whole new level, and my overall experience with it inspired me to write this book, whose purpose is to clear away all the theoretical, scientific, and technological junk that Western runners are exposed to and reveal a much more reliable way to run better and with greater fulfillment: by listening to and learning from the body.

It may seem self-evident that runners do not need to be shown how to effectively listen to their bodies, but nothing is further from the truth. While every runner gains a degree of mind-body competence automatically, developing an exceptional capacity to run by feel is difficult and rare, and the likes of Haile Gebrselassie, who figure it all out on their own, represent one-in-a-million anomalies. I believe that even the most serious competitive runners never realize their full potential largely because they never fully develop their capacity to run by feel.

Mindfulness must be trained in running just as it must be cultivated in life. In life, doing what feels good leads to happiness only if a person has become mindful enough to recognize what feels best in the long term. For example, indulging anger may feel good momentarily, but in the long term it can poison relationships and prevent the angry person from developing better emotional coping and communication skills. Similarly, runners, fearing the prospect of experimenting with different methods, might find that it feels good to blindly follow training plans or at least a general training system created by some great expert. But if they bite the bullet and experiment anyway, they can ultimately create a whole new and better comfort zone of training customized to their unique physiology and personality.

Running by feel is the best way to run. However, you cannot always trust your feel for running in any given moment. Often, you may feel multiple sensations simultaneously, some of which are mutually contradictory. For example, the pain of an incipient injury might tell you to stop, while your work ethic and your addiction to running might tell you to keep going. To consistently choose the right feeling to trust, you must cultivate the capacity to step back and observe yourself objectively—or, if not objectively, then from a perspective based on accumulated wisdom. You must cultivate mindfulness. This process will proceed most rapidly and efficiently if you make a conscious commitment to it, but a good guide can help it along.

In this book, I will be your teacher of mindful, or mind-body, running. It's not that I am such a great expert in the practice. I will be the first to admit that Haile Gebrselassie, Steve Jones, and Alberto Salazar have mastered this skill much more fully than I ever will. I make many mistakes, am still learning, and have a lot more to learn. There is a difference between a role model and a guide, however. While my contact with great runners and coaches who have mastered the practice of mind-body running and my study of the brain's role in running enable me to volunteer myself as your guide to running by feel, it is the runners and coaches who have figured it out for themselves, each in his or her own way, who will be your primary role models in these pages.

Running by feel is a rebellion against our modern traditions of training for distance running. Fittingly, then, this book is not a conventional running book. What follows is not the usual concatenation of tips culminating in the one-size-fits-all training plans found in many running books. Instead, this book presents a collection of essays that explore broad ideas touching on various aspects of what I hope emerges as a coherent run-by-feel philosophy. If you are looking for "First do this, then do that" guidelines, you will be disappointed. In mind-body running, you are ultimately on your own. Only you can feel your way to better running. All I can do here is to create a clear and solid conceptual framework that you can use to find your own way. But I would like to think that the limited service this book provides (like the limited service that the best running coaches provide their best runners) will do more to improve your running than the more traditional running book, which does all of the thinking for you and ignores the *feeling*.

ENHANCING THE CAPACITY TO FEEL

Japanese novelist and runner Haruki Murakami wrote a memoir, entitled *What I Talk About When I Talk About Running*, that captures a common fantasy among runners. In this slender volume, Murakami tells the story of running his first (and only) ultramarathon. Initially, he says, it was easy. But the going got rough after 50 km, and Murakami had to try every psychological trick in the book to force himself to keep running despite the astonishing pain and suffering he was experiencing. Eventually, he told himself: "I'm not a human. I'm a piece of machinery. I don't need to feel a thing. I just forge on ahead." Then a funny thing happened: It worked. Murakami did not, of course, turn into a machine, nor did he cease to feel anything, but somehow the very repetition of this thought enabled him to find a certain peace with his pain and suffering and catch a second wind. "My muscles silently accepted this exhaustion now as a historical inevitability, an ineluctable outcome of the revolution," he wrote. "I had been transformed into a being on autopilot, whose sole purpose was to rhythmically swing his arms back and forth, move his legs forward one step at a time." Now fully "in the zone," Murakami found himself easily passing the scores of runners who had passed him in his earlier rough patch. "It's weird, but at the end I hardly knew who I was or what I was doing," he recounted. "By then running had entered the realm of the metaphysical. First there came the action of running, and accompanying it there was this entity known as me. I run; therefore I am."

I love this passage because it describes every competitive runner's occasional fantasy: to be numb. In some moments each of us wishes to be a robot running without feeling. After all, this metamorphosis would spare us a lot of pain and enable us to run better, because suffering slows us down, right? Murakami's story seems to validate this wish. He slowed down as he suffered; then he numbed himself and sped up. But Murakami did not really eliminate feeling in the way that a robot has no feeling. While he viewed his brain as the problem during his rough patch and wished to solve the problem by essentially shutting his brain off, it was actually his brain that turned things around for him. He did not incapacitate his feelings; instead, he used his capacity to feel to identify a problem and fix it—ironically, by cooperating with his conscious mind to create a fantasy of incapacitating his feelings.

It is natural to sometimes wish you could run without your brain, yet this is the vainest of wishes, because your brain does absolutely everything when you run. It is responsible for every contraction of every fiber of every muscle on every stride. It makes your heart beat and your lungs fill and empty in the right rhythm. It regulates your fuel supply. It lets you see where you are going. The notion of running without a brain is not just funny; it's laughable. The only reason a nervous system even exists at all in any animal is to enable movement. There is a very primitive species of sea creature with a very primitive nervous system; the creature swims around a bit in the first part of its life and then plants itself and remains stationary for the second part of its life. And as soon as the self-implantation occurs, the creature devours its own brain. No movement, no brain; no brain, no movement.

Of course, what we really mean when we say we wish we could run brainlessly is that we wish we could run without feeling. But that is part of the package. The big difference between a human and a robot is that humans are alive. All living things want to stay alive, and feelings help us stay alive by doing things like signaling harm. Our capacity to feel does not always produce pleasant results when we run, but it keeps us from running ourselves to death. Don't think for a minute that the capacity to feel holds anyone back, though: A dead runner, or even a dying one, cannot run very fast.

Recent exercise science has clearly demonstrated that at the point of exhaustion, athletes always have reserve capacity left in their muscles and that the amount of reserve capacity left is variable. Factors such as experience, training, and motivation affect how close athletes are able to come to true physiological limits before fatiguing. As athletes, we covet that knowledge of how close we are to our limits. When it comes time to race, we would like to tap this reserve, taking our performance as close to those limits as is physically possible. Imagine the advantage of having a "dashboard" to look to, giving feedback on where this reserve stood. The brain is the window to this feedback, the key to unlocking more of that reserve (although, again, there is always going to be some reserve).

The physiology of running performance is incredibly complex. There is no single factor that determines how fast and how far we can go. Dozens of interdependent factors conspire to influence this determination. It is the brain that ultimately decides, however, basing its calculation largely on a synthesis of data extracted from ongoing monitoring of all the relevant physiological factors. The brain is, of course, part of the body and coevolved with it over millions of years. It is exquisitely designed for the function of maximizing running performance (among many other functions, of course). In fact, the brain cannot possibly be improved on. No humanmade instrument could ever do a more superior job than the brain of enabling a human runner to perform better.

In this book we will explore how you can use the emotions of confidence and enjoyment to shape your future training; learn from how your body responds to training and develop your personal magic training formula; use repetition in training to cultivate a performance-enhancing force called psychological momentum; manipulate your brain to enable you to run harder (hence faster) in key workouts and races; train without the use of training plans; use fear, anger, and even injuries to run better; and improve communication between your brain and muscles to reduce your injury susceptibility and improve your stride.

Much of this work is performed on a subconscious level. But much of the feedback that the brain receives from the body and interprets becomes conscious feeling—the feeling of rhythmically contracting and relaxing muscles, the feeling of burning lungs, the feeling of "God this hurts, but I still think I have enough left to outkick this guy to the finish line," and so forth. Thus, it is largely because of the capacity to feel that no humanmade instrument will ever be capable of regulating running performance better than the brain. This is a fact. But beyond being true, isn't that also great? Isn't it just great that nothing that comes in a box can enhance running performance more than communication between the brain and the rest of the body? Who would want it any other way?

PART I

LEARNING TO LISTEN

ONE

PHYSICAL CONFIDENCE

Training gives me proof.

—John Litei

PERFORMANCE-ENHANCING DRUGS have tarnished world championships and disqualified record-breaking performances. Nevertheless, drug-free elite runners can, and do, win world championships and break world records. But there are those who maintain a more cynical view of the ability of clean runners to compete against dopers. Renowned South African exercise physiologist Tim Noakes is among them, and several years ago he agreed to debate this topic with me.

I challenged some of Noakes's stated beliefs, and I was able to persuade him to concede a few of my points. For example, I pressed him to confess it unlikely that women's marathon world record holder Paula Radcliffe was a doper, given that she had requested that her blood samples be frozen so that they could be proved clean by more advanced testing methods developed in the future.

"I absolutely agree with you," Noakes said. "Paula Radcliffe has gone out of her way to prove that she is not doping, which would be utterly reckless if she were."

"And if Paula Radcliffe is clean," I said, "is that alone not proof that performance-enhancing drugs do not provide an insurmountable advantage?"

"If you could prove that, for example, Paula Radcliffe is not using drugs," Noakes granted, "that would make a strong case that others could compete without doing it as well. But it works both ways," he added. "If you can prove that even one record-setter gained an advantage from doping, what message does that send to the clean athletes competing against him?"

Touché.

My last question for Noakes was more personal, hence even more aggressively challenging to his viewpoint, if less directly so.

"What would you do," I asked, "if you had a son who demonstrated a special talent for distance running and who told you that his dream was to break a world record some day—without drugs, of course?" I was intentionally putting Noakes in a position where he would either have to tell me that he would coldly quash his child's dream by saying he had no hope of breaking a world record without cheating—as this was the answer that would have been most consistent with his viewpoint—or surprise me with another answer. He surprised me.

"The first thing I would do," he said, "is get my son a coach who believed he could break a world record."

BELIEF AND THE BRAIN

If someone else had spoken these words, I might have dismissed them as so much mush-headed greeting-card philosophy. But Tim Noakes is not a mush head. He is perhaps the greatest exercise scientist of his generation— or any generation. And I knew that on his tongue, these words expressed a very particular thought, one based on decades of ingenious scientific inquiry.

Noakes is the chief architect of a new model of exercise performance that sees the brain as the source of all our capacities and all our limitations. Even though the muscles and blood and heart and lungs are important, Noakes has shown that it is the brain that ultimately determines what we can do as athletes. It is the brain that determines when we can run faster or farther and when we cannot.

One of the most often repeated sayings in sports is this: "What you believe, you can achieve." Next time you hear an athlete or coach use this expression, ask why it is so. Chances are he or she will not be able to articulate a clear reason, but will probably make some reference to the power of the mind to overcome physical limitations. But Noakes understands that the mind is nothing more than an epiphenomenon of the brain's operations and that the brain is every bit as physical as the rest of the body. Noakes knows why athletes often—not always, but often—are able to achieve what they believe. He knows that our beliefs about what we can do as runners are the products of evidence-based calculations of our capabilities performed by the brain on a largely subconscious level.

The evidence used in these calculations comes from two sources: the body and conscious experience. During running, the brain constantly monitors feedback from the body (either directly, by monitoring muscle fuel levels and so forth; indirectly, by monitoring the intensity of the brain's own efforts to activate the muscles; or both—there is scientific disagreement about this) and in doing so learns the body states that correspond with performance limits. But the body changes through training, and as the body changes, the brain is required to make new projections about what a runner can do. For example, at the beginning of the training process, the body might reach the state that the brain associates with its limits after 1 mile covered in 8 minutes. But after several weeks of training, the same runner's body might be in a much less extreme state of stress after covering 1 mile in 8 minutes. Based on this new feedback, the brain might calculate that the runner now must run 1 mile somewhat faster than 8 minutes to reach the same limiting state. This subconscious calculation would then generate a conscious belief in the runner that he or she should now set a goal to run 1 mile in, say, 7:30.

So that's the sort of biological evidence on which performance beliefs are based. As for the experiential evidence, imagine two runners, Susan and Liz, of roughly equal ability. Susan and Liz race each other over a distance of 5K, and Liz finishes 5 seconds ahead of Susan with a time of 20:12. Two weeks later, Susan runs another 5K race, in which Liz does not participate, and cracks the 20-minute barrier, running 19:56. Upon finding out about this performance, Liz, who until that time did not believe she could run a sub-20-minute 5K, recalculates her potential. Knowing that she can run faster than Susan, and now also knowing that Susan can run faster than

20:00, Liz embraces the belief that she, too, can run faster than 20:00. Sure enough, in another 5K race the very next week, Liz matches Susan's time of 19:56.

Tim Noakes had this type of experiential evidence in mind when he suggested that the first thing he would do with a son who dreamed of breaking a world record was to find him a coach who believed Noakes's son could break a world record. A coach who believed that this boy could break a world record might be able to cultivate this belief in the child in much the same way that Susan's 19:56 5K performance cultivated in Liz the belief that she could break the 20-minute barrier as well.

Noakes told me he had lost count of the number of times he had asked elite runners how they achieved a certain performance and had received the answer, "My coach said I could."

I can cite a few examples as well. Here's one: In 2009, only 10 weeks after switching to a new coach (Alberto Salazar) at a low point in his career, Dathan Ritzenhein broke the American record for 5,000 m, running 12:56.28. When I asked Ritz how he did it, he said that Salazar's expressed beliefs about what he was capable of doing were a major factor. "When your coach is as accomplished a runner as Alberto was and he tells you how well you're doing and these goals that you are on track toward, that just makes a huge difference," he said. "If he sees and believes, then I can, too."

I must point out here that Salazar did not tell Ritzenhein that he was ready to run a record-breaking 5K simply for the sake of building Ritzenhein's confidence. He did it because he truly believed that Ritz could run a record-breaking 5K. Nor did Noakes say that he would find a coach who would tell his son he could break a world record whether the coach actually believed it or not. He said he would find a coach who really believed it. No runner can go out and break a record simply because a coach says he can. While experiences such as confidence-building pep talks from coaches can influence the brain's calculations about what the body can do, the most influential calculations by far occur during the runs themselves, when biological feedback, which cannot lie, has the final say. This is why experiments in which athletes are given false information about their pace in time trial efforts (specifically, they are told they are going slower than they really are) have no effect on their performance.[1] While an athlete in such an experiment may know that, for example, she can pedal a stationary bike at 200 watts for one hour, she cannot suddenly increase her power output to 210 watts and sustain it for the remainder of an hour just because a man in a lab coat falsely tells her she is pedaling at 190 watts when in fact she is already churning out 200 watts and her body knows it. Thanks to organic communications with the muscles, the unconscious brain is already aware that the body is at its limit, and this always trumps consciously received information in the end.

In this regard there is an important distinction to be drawn between *willing* a performance and *believing in* it in the specific sense of "believing" that applies to this discussion. Willing is wanting. It is an overt effort to believe that a coveted goal will be achieved. It is what we might call a top-down phenomenon. A goal is born at the conscious level, and then the mind tries to make the body believe it can physically realize that goal, yet the body may know itself to be quite incapable of satisfying the mind in a given case. Every athlete on the starting line of the women's 1,500 m final of the Olympic Games believes she can win the gold medal in the sense of wanting to believe it—willing it. But only a few of them believe it in their bodies; only a few believe it in the sense of being confident that it can happen.

Believing in this second sense is a bottom-up phenomenon. Through the practice of running, the body learns what it can do. This learning is experienced as a warm feeling of self-efficacy as a runner embarks upon a performance in pursuit of a particular goal consonant with the body's self-knowledge. In rare, special moments, training goes so well that a runner's brain-based performance calculation mechanism (with the help of experiential feedback in the form of speed and distance, or performance, information gathered in key workouts) comes to believe that the runner is capable of doing things he has never done before. Dathan Ritzenhein experienced one such moment in his preparation for the two track races he ran in the summer of 2009—the World Championships 10,000 m (where he finished sixth in a personal-best time of 27:22.28) and the 5,000 m in Zurich, where he set his American record. "I knew that I was doing things I hadn't done before," he said of the workouts he completed at a Nike Oregon Project

training camp in the Swiss Alps that summer. "I was doing workouts that
I could not have replicated when I was at my best before. That gave me
confidence."

This concept is critical: The actions of Ritzenhein's body told him he
could run some spectacular races, and sure enough he went out and did exactly what his body told him it could do. Confidence is not some nonphysical
quality snatched from the spiritual dimension and installed in the mind. It
is the feeling that arises when the body's knowledge of itself is in harmony
with a person's dreams.

Confidence is really the runner's best guide through the training process toward race goals. Workout split times are great, but only inasmuch
as they build confidence, which is also influenced by experience, like Liz's
experience of learning that her rival Susan had run a 19:56 5K. Runners are
typically taught to believe that the primary objective of training is to stimulate the physiological adaptations that will enable them to achieve their
race goals. But what exactly are those adaptations, and what is needed to
stimulate them? It does not really matter. What matters is that the unconscious brain knows when the body is capable of achieving the goals of the
conscious mind and communicates this knowledge to consciousness in the
form of the feeling of confidence. Therefore, the primary objective of training for every competitive runner should be to develop confidence in her
ability to achieve her race goals. It is much easier for a runner to know that
she has trained in a way that makes her confident that she can perform at
the level of her aspirations than to know that she has stimulated the physiological adaptations that will enable her to perform at this level.

The most advanced runners are led by their sense of confidence, whether
they think about it this way or not. They are very aware of their confidence
level, and they instinctively make decisions that promise to increase their
confidence and mute their doubt. This is what Dathan Ritzenhein did in deciding to switch coaches and turn his competitive focus from the marathon
back to the track for a while after a disappointing performance in the 2009
London Marathon, in which he finished 11th in a time of 2:10:00. Of the
thought process that preceded those decisions, he said: "I just realized one
day that I wasn't as tough as I used to be. I used to be known for that when
I was racing and training. I still would work hard, but I didn't have the edge.

It wasn't that I was unhappy doing it, but I didn't have the real spark and passion that I used to have."

On a pure performance level, the core of Ritz's problem was that he arrived at starting lines without confidence. Specifically, his body told him it was not fast enough. "That was an underlying issue with me going into some of the races," he said. "I didn't feel I was prepared enough in that way."

If it does nothing else, a runner's training must make him feel prepared, because if he *feels* prepared, he *is* prepared, and if he doesn't, he isn't. To fix the problem, Ritz decided to train for lifetime-best performances in the 5,000 m and 10,000 m, not so much to develop a scientifically calculated increase in speed as to recapture that feeling of toughness and preparedness that he would need to achieve his marathon dreams. He came away from his sixth-place finish at the World Championships and his third-place finish in Zurich, just 4 seconds (and closing) behind world record holder Kenenisa Bekele, with more speed and a warm feeling about how it would affect his next marathon starting line experience. "Hopefully, what happens is that I show up and I feel confident that I'm ready to run with anybody," he said. "Now I feel I can run with anyone in the world on the track, so why can't I do it in the marathon?"

MENTAL AND PHYSICAL CONFIDENCE

There are two types of confidence: physical and mental. Physical confidence is the unconscious brain's calculations of what the body can do. Mental confidence is the conscious feeling that follows physical confidence. While, as we have seen, mental confidence is affected by experience in training and racing, it is most strongly influenced by physiological feedback to the unconscious brain from the body.

Mental confidence is confidence as we all know it: a belief that we are capable of performing specific tasks or achieving specific goals. Physical confidence is a subconscious calculation that *predicts* our physical limits with respect to a specific task. In cruder terms, mental confidence is what the mind *thinks* the body can do. Physical confidence is what the body itself *knows* it can do.

Both mental confidence and physical confidence are important, but physical confidence is probably more important because it is usually more accurate and it is also the primary source of mental confidence. Fully appreciating the importance of physical confidence means first understanding how science now looks at the role of the brain in regulating exercise performance.

MIND-BODY RUNNING

Make it your primary objective in training to develop confidence in your ability to achieve your specific race goals.

One of the leading researchers in this area is Samuele Marcora of the University of Bangor, Wales. In a series of elegant studies, Marcora singlehandedly exploded the traditional, cardiovascular/muscular explanation of endurance performance and fatigue and replaced it with a brain-based alternative. In one of these studies, ten members of the university rugby team were recruited as subjects. Each performed a maximal voluntary cycling power (MVCP) test, which consisted of an all-out 5-second effort on a stationary bike. After a period of rest, the subjects were then required to pedal the same bikes as long as possible at a fixed wattage that corresponded to 90 percent of their individual VO_2max values, which were obtained from previous testing. On average, the subjects were able to continue for roughly 12 minutes at 242 watts before giving in to exhaustion. Immediately after "bonking" in this high-intensity endurance ride to exhaustion, the subjects repeated the 5-second MVCP test.

As you might expect, the subjects were not able to produce as much power in the second MVCP test, done in a fatigued state, as in the first, done in a rested state. In fact their power dropped by about 30 percent, from an average of 1,075 watts in the first test to 731 watts in the second.

What's interesting about this finding is that it cannot be explained by the conventional model of endurance fatigue, which proposes that the involuntary decline in performance that defines bonking occurs when some physiological limitation is encountered—for example, acid buildup in the muscles causes the muscles to essentially stop functioning. But this model predicts that if athletes cycle to the point of failure at 242 watts, they cannot possibly produce 731 watts for 5 seconds immediately afterward. The fact that these rugby players were able to briefly triple their power output in the second MVCP test relative to the ride to exhaustion clearly shows that, physiologically, they were capable of riding much longer in that ride to exhaustion than they actually did.

So if it wasn't a physiological limit that caused the subjects to quit their high-intensity endurance ride after roughly 12 minutes, what was it? In a paper about the study, Marcora proposed, "The most likely explanation for the very high MVCP produced immediately after exhaustion is psychological. Subjects knew that the final MVCP test was going to last only 5 [seconds], and such knowledge motivated them to exert further effort after the time to exhaustion test, which had a longer and unknown duration."

This psychological explanation can be valid only if perception of effort is the true cause of exhaustion, and that is exactly what Marcora believes. This belief is supported by the finding that ratings of perceived effort are always near maximal in research subjects (in this study and many others) at the point of exhaustion. Marcora argues that perception of effort is based primarily on how hard the brain has to drive the muscles to maintain a desired level of performance. As the muscles and cardiovascular system approach their limits during sustained exercise, the brain has to drive the muscles harder and harder to sustain the desired level of performance, so the perception of effort goes up and up.

At the point of bonking, the muscles and cardiovascular system still have not reached their limits, but the athlete's tolerance for suffering has. "What we call exhaustion is not the inability to continue," Marcora explained to me in an interview. "My idea is that perception of effort is basically a safety mechanism like many other sensations. Think about thirst or hunger or pain. All these sensations are there to make us do something that is beneficial for our survival, and I think perception of effort does the same."

Marcora notes that many of his exercise colleagues reject his new model of endurance fatigue on the grounds that mere perceptions are not powerful enough to set performance limits that highly motivated athletes cannot simply override through conscious will. He counters that this notion is an unfounded prejudice that subjugates the psychological to the physiological. Look around and you'll see many examples of perceptions completely controlling human behavior. Or try setting a marathon PR with a small, sharp pebble in your shoe. That pebble will do little physical harm, but the pain will cripple you no matter how much willpower you might have.

Just as pain often sets in when serious damage to the body is imminent but not yet actual, the feeling of fatigue sets in when the body's physiological limits are being approached but have not yet been reached. Thus, it is not the body's limitations that limit running performance but rather the mind's perception of those limits. Somehow the mind is able to know what the body can and cannot safely do in exercise and uses perceptions to make its calculations of the body's limitations known to the mind, which then enforces limits by making the runner slow down or stop when the level of suffering becomes too great. In short, these calculations and the perception of effort they yield function as an exercise pacing mechanism.

MIND-BODY RUNNING

Ask yourself, "What sorts of training experiences would give me the most confidence to enable me to achieve my goal?" Then do whatever intuition gives you in response.

Some researchers, including Ross Tucker, another South African exercise physiologist who happens to also be a protégé of Tim Noakes, believe that the mind calculates the body's limitations by monitoring "afferent" feedback from the body that provides information on muscle energy and acidity levels, core body temperature, and so forth. But Marcora's research suggests that the mind neither needs nor uses such feedback to perceive effort. Rather, this perception is based on the intensity of the brain's efforts to drive the muscles and on conscious awareness of how far away the finish line is. Changes that occur from the neck down during exercise influence perception of effort only indirectly by increasing the intensity with which the brain must drive the muscles to keep them working at a desired level of output.

However it is that the mind calculates the body's limitations, it clearly does so, and quite accurately. Tucker's preferred name for the physiological pacing mechanism is "anticipatory regulation" because it's based on an anticipated endpoint of exercise—the finish line, in the case of running races. "The whole premise for pacing is that the brain is regulating exercise performance in order to protect the body from reaching a limit or a failure point or a potentially harmful level before the end of exercise," Tucker told me.

Anticipatory regulation works better in experienced runners than in beginners, because this mechanism uses past training and racing experiences to make accurate calculations about how fast the runner can go without either bonking or finishing with too much left in the tank. Even in the most experienced athletes, these calculations aren't perfect—and thus a perfectly paced race is a rarity—but they are very reliable.

Because physical confidence generates mental confidence, which is more accessible to consciousness, runners should engage in those training practices that make them most consciously confident of their ability to achieve their race goals. If training gives a runner mental confidence, she can be sure that it is also developing physical confidence by providing her anticipatory regulation mechanism with the information needed to calculate that her body is ready to race well. Following any sensible training plan that adheres to the conventional principles and methods of run training will increase confidence. But what if, instead of following a scripted training plan, the runner simply asks herself, *"What sorts of training experiences would give me the most confidence about being able to achieve my race goal?"* Experienced runners can get better results by using this question to determine the course of their training than they can by consciously and deliberately planning their training according to established rules. We will return to this idea later in this chapter and again in Chapter 6 (aptly titled "Winging It").

INTUITION-GUIDED TRAINING

The question I just posed is essentially an invitation to make intuition-based training decisions. High-performing experts in almost every field of endeavor use intuition more than logic and ratiocination to make decisions, because most of the knowledge we accumulate through experience in any field of endeavor is stored in unconscious brain regions. In other words, most of the learning we do in our jobs, hobbies, and relationships is implicit rather than explicit. The unconscious brain regions that are the seat of implicit learning, which include the basal ganglia, are often able to make faster, more accurate judgments and better decisions than our minds can through the conscious application of explicit learning. The only problem is that the basal ganglia are too primitive to communicate with consciousness in plain English. Instead, they communicate through feelings, hunches, and intuitions.

As a runner, you learn a lot more implicitly through training itself than you do explicitly through learning how to train from coaches, books, and Web sites. And you will make better predictions about the sorts of training experiences that will build your confidence—which itself is the best predictor of racing success—by using intuition than by engaging in overthinking.

In our highly rationalized, science-dominated modern society, intuition is frequently—and wrongly—dismissed as being too primitive to be trusted in decision-making. Ironically, though, contemporary neuropsychology has elevated the status of intuition by explaining how it works and how well it works. "Intuition is seen as mysterious and unexplainable at best and as something inaccurate, hokey, or epiphenomenological at worst," wrote Harvard psychologist Matthew Lieberman in a scientific paper on intuition.[2] In this paper, Lieberman argued that intuition is a valuable source of information produced by subconscious calculations involving patterns learned implicitly through experience. "When one relies on intuition," he wrote, "one has no sense of alternatives being weighted algebraically or a cost-benefit analysis being undertaken." However, he said, "in recent years, research on implicit learning has suggested that our behavior can be rule-like and adaptive without concomitant conscious insight into the nature of the rules being used." Unconscious parts of our brain are able to make sophisticated predictive calculations regarding what is likely to happen without our conscious minds having any sense of the process. Only the results of these calculations reach consciousness, as intuitive feelings. Anticipatory regulation is a great example of this phenomenon. The feeling that you are running too fast and the feeling that you could run faster are intuitions—very smart intuitions, in most experienced runners—that come to consciousness as the fruit of extremely complex, experience-based calculations. No amount of conscious calculation could do a better job of telling you how fast you can run in a given workout or race on a given day.

Malcolm Gladwell's *Blink: The Power of Thinking Without Thinking* is essentially a book about intuition. In it, Gladwell mentioned another book, called *Sources of Power*, by Gary Klein, that discusses how high-performing professionals in various fields rely on intuition to make good decisions. Gladwell told a story he had heard from Gary Klein about a fire-fighter who thought he had ESP because he often knew what was going to happen on the job before it happened. One night he and his men were bat-tling a kitchen fire when he suddenly ordered everyone out of the house. He did not know why; he just did it. As soon as they had escaped, the floor they had been standing on collapsed. No wonder the firefighter thought he had ESP! But Gary Klein's in-depth interview with the firefighter, in which he was asked to recall every detail of the situation, revealed that the firefighter had subconsciously registered various cues that the source of the fire his company was trying to put out was not in the kitchen itself but in the base-ment beneath them. Through experience on the job he had learned the pat-terns of different types of fires. And on that night his unconscious seat of implicit learning was able to recognize the pattern of a basement fire and deliver to the firefighter's consciousness an urgent, intuitive feeling that he and his men were in serious danger and had to flee the home immediately.

This story gives us an idea about how we should make intuitive de-cisions to build confidence through training as runners. The fireman who saved himself and his men by acting on intuition was, of course, extensively trained in fighting fires and brought a system of firefighting techniques to bear in fighting each fire. Nevertheless, most of what he really knew about fighting fires he learned implicitly through experience on the job. This knowledge existed in his unconscious as a capacity to recognize certain pat-terns before his conscious faculties did, make predictions based on them, and signal these predictions to his consciousness in the form of gut feelings. Similarly, every runner must learn and apply the principles and methods of training that have evolved over many generations as best practices. There are specific ways of training that are generally more effective than others for all runners, just as there are more and less effective ways to fight fires. But each runner is unique, and every day in the life of a runner presents a novel challenge in the quest to improve. Only by learning through experi-ence can the individual runner gain proficiency in customizing the applica-tion of the proven principles and methods of training and in making good predictions about how specific training decisions will affect fitness devel-opment. And most of this learning is implicit, as it was with the firefighter in Gladwell's book. The runner's subconscious faculties are usually first to figure out what the runner should do next and communicate their conclusions to consciousness as feelings and hunches.

In *Blink*, Gladwell used the phrase "creating structure for spontaneity" to describe how the best decisions are made spontaneously, through intuition, but within a framework that ensures intuitions serve a defined purpose. Intuitions are most likely to be relevant and useful when a specific goal has been internalized, so that the goal can operate on a subconscious level and give direction to the calculations of the unconscious. A marine general who is a master of intuitive decision-making and whom Gladwell wrote about in his book called this guiding force that creates structure for spontaneity "intent." In explaining how in 2000 he shocked the highest brass of the U.S. military by using an improvisational strategy to command an "enemy" force to victory against a far superior force in the largest war games ever staged, this general said: "The overall guidance and the intent were provided by me and the senior leadership, but the forces in the field wouldn't depend on intricate orders coming from the top. They would use their own initiative and be innovative as they went forward."

In these words lies a metaphor for individual goal-directed intuitive decision-making. The senior leadership is the conscious mind, which sets the goals and applies explicit knowledge—about warfare in the case of a military commander and about training methods in the case of a runner. The forces in the field are the unconscious, which has the capacity to use its own initiative and innovate through the application of implicit learning. And the specific intent that best creates structure for spontaneity in the runner is confidence. The surest way for a runner to make the best decisions for improvement is to internalize the intent of building confidence, so that the unconscious reliably supplies hunches about things to do to increase confidence and things to do to avoid sabotaging confidence.

Kenyan runner John Litei summarized this philosophy beautifully in a quote included by Toby Tanser in his book *More Fire*. Litei said: "Training gives me proof. I can't go to the competition without proof; it gives me the knowledge and the belief. I know in my heart I will succeed."

The ability to achieve race goals is determined by a very sophisticated calculator in the unconscious brain: anticipatory regulation. This calculator cannot be fooled. It requires proof. The feeling that your mental confidence is increasing is a reliable indicator that your training experiences are proving to your unconscious that you will be able to achieve your goals—in other words, that your training experiences are cultivating physical confidence. You cannot maximize confidence-building training experiences by making plans and sticking to them. The true best course to take in your training is influenced by innumerable factors that are constantly changing, creating a need for continual improvisation. The unconscious is a better improviser than consciousness, which receives the predictions of the unconscious as intuitions.

An important implication of the experience-based nature of implicit learning is that inexperienced runners lack the wherewithal to let their intuitions direct the course of their training. Beginners must learn and apply the proven, general best practices of training, relying on such authoritative knowledge almost entirely to direct the course of their training until they have gathered enough experience to begin receiving intuitions. The more experienced they become, the more they can rely on intuition and the less they need to rely on explicit learning. But even fairly new runners experience some good hunches about what to do. The problem is that coaches and experts tend to discourage runners from relying on intuition, so that only those runners who instinctively trust their hunches develop their intuitive capacity to full maturity.

MIND-BODY RUNNING

Intuition becomes refined with experience, so as a beginner, rely largely on established principles and methods to guide your training. As you gain experience, rely more on your own hunches than on what others do.

Tracking Confidence

Most runs will not affect your confidence one way or the other. A few, however, will boost your confidence, and inevitably a few (hopefully fewer) will weaken your confidence. I recommend that you note every run that increases or decreases your confidence in your training journal. Such notations could be as simple as the phrases "Confidence Up" and "Confidence

Down" appended to the relevant day's journal entry. This practice will serve two purposes. First, it will help you internalize the intent of training overtly to maximize your confidence. It will get you into the habit of paying attention to your confidence and instill in you a confidence-focused mind-set. Second, this notation will help you identify cause-effect relationships between your workouts and your confidence level. You will begin to see patterns in terms of the types of workouts that tend to increase or reduce your confidence, the training patterns that anticipate a rise or a dip in confidence, and so forth.

Over time, the mindfulness that you bring to bear on these cause-effect relationships will refine your intuitions so that you receive frequent and reliable hunches about how best to increase your confidence level through your training. I cannot tell you where your intuitions will lead you as a runner. But I can tell you that if you commit to becoming an intuitive runner, you will become a better runner than you would by always doing only what the experts tell you to do.

MIND-BODY RUNNING

Optimize intuition in training by choosing peak workout formats, identifying which training practices work, making daily adjustments, and addressing any problems encountered.

Intuition's Role in Training Decisions

Many mindful elite runners plan by intuition what I call "peak workouts." These workouts are the most challenging race-specific workouts you do at the end of a training cycle, just before you taper for a peak race. As such, peak workouts provide the most direct proof that your body is ready to perform at the level required to achieve your race goals. There is no single peak workout format that is clearly best for a race of any given distance, even in purely physiological terms. I believe that the best way to plan peak workouts is to ask yourself what sorts of peak workout experiences would give you the greatest amount of confidence going into your peak race. The idea is to walk away from your peak workouts thinking, "If I can do X, I know I can do Y." As Kara Goucher told me, "If you can't do workouts that predict that you can run a certain time, then you're probably not going to run that time."

Dathan Ritzenhein's peak workout before his two triumphant European track races in the summer of 2009 was a 5,000 m solo time trial run in 13:44 at high altitude. "I felt great and it gave me a lot of confidence going into Berlin," he wrote of that workout on his blog. But a very different sort of workout might have done the job just as well or done a better job for a different runner in the same circumstances. Some runners have a favorite interval set that they like to do as a peak workout before a 5K or 10K race. Others like to do an actual tune-up race as a peak workout before a peak race. Whatever works is justified.

I will say more about peak workouts in the context of a discussion on training without a plan in Chapter 6.

Intuition will also help you develop a personal training system over time. As you practice training methods that you pick up from a trusted source, such as a coach or book author, you will notice fluctuations in your confidence level. Then you will develop intuitions about the sources of these fluctuations, both positive and negative.

For example, in paying attention to her confidence level, marathon American record holder Deena Kastor noticed that her confidence benefited most from extended stretches of uninterrupted intensive training. "I really gain the greatest confidence from putting together weeks upon weeks of solid training," she told me. "It's not really a matter of walking away from a session of mile repeats and saying, 'Wow, I'm ready.' It's running a session of mile repeats two days after a 24-mile-long run and following that up with a tempo run just under race pace—it's putting in the work week in and week out that's really what I thrive on." This grinding approach to training is different from the "pick your spots" approach that works best for some other runners.

The feeling of confidence that Kastor derives from grinding it out in training is probably her intuition's way of telling her that her body responds well to that approach and that it is a good fit for her routine-loving personality. Kastor's self-awareness in this regard has led her to make crucially beneficial training and lifestyle decisions, such as planning long blocks of heavy training, strictly limiting her racing and travel during important training periods, not placing too much emphasis on individual workouts, and being fanatical about recovery so that her body can handle those long stretches of heavy training.

Another way to let intuition guide you through the training process is with day-to-day improvisations that take advantage of unforeseen opportunities to boost your confidence and steer around potential hits to your confidence. A runner's confidence often takes a hit when he runs a scheduled high-intensity workout at a time when his body is not ready for it, perhaps because of lingering fatigue from previous training. In these cases, experience-based hunches can tell you when you need to improvise a change and suggest specifically what to do instead of what you had intended to do. "I would say that two-thirds of the time everything goes as planned," Kara Goucher told me. "But as often as one out of every three workouts won't go as planned." When this happens, Goucher and her coach, Alberto Salazar, must improvise. Sometimes they choose to scrap the workout and try again another day. This happened during an 8 × 1 mile track workout that Goucher was attempting in training for the 2009 World Championships Marathon in Berlin. Just three laps into the workout, Salazar pulled Goucher off the track and instructed her to go home and take a nap. He knew she was not ready. "We just completely stopped it, and I did it the next day and had great success," Goucher said.

If dealing with unexpected flatness on the day of a planned hard workout were always as simple as going easy instead, then it would not take a lot of experience to make the right call. But sometimes it is best to push through the planned session, making only small adjustments to accommodate your unexpected flatness, because failing to do the work would deal a heavier blow to your race confidence. When training for the 2009 Boston Marathon, Kara Goucher set out to run a very similar workout to the abandoned session just described: 9 × 1 mile at a little faster than marathon pace. As in the previous described workout, Goucher struggled from the start. But this time, instead of calling off the workout, her coach (it was actually Alberto Salazar's assistant, Jerry Schumacher, who monitored her workout that day) modified it on the fly, because she needed the work and

MIND-BODY RUNNING

Intuition is not always right, and it is not always easy to distinguish the voice of wise intuition from those of insecurity and habit. Don't follow hunches blindly.

could not push it back since she was running out of days and needed the next couple to recover. Schumacher first cut her intervals from four laps to three laps each (1,200 m). Still she struggled, so he cut the intervals to two laps (800 m). But he also added intervals to the workout, and he kept her pace target the same. "It was important that day that I ran a certain volume at a certain pace," Goucher explained, "so I just had to push through it, but we made these little adjustments along the way so that I could still succeed in the workout even though I was having a tough day. When it was all said and done, I did get the distance I needed at the pace I needed; it just wasn't what we thought it was going to be at the beginning."

Finally, intuition is a terrific tool for addressing weaknesses and solving problems encountered in training. For example, suppose you run up against the common problem of fading after mile 20 every time you run a marathon. There are a variety of training experiences you might try to address this issue. Focusing on peak workouts only, you could do one or more overdistance (27–30-mile) long runs, doing longer runs at marathon goal pace (14–16 miles), and doing back-to-back 20-milers on consecutive days. Choose whichever solution you think would give you the most confidence of breaking through your bonking problem and try it. Don't worry so much about identifying the precise physiological cause of your bonks and then identifying the right workout or workouts to stimulate the appropriate physiological adaptation to address this cause. Focus on confidence, because the training experiences that give you confidence that you will break through the wall are likely to provide the right physiological stimuli.

I had the problem of bonking late in marathons myself and once chose to address it by actually running a full marathon tune-up race at about 94 percent effort. Conventional wisdom would call this move crazy, but guess what? It worked. Three weeks later I ran a 5-minute PR in another marathon. The brain knows best.

Dathan Ritzenhein used intuition to solve the problem of his disappointing performances at the marathon distance. Intuition told him that he lacked the toughness needed to push harder in marathons. Intuition told him that going down in distance and racing some 5,000s and 10,000s on the track would be a good way to relearn the capacity to "go to the wall" in competition. He followed his intuition, and it worked.

False Intuition and Other Voices

Intuition is not always right. What's more, it is not always easy to distinguish the trusted voice of implicit learning, trained to improvise within the structure of a specific intent, from other internal voices, some of which are a lot less trustworthy. Runners are often led into a vicious circle of confidence self-sabotage by an internal voice of insecurity operating under the influence of a prejudicial conviction that doing more is the only way to do better. All too often, when a runner doubts his fitness, his knee-jerk response is to train harder to restore confidence. If, as is often the case, not doing enough was not the cause of the runner's doubts, then doing more only makes matters worse. Confidence drops even further, causing the runner to train even harder to restore it. Runners must keep a constant lookout for bad intuitions and those other voices.

Ryan Hall, the men's half-marathon American record holder, has been down the path of confidence self-sabotage before. But he has heeded his intuition, and he probably will not go down that path again. "I have found that I improve much more," Hall wrote on his blog, "especially over the long run, when I let the training come out and am not out there trying to really force something special to happen. It's interesting that I maximize my potential when I just let it come out rather than by trying harder. The great thing about letting my fitness come is that it makes training very enjoyable and puts me at peace with where I am ... while realizing that my fitness will continue to increase. This mindset allows me to always be successful and really enjoy both the process and the outcome."

The feeling of enjoyment that Hall speaks of here is another product of mind-body communication that can guide runners toward consistent performance improvement. It is perhaps even more important than the feeling of confidence, and it is the topic of the next chapter.

TWO

RUN HAPPY

When I am running well I am happy,
and when I am happy I run well.

—Ian Thompson

IN THE SUMMER OF 2007, I served as a support crewmember for Dean Karnazes in the Badwater Ultramarathon. Known as the world's toughest footrace, Badwater starts on the floor of Death Valley, typically in 120 degrees of heat, and finishes 135 miles away, halfway up Mt. Whitney. I drove down from my home in northern California on the Saturday before the Monday race start. I found Dean in his room at the camplike resort that served as race headquarters. It was unbearably hot outside. I was surprised to discover that it was unbearably hot inside Dean's room, too.

"I keep the AC off to acclimatize," he said brightly.

It was strange to finally meet him in person. For the preceding few months, I had been helping Dean write *50/50*, his second book and the follow-up to the runaway best seller *Ultramarathon Man*, which had elevated his status from cult figure in the ultrarunning counterculture to international celebrity, *Tonight Show* guest, ESPY Award winner, and one of *Time* magazine's 100 most influential people in the world. I had seen him on *Good Morning America*. I had talked to him by phone dozens of times. But I had never before met him face-to-face.

Badwater participants are allowed to have four supporters in two vehicles, and that's what Dean had. One of the major duties of supporters is to take turns pacing their runner. Because Dean had hired me to write in his voice for *50/50*, which chronicled his running of 50 marathons in 50 days, one in each of the 50 American states, the previous summer, I wanted to experience the event through Dean's eyes and get a small taste of what it's like to be the real Forrest Gump, so I volunteered to take the first shift in pacing Dean, when the sun was still high and we were still below sea level, baking in nature's perfect terrestrial furnace.

I ran 25 miles with him. Our pace was slow, about 10 minutes per mile, and we stopped once every mile, where the support vans awaited us with cold drinks, ice baths, and whatever else we might need. I have always gotten my kicks from trying to run fast over moderate distances. Dean gets his kicks from running far—very far—which is necessarily done slowly. Initially, as I ran beside Dean, I chafed against the dawdling pace, despite the intense heat, but after a few miles my body fell into a comfortable rhythm and my mind found a happy place, divided between absorption in the physical experience and faraway thoughts.

Another crewmember took my place just as Dean was starting the first big climb of the race. Things started to go south for him soon afterward. His body mutinied, and he was forced to walk for long stretches. His one-mile pit stops grew longer and longer. Then they turned weird. Becoming delirious with fatigue and sleep deprivation, Dean became fixated on the idea that his wardrobe was the cause of his collapse. He changed his shoes at one stop, his shirt at another, his shorts at yet another. He requested items of clothing that were packed deep inside his luggage in one of the vans— stuff he had never intended to use in the race and did not really need now. When those measures failed, he asked one of my fellow crewmembers for *his* shorts. Then he asked us to make new clothing. We had to cut off the legs of a pair of sweatpants to make shorts out of them.

After a few hours of this madness, our most experienced crewmember, Jason Koop of Carmichael Training Systems, forced Dean to take a seven-minute nap. (Apparently, seven minutes of sleep are just enough to restore the body and mind to seminormal functioning under such circumstances.) Dean did get a bit of a bounce from the brief enforced slumber, but he never fully recovered. It was a bad race. He finished 10th—disappointing for a man who had won the race three years before. Afterward, I teasingly informed him that the race winner, Valmir Nunes, had not so much as changed his socks en route to setting a new Badwater course record of 22:51:29.

We crewmembers had a lot of time to talk in the support vehicles during the race, and after Dean hit the wall, we spent some of that time speculating about the cause of his poor performance. Koop, who had accompanied Dean throughout the Endurance 50, suggested that Dean simply ran too much to achieve peak performance in any single event.

"He doesn't even really train," Koop said. "He just goes from one event to the next without any rest or any chance to focus his training on one race."

These words made sense to me at the time, and they still make sense on one level. But upon reflection I decided I was not so sure that Dean would perform better if he took a different approach to his running. He loves the utterly original approach to running that he has created. He enjoys running as much as any runner has ever enjoyed running, and any change he might make to his formula for the sake of performing better in this or that race would almost certainly hurt his performance in the long run, because it would make running less fun for him, and I believe that enjoyment and performance are tightly connected.

DEAN KARNAZES, JOYFUL RUNNER

Throughout his life as a runner, Dean Karnazes has been exceptionally insistent on running in the way that gives him the greatest enjoyment. It just so happens that his way of enjoying running is very different from that of most competitive runners—even from that of most ultrarunners—and yet remarkably successful. In *50/50*, Dean said, concerning a crucial stage in his development as a runner:

> As much as I enjoyed taking part in structured events like the Western States 100, they were no longer enough for me. I felt a deep yearning to go even further, to break free from the wildly loose confines of periodic course markers, sporadic aid stations, and occasional support found in most ultramarathons, and to try something really over-the-top. So I started doing my own thing. I ran a 199-mile, 12-person relay

race alone as a team of one. I'd sometimes run unsupported through the mountains for days. Sure, it was extreme, and it was unusual, but it was me, and it made me happy. It was what I loved to do, my way of following my heart. That's probably why I'm still at it.

Dean has never followed a structured training plan in his life because, he said, "it reduces the run to a training stimulus, and I want it to be an adventure." He runs 80 to 120 miles in a typical week, but not the way others do. One day he might run 5 miles, the next day 50 miles—whatever he has time for. He does not follow the principle of alternating hard days and easy days; instead, he runs more or less as hard as he can relative to the distance he covers every time he heads out the door. He competes in races and participates in other noncompetitive running events almost every weekend (and often during the week) year round. He does all of these things because he enjoys them, and indeed the pursuit of enjoyment is his one and only explicit training principle, which, he and I agree, should be every runner's guiding principle. "If you don't enjoy training, you're doing something wrong," he says.

Being competitive, chasing personal records, and relying on structured training are not inimical to the objective of maximizing enjoyment in running. To the contrary, most serious runners enjoy running most when they are competitive, obsess over their workout and race times, and base their training on proven, conventional practices. But most runners fail to consciously manipulate their approach to running to maximize their enjoyment. This failure limits their improvement, which further limits their enjoyment, because improvement is the greatest source of enjoyment in running.

The feeling of enjoyment in running is one of the best clues that what you are doing is working, and the feelings of boredom and burnout are among the best clues that what you are doing is not working and should be changed. Furthermore, the sense that you would enjoy doing something new in your training is intuition's way of telling you that taking a leap of faith and trying that something are very likely to help you improve.

Let me be clear: You should pursue enjoyment in running not only for its own sake (because enjoyment is enjoyable), but also for the sake of getting faster (or going farther, if you are cut in the mold of Dean Karnazes). Indeed,

Dean might not be the best example of the benefits of training for enjoyment because he is not a typical performance runner, but there are countless other, more typical examples available. You might be quite shocked to learn how many successful elite runners base important training decisions on emotional, rather than physiological, rationales.

Take Torsten Abel, a German professional triathlete and coach to world champion triathlete Leanda Cave, among others. Like every other serious triathlete, Abel includes bricks, or combined bike-run workouts, in his training. But whereas most coaches urge triathletes to do these workouts often, to maximize the physiological adaptations needed for efficient off-the-bike running in races, Abel puts off this type of training as long as possible—until just six or eight weeks before a major race. Why? "It's like shaving my legs," he told me. "When I shave my legs, I get so excited I get goose bumps, because it means it's almost time to race. It's the same with brick workouts. I wait to do them until I can't wait any longer, and that makes them very special and exciting."

Abel does not tell the athletes he coaches to automatically do the same, however. He just encourages them to do whatever gets them most excited about their training, regardless of whether it defies physiological common sense. "You have to enjoy it," he said. "Having fun gives you wings, and then there's no stopping you."

SLAVES TO RUNNING

Very few runners allow themselves to pursue enjoyment as freely and instinctively as Dean Karnazes and Torsten Abel do. As Dean and Torsten tell their stories, it's hard to know which came first—enjoyment or improvement. Too many runners lose sight of enjoyment and become slaves to training. This is why so many runners fail to realize their full performance potential. Brian Sell might serve as an example of a running career limited by insufficient fun. Sell accomplished quite a lot in his career. He finished fourth in the 2006 Boston Marathon and sixth in the 2006 Chicago Marathon with a sizzling personal-best time of 2:10:47. The following year, he finished third in the U.S. Olympic Trials Marathon and realized his dream of competing in the 2008 Beijing Olympics. After Beijing, however, Sell showed signs of intensifying burnout, his performances tanked, and in 2009 he retired at just 31 years of age, a shell of his former self.

It's entirely possible that Sell's premature physical and mental decline as a runner was a result of his approach to training. Sell was coached by brothers Keith and Kevin Hanson, who come from the ultrahigh-mileage school of running. There isn't anything inherently wrong with ultrahigh mileage; it's just not right for every runner, and I suspect it was never right for Sell. Yes, he accomplished a lot with high mileage, but he might have accomplished more and certainly maintained his peak performance level longer if he had listened to and heeded the feeling of burnout that cast a shadow on some of his interviews over the course of his decline.

"I can definitely feel, I think, my age creeping up on me," he said in one of these interviews, which took place when he was 30, shortly before the Beijing Olympics. "In the mornings, it seems like every year I have to get up about ten minutes earlier than I did the year before just to get warmed up and ready to go. But as far as feeling fresh, it's always been just a kind of calloused, dull feeling in the middle of these 160-, 170-mile weeks where I never feel great but I never feel like just stopping and walking either. Yeah, it's been about the same for the past five years or so."

These are not the words of a man who is enjoying his training. When I read them, I thought that Sell would not run particularly well in the Olympics, and he did not. But he was so committed to his high-mileage training and so accustomed to tuning out the voice of intuition within him that he changed nothing afterward. As he prepared for the Boston Marathon the following spring, he was interviewed again, and he sounded much the same, maybe worse.

"I'm definitely feeling wearier," he said. "The beginning of this segment was one of the hardest ones that I've had in a while. I think it was a little bit of a mental letdown after the Olympics and so forth. Physically, too, in dog years, I'm 60 years old as far as mileage goes. I mean, I've been averaging 140 miles a week for the last five, six, seven years. I'm definitely feeling that I'm getting towards the end in my career here."

Any runner reading these words might surmise that Sell would not run particularly well in Boston. I don't intend to pick on Brian Sell. He is an accomplished runner, and he got some great results from his training. I could be wrong to speculate that Sell could have run better, or run well longer, by changing up his training so that he enjoyed it more. But I don't think so.

It bears mentioning that while Sell felt weary and old at age 30 in the Olympic Marathon, the winner of the women's marathon in Beijing, Constantina Dita-Tomescu, whom I will mention again in Chapter 4, was 38, and the silver medalist behind her, Catherine Ndereba, was 36. Interestingly, Ndereba, the most accomplished female marathon runner in history, runs less mileage than most elite marathoners and significantly less than Sell, peaking at 100 miles per week. In a 2007 interview for the New York Road Runners Web site, Ndereba said: "What I do is what is comfortable. I can only handle what I can handle. It doesn't bother me that my opponents are running 120 or 130 miles. There are different amounts of mileage that each individual can handle. . . . If I go over 100 miles in one week, the following week I feel like, 'Wow, I'm done.'"

The key difference between Brian Sell and Catherine Ndereba is not the amount of mileage their individual bodies can handle. It is how they respond to the messages that their bodies send them. When in the past Ndereba ran more than 100 miles per week, she felt uncomfortable and deemed that feeling unacceptable, so she set a 100-miles-per-week cap on her running volume. Judging by his own remarks, Sell is not any more comfortable running 140 to 160 miles per week than Ndereba was at 105 or 110. But apparently the idea that he would run better if his training made him less miserable did not cross his mind. Ndereba kept her training enjoyable and has kept running at her peak level into her late 30s. Sell seems to have allowed himself to not enjoy his training much for weeks or months at a time, and his prime ended before his 20s did.

ENJOYMENT AND IMPROVEMENT

To further illustrate the correlation between performance and enjoyment, imagine we could conduct an experiment as follows: A sports psychologist puts the members of an adult running team through a performance test such as a 5 km time trial or a VO_2max (maximum rate of oxygen consumption during exercise) test once every 4 weeks for a total period of 20 weeks as the runners engage in their normal training. He also asks all of the runners to keep detailed training logs that include an enjoyment rating for each run and an overall training enjoyment rating at the end of each week. I would bet my life savings that the sports psychologist leading this study would find a very strong mathematical correlation between the rate of improvement in fitness and the level of training enjoyment for individual runners. And I believe he might also find that this correlation was causal in both directions. That is, he might observe that increasing or high levels of enjoyment were as likely to predict improved performance as vice versa, indicating that enjoyment influences fitness improvement as much as fitness improvement influences enjoyment.

MIND-BODY RUNNING

Do more of what you enjoy most and less of what you enjoy least in training. The feeling of enjoyment is your body's way of telling you that your training is working.

The real-world experience of every runner conforms to this projection. In my 20-plus years as a runner, I have always known my enjoyment of running to grow or shrink as my performance climbed or declined, and I have never known a competitive runner who enjoyed his or her running when it was going badly.

Those runners who perform most consistently well over the long term are those who insist on enjoying their running and do not allow coaches, performance pressures, or any other controllable factors to spoil their fun. There may be no better example than Joan Benoit Samuelson. She won her first Boston Marathon at age 22, won an Olympic gold medal at 27, set an American marathon record at 28, finished ninth in the 2000 Olympic Trials Marathon at age 43, qualified for the Olympic Trials Marathon again at age 50, and set an age-group national marathon record of 2:49:09 at age 52. Throughout her long and illustrious running life, Samuelson has always done things her way. She turned down an opportunity to relocate to the running mecca of Eugene, Oregon, and continued to live and train in her home state of Maine, despite the harsh winters, because she was comfortable there. "Becoming a champion requires that you are comfortable when and where you are training," she said in a 2007 speech at the Maine Running Company. We will return to this important idea of comfort zones in Chapter 4.

Samuelson stepped back from racing in her very prime, even forgoing the opportunity to defend her Olympic gold medal in 1988, to have children because she wanted to be a mother. In her peak years she seldom trained with other runners, despite the purported benefits of group training, because she had more fun training alone. And as she often says, she has always trained "by the seat of my pants." Even in her finest hours, her training schedules were never more specific than calling for a long run on a certain day, a tempo run on another day, and so forth. The details were always filled in on the fly. If she felt good, she ran longer or faster, and if she felt lousy, she ran shorter or slower. Whatever felt right at the moment was what she did.

Running is the simplest of pursuits for Samuelson, all about the joy of the activity itself and the purity of mano-a-mano competition. She has never used a heart-rate monitor. She has never even been comfortable with making money from the sport. In 2007 Samuelson watched a Division III college cross-country race and came away thinking, "That is pure sport." No scholarships, no hope of future shoe contracts, just good old-fashioned passion and competition. In her Maine Running Company speech, Samuelson said that passion is the most important characteristic of a champion. But, as she rightly pointed out, "passion cannot be instilled; it is either there or it is not."

Passion with Balance

Surprisingly, many elite runners allow their passion for running to get lost or ruined. Brian Sell is not alone in this experience. Alan Webb is perhaps the poster boy of the phenomenon. His career thus far has had two distinct happy phases and two very unhappy ones. The first happy phase was the high school years, which culminated in Webb's demolishing the U.S. national high school mile record, running 3:53.43. Then two years of poor performance set in; he suffered from excessive pre-race anxiety caused by the pressure he felt to live up to the towering standard he had set in high school. He dropped out of college after one lackluster year there, turned professional, and stopped having fun. "All of that pressure, I just got so worked up about it," Webb said in an interview. "The nerves killed me. Before a race, my stomach would be a knot. I couldn't relax, because I felt like I had to win."

Webb bottomed out at the 2003 U.S. Outdoor Track and Field Championships, where he finished 10th in the 1,500 m. A week later his appendix burst. But it was a blessing in disguise. Webb decided to take a full month off from running. He used that month for deep introspection and came out of it knowing that he still loved running and still wanted to run for all the old reasons that had nothing to do with being a professional under heavy pressure to live up to his own name. He came back strong the following year and just got better and better until, in 2007, he broke Steve Scott's 25-year-old American record in the mile, running 3:46.91.

It seemed that Webb had figured it all out and now had the kind of momentum that could not be stopped. But in 2008 he crashed to earth again, failing to qualify for the Beijing Olympics. The following autumn, after another bad year interrupted by injury, Webb abruptly left his longtime coach, Scott Raczko, and moved from Virginia to Portland, Oregon, to join Alberto Salazar's Nike Oregon Project.

A few months before that rupture occurred, I had the opportunity to interview Steve Scott. I first asked him what he had learned as a coach—Scott is now a coach at Cal State San Marcos—that he wished he had understood when he was competing. Scott talked about how his athletes treated their big races as though they were judgment day and how this self-imposed pressure made them miserable and restricted their running.

"Performance is all about relaxation," he said. "Nerves kill performance. I wish I could go back and not have that life-and-death attitude that I often brought to races."

I then asked Steve Scott what the heck was wrong with Alan Webb.

"I think he's overtrained," Scott said. "I went through the whole overtraining thing from '89 until the end of my career, so I know his frustration. In the beginning you don't think it's overtraining. And when you're overtrained, the only thing that can get you back to where you were is rest—prolonged rest. I'm talking three months, six months, maybe even a year."

Webb himself had already confessed to overtraining the previous year, but he had not given himself the sort of prolonged rest that Scott advised. Overtraining syndrome has been heavily researched, and exercise scientists have unanimously concluded that loss of enjoyment in training is the earliest reliable warning sign of the condition.[1] By the time the athlete's performance plummets and hormonal markers of overtraining emerge, it is already too late. Prolonged rest is needed. But the runner who consciously guides his or her training by the feeling of enjoyment can catch the problem early and avoid a major setback. Perhaps Alan Webb has not yet learned to adequately trust his emotions to guide his training, but in this regard I think he made a smart move in joining the Nike Oregon Project. I know from my own conversations with Alberto Salazar, who struggled with overtraining during his competitive career, that he believes strongly in the importance of enjoyment in training and racing and in keeping the fun in running by maintaining a healthy perspective. Salazar told me, "I tell my runners, 'This is just a small part of life. I'm going to do my best for you, and you do your best, and whatever happens, happens. It's not the end of the world, no matter what.'"

Although this may seem paradoxical, keeping perspective and balancing running with the rest of life are good for a runner's enjoyment of running and for running performance. Such perspective and balance—as exhibited in her decision to stay put in Maine, for example—were keys to Joan Samuelson's long-term success. My all-time favorite quote about the enjoyment-performance connection in running comes from Ian Thompson, a great British marathon runner of the 1970s, who said, "When I am running well I am happy, and when I am happy I run well." Here the enjoyment-improvement formula encompasses all of life, and correctly so. Runners not only train and race better when they enjoy their training, and enjoy their training more when they perform well, but they are also better partners in their relationships and more effective workers when their running is going well, and they run poorly when they are not getting along with their partners or their jobs are not going well.

Proof and Performance

The scientific research on exercise enjoyment teaches us what we already know from real-world experience, which is that enjoyment and performance go hand in hand. One finding of the research is that the more a person enjoys exercise, the more likely she is to continue exercising. In one study, Beth Lewis, an exercise and sports psychologist at the University of

Minnesota, had a group of sedentary adults complete a moderate-intensity workout and then a questionnaire designed to determine its effect on their mood. The participants were then encouraged to maintain a regular exercise program. Lewis found that those who most enjoyed their first workout were significantly more likely to still be exercising six months and then one year later.[2]

Interpreted more broadly, this result suggests that we invest more effort in exercise when we enjoy it. For the beginner, investing more effort means not quitting. But for the competitive runner, it means pushing just a little harder in key workouts. It's a much subtler difference than the difference between maintaining a new exercise habit and returning to the couch, but that extra 1 or 2 percent effort that the runner who is having fun in training gives in tougher training sessions may easily add up to measurable differences in races.

MIND-BODY RUNNING

Improvement makes running more enjoyable, and enjoyment stimulates improvement, so arrange your training to make your improvement more evident.

Exercise psychology has also shown that aerobic fitness is related to enjoyment of aerobic exercise. Fitter individuals enjoy exercise more than less fit persons because the balance of positive and negative affect (pleasure and pain) during exercise appears to be determined primarily by a person's proximity to exhaustion, and less fit individuals are closer to exhaustion earlier in exercise and at lower intensities. Put another way, exercise enjoyment is essentially the feeling of exercise capacity, so that the more this capacity grows (i.e., the fitter a person gets), the greater the enjoyment of exercise becomes. In a fundamental sense, the world's greatest runners are able to enjoy running more than the rest of us can. The sensation of speed is thrilling, and the feeling of running effortlessly is pleasurable. Only in the greatest runners are the thrill of speed and the pleasure of running effortlessly combined in the highest degree. Fortunately, though, all runners are equally capable of increasing their enjoyment of running by improving their fitness. Again, even though the pattern of exercise enjoyment corresponding to increased exercise enjoyment has been demonstrated only in untrained populations,[3] every experienced runner knows that this pattern applies to the trained athlete, too. Speaking for myself, I have always enjoyed running the most when my fitness level has been highest.

In this regard, running is no different from other activities, such as playing the violin and solving math problems. We most enjoy the things we do with the greatest competence. Psychologists use the term "self-efficacy" to denote the feeling of task-specific competence. The relationship between self-efficacy and enjoyment in exercise is well demonstrated. A number of studies have shown that the increase in exercise enjoyment that many people experience when they stick with a new exercise program long enough to get measurable results is largely mediated by self-efficacy.[4] In other words, people enjoy exercise more largely because they feel a greater sense of mastery of whatever form of exercise they are practicing.

Exercise self-efficacy and fitness are not identical. Whereas fitness contributes to exercise enjoyment primarily through bodily sensations, exercise self-efficacy contributes to exercise enjoyment more through objective performance feedback. This distinction is important, because it suggests that runners can consciously set up their training to provide the best and most consistent evidence of their improvement and thereby maximize their enjoyment of running, which will in turn promote further improvement. The potential for performance feedback to influence self-efficacy, and thus enjoyment, for better or worse was highlighted in an interesting study at the University of Illinois. A pool of 46 college women was separated into two groups, each of which completed a certain exercise task and received feedback on performance throughout it. Without the participants' knowledge, however, the performance feedback was manipulated so that members of one group seemed to fail miserably while members of the second group seemed to succeed gloriously. Questionnaires completed afterward revealed that members of the second group enjoyed the exercise task much more and rated their self-efficacy much higher than did members of the first group, even though the actual performance of both groups was the same.[5]

The lesson of this study is not that we can maximize self-efficacy, enjoyment, and improvement in our training by tricking ourselves into believing that we are performing better than we are—and yet the lesson is not far off from that. What the Illinois study really tells runners is that we should feel free to arrange our training in whichever way makes our improvement most evident. The one thing every runner must do is collect relevant objective performance feedback—mileage, pace, heart rate, and so forth. But it's up to the individual runner to determine the particular types of workouts and the ways of sequencing them that yield the best evidence of improvement.

A certain amount of repetition in training is required for proof of improvement. If you never perform the same workout twice—and especially if you never perform the same hard workout twice—you have no basis for apples-to-apples performance comparisons. But if there is too much repetition in your training, there is no stimulus for improvement. Also, when the variation in training is progressive in nature—for example, your long run this week is 10 miles, and your long run next week is 12 miles—that in itself is evidence of improvement. So it's important to balance repetition and progressive variation in training.

MEASURING ENJOYMENT

Alongside measuring confidence, as discussed in the previous chapter, one of the best ways to figure out the balance of repetition and variation that is right for you—as well as the optimal weekly mileage, volume of high-intensity training, frequency of recovery weeks, and so forth—is to continually monitor your enjoyment of training, because enjoyment (alongside confidence) is the primary experiential evidence that your training is effective, while lack of enjoyment is your unconscious brain's way of telling you that your training is not working.

I use a very simple system for monitoring training enjoyment in my own training; perhaps it will work for you: After completing each run, assign it an enjoyment score of 1, 2, or 3. Rate the run a "1" if it was, on balance, not enjoyable. I say "on balance" because most runs have both pleasant and unpleasant aspects. So a score of "1" indicates not that the run was completely unpleasant, but that its unpleasant moments or aspects outweighed its pleasant ones. Rate the run a "2" if it was about equally pleasant and unpleasant. Rate the run a "3" if it was, on balance, enjoyable.

It is important that you score every run, because you will need a complete data set to make accurate connections between particular training inputs (mileage, rate of mileage increase, and so forth) and this affective output. In using this system, you will quickly find that your ratings reflect how your actual feelings (of effort, fitness, and the like) during a run compare to your expectations for that run. Research has shown that exercise enjoyment is broadly determined by these types of comparisons. For example, in a study that Ross Tucker (mentioned in the previous chapter) conducted at the University of Cape Town, South Africa, runners reported their subjective rating of perceived exertion (RPE) once each minute throughout a series of moderate-intensity treadmill runs.[6] In one of these runs, they were told to run for 10 minutes, but at the end of 10 minutes they were told to run for another 10 minutes. There was a sudden spike in RPE in the 11th minute of this test. That is, when the runners' expectations for the difficulty of the workout were thwarted, it suddenly felt more difficult. In the second run, the runners were told to run for 20 minutes at the same intensity. There was no spike in RPE at any point in this second run, although it was in fact structurally identical to the first run. The only difference was that this second conformed to their expectations. The mere fact that the first workout was harder than expected made it actually harder.

> **MIND-BODY RUNNING**
>
> Rate your daily enjoyment level for each run. Also track weekly and 28-day averages. Look for the cause-effect relationships between enjoyment and running performance, and modify your training to enhance both.

This is one reason that very hard workouts can be enjoyable and easy ones can be no fun at all. A nonrunner or inexperienced runner might assume that a running program shaped by enjoyment would consist of nothing but short, slow runs. But this is not the case, because competitive runners expect the feeling of fitness and their running self-efficacy to gradually increase through the training process as they work toward a peak race, and these results will not manifest if every run is easy. Building fitness and self-efficacy requires that hard workouts be done, and with these workouts comes an expectation of suffering that actually increases the possibility that the hard workouts can be enjoyed.

In addition to scoring individual runs, create a weekly tally, and divide this number by the number of runs you complete in the week to generate a weekly average. Suppose that in a given week your Monday run is a 2, your Tuesday run is a 3, your Wednesday run is a 1, your Thursday run is a 2, your Friday run is a 2, you take Saturday off, and your Sunday run is a 3. In this case your average enjoyment index for the week is 2.17 (13 ÷ 6). Generate 28-day (monthly) enjoyment averages as well. Doing these three levels of enjoyment monitoring will help you identify different types of cause-effect patterns in your training.

There is no limit to the variety of patterns you might find. Don't let this prospect intimidate you. Just pay attention to the training input variables that matter to you, keep monitoring your enjoyment, and patterns will reveal themselves one by one. You will never even come close to identifying every factor that affects your running enjoyment, but each factor you do identify will be valuable and will be one more factor than you would have identified if you had not performed this type of analysis.

Start by trying to determine if you tend to enjoy certain types of workouts more than others. If you do, think about why this is the case and if anything needs to be done about it. The right answer will seldom be obvious. A pattern of not enjoying a particular type of workout as much as others may indicate that your expectations for it are unrealistic. It may indicate that you are doing that type of workout too often (and thus ceasing to benefit from it) or not often enough (and thus failing to get comfortable with the sort of stress it imposes). Start with your first hunch, test it out, and if it doesn't work, move on to the next hunch. It is a blind process, but one in which you are guaranteed to learn lessons that will help you get more enjoyment out of your training and better results.

No pattern is too trivial to note. For example, in my own use of this system I discovered that I never experienced a 3 (enjoyable) run right after a 1 (bad) run. In the best case, there was always at least one 2 that served as a bridge between them. Since discovering this pattern, I have been able to adjust my expectations for the next run or two after a bad run so that I don't freak out as much when they aren't great.

Some of the most valuable patterns you will find will be on the macro level. Pay attention to how your enjoyment level changes as the training process unfolds. After monitoring your enjoyment level through a few training cycles, you might find that your enjoyment level begins to slide after, say, 16 weeks of focused training for a peak race. If there are indications that your performance plateaus at approximately the same time, you have pretty good evidence that you need to shorten your training cycles to avoid peaking early and becoming "stale" before race day.

Be aware that dips in enjoyment are not always bad. A dip is bad only if it is connected to a dip in performance. While your performance will never improve according to your expectations during protracted periods of low running enjoyment, suffering through a brief period of low enjoyment now may enable you to enjoy training more later and perform better. Many competitive runners benefit from periods of overreaching, when they train a little harder than their bodies can handle but then cut back and recover just before the excessive training causes a precipitous performance decline. Because of the fatigue that steadily accumulates during overreaching, these periods are typically unpleasant, but when they are done right, there is a big payoff of enjoyment and performance improvement on the other side.

Lastly, do not limit yourself with preconceptions about where enjoyment can and cannot lead you in your training. Who cares if it leads you to run more or less or slower (except in races, of course) or faster than anyone else you know? Always trust that the more you enjoy your running, the better you will run. There is a Portuguese expression I learned from Dean Karnazes that captures this idea perfectly: "Who runs for pleasure never gets tired."

THREE

FINDING A MAGIC FORMULA

There is a magic formula.... It's just that
the magic is different for everyone.

—Keith Dowling

FIVE MILES INTO THE 2008 NCAA Division I Cross Country Championships, Oklahoma State University freshman German Fernandez suddenly
dropped to the ground as if he had been shot and began writhing in agony,
grabbing his right Achilles tendon. He took a few weeks off from running
and underwent intensive rehabilitation.

Fernandez had only a few weeks of light training in his legs when he
ran his next race, an indoor mile. He broke the junior world record for that
event, running 3:56.50. (He broke that mark a month later, running 3:55.02.)
All observers were shocked by the performance, including Fernandez and
his coach, Dave Smith. "He looked as smooth as ever," Smith gushed after
the race. Although it was already well established that Fernandez was a su-
premely gifted runner (he had broken a long-standing national high school
record for 2 miles the previous spring), no one knew that he had a second
gift layered on top of the first: the gift of gaining fitness extremely quickly in
response to training. Even among the very few runners who can run as fast
as Fernandez in peak shape, only a small minority are able to get in shape
that fast. The genes that give individuals natural talent for running certainly
overlap with those that make them responsive to training, but they are distinct. Only the rarest of talents have both sets of genes in full measure.

Scientists are only beginning to identify the genes that influence individual responses to exercise training. For example, researchers have identified a polymorphism in a gene called INSIG2 (a genetic polymorphism is one form among two or more possible forms that a particular gene can take) that tends to limit muscular adaptations to resistance training in men.[1] We might call this the "hard-gainer gene" because men with it have a harder time gaining muscle mass and strength through weightlifting. (Why such a gene exists, I don't know, but it does.) Other genetic polymorphisms are known to have the opposite effect.

Traditional studies in exercise science that look at the group effects of exercise protocols often mask the tremendous degree of variation in individual responses to training because they highlight averaged results. A good example of this phenomenon is the HERITAGE Family Study, which investigated the effects of a 20-week walking program on VO_2max in a large population of previously sedentary men and women.[2] The average increase in VO_2max after 20 weeks was 16 percent. However, in some individuals the increase was as great as 40 percent, whereas in a few others there was virtually no change in VO_2max.

Because the study population consisted of 481 persons from 98 two-generation families, the researchers were able to generate evidence of a genetic influence in responsiveness to low-intensity aerobic training. Specifically, the "responders" to training, who experienced large increases in VO_2max, tended to be from the same family but were not necessarily the individuals who had high VO_2max values to begin with. In other words, the capacity to adapt to training is genetically determined but is not influenced in the same way as the genetically determined baseline. Not only do genes influence the starting level for aerobic capacity, but they also independently affect how responsive the cardiorespiratory system is to endurance training. This may explain why my friend Mike ran no better than I did when we were both untrained, yet he got fitter in response to training much faster than I did.

Genetic diversity affects more than just the general VO_2max response to aerobic exercise. It is also known to affect the individual response to altitude training. In 2005 researchers from the University of Heidelberg, Germany, found significant interindividual differences in how much blood levels of erythropoietin, the hormone responsible for generating new red blood cells, increased among elite-level junior swimmers during three weeks of altitude training.[3] These differences are definitely genetically rooted.

Individual differences in the rate of recovery from exercise training are also gene based. A 2007 study published in the *Journal of Applied Physiology* reported that individuals with certain polymorphisms in the IGF-II gene region lost more strength, experienced higher levels of muscle soreness, and suffered higher levels of muscle damage after weightlifting than did persons lacking those polymorphisms.[4]

Among the many other physiological responses to exercise where a high degree of variation between individuals is seen is weight loss. Genes appear to control both metabolic and behavioral responses to aerobic exercise in ways that facilitate weight loss in some and inhibit it in others.[5] Some scientists believe that we will eventually know enough about all of the genes that influence the body's adaptations to exercise training to develop customized exercise regimens based on the individual athlete's or exerciser's genetic makeup. Nice idea, but it will be a long time before we have the capability to effectively individualize training prescriptions based on individual genomics, and I think it likely that genetic analysis will never surpass real-world experience as a means of determining what works and what does not work for an individual endurance athlete, as genes do not tell the whole story. Nevertheless, most runners fall far short of exploiting the full power of real-world experience to develop their personal optimal training formulas. I believe this is true in part because it takes a lot of mindfulness, creativity, and self-trust to learn from training experience and apply the lessons learned, and in part because the average runner does not understand just how differently individual athletes respond to the same training practices and hence how important it is to find her or his own recipe.

As 2:13 marathoner Keith Dowling said, "Some say there's no magic formula. I say there is. It's just that the magic is different for everyone." I believe that even most seriously competitive runners fail to realize their full performance potential primarily because they fall short of developing their optimal training formula. The most successful runners are not always more gifted than those who finish a few steps behind them in races. Often their true advantage is that, whether by luck or by their own wherewithal, they have found their best way to train and thus get more out of their talent.

One of the best ways to appreciate just how disparate optimal training formulas can be is to consider the training methods of world beaters whose optimal training formula is especially unusual. Ethiopian runner Tirunesh Dibaba, who holds the women's world records for 5,000 m on the track and 15 km on the road, is such an athlete. Dibaba trains far more lightly than almost every other world-class runner of her generation. Her longest runs are 80 minutes. She hits the track twice a week, but her interval sessions are almost shockingly mild—just a handful of short intervals (150 to 400 m) at very high speeds with short recoveries. This formula obviously works for her, because no woman in history has ever run faster than she does at her specialty distance. But her closest rivals would probably not move any closer to Dibaba by copying her methods. They have their own magic formulas. Whether or not they ever discover them is another matter.

CONNECTING CAUSE AND EFFECT

How do you discover your own optimal training formula? You continually pay close attention to your training and your body, connecting cause and effect so that you can then discard training patterns that yield poor results and retain training patterns that yield good results. This is easier said than done, as there are myriad factors that affect how you feel and perform in training and races, but the three most important factors by far are overall volume, high-intensity training, and periodization system.

There are two distinct types of results that you can use to evaluate the effectiveness of your training and make your training more effective. The first type is your performance in workouts and, especially, in races. A training method that makes you faster is clearly more effective than one that does not. Likewise, a training method that causes your performance to improve steadily over a long period of time is more effective than one that causes your performance to improve for only a short time before it stops yielding results.

The second type is affective results, or how your training makes you feel. In particular, as discussed in the preceding chapters, be mindful of how much you enjoy your training and of how your training affects your confidence. These feelings indicate the proper direction for your future training as reliably as hard pace data do, provided you trust and know how to interpret your feelings. A new movement in exercise psychology advocates a self-guided approach to regulating exercise intensity on the grounds that this approach yields better long-term outcomes than using prescribed exercise intensities based on one-size-fits-all scientific rules of effectiveness. David Williams at Brown University and other researchers have pointed out that people enjoy exercise most when they choose their own pace, they exercise most consistently when they most enjoy exercise, and they get the greatest results when they exercise most consistently.[6] Thus, there is no need to prescribe exercise intensity with scientifically based guidelines, and most people self-select exercise intensities that are within physiology-based American College of Sports Medicine guidelines, anyway.[7]

Now, competitive runners are different from the overweight, sedentary, and elderly populations that are the targets of this self-paced exercise movement—but not so different. Obviously, an overweight and previously sedentary individual will not self-pace her way toward developing a personal training regimen that includes lactate interval sessions, threshold runs, and other such workouts arranged in a progressive series that culminates in a planned, short-term performance peak. In other words, the noncompetitive exerciser who follows the path of maximum enjoyment will not reinvent the training methods commonly used by competitive runners, which are those methods that have tended to yield the best performance results over many generations of trial and error undertaken by runners all around the world. Nor would the individual competitive runner reinvent these methods within a single lifetime if guided only by his affective response to methods initially chosen arbitrarily. Instead, the individual competitive runner must use his emotions and performance results together to choose his way forward in training. This process occurs in two steps.

Step 1. Use your emotions to select a specific approach to training from among the various proven methods. Avoid the temptation to reinvent the proverbial wheel; there is more than one effective way to train. Naturally, when you are just beginning as a runner, you don't have personal performance results for determining what works for you and what doesn't. But you do have available the collective performance results codified in today's standard training methods. While there is a family resemblance in the training methods used by all successful runners at every level of the sport, there are great differences at the level of details. Here your emotions become valuable tools in selecting the specific methods you wish to try first, before you have put them to the test and get performance results from them, good or bad. I believe that the specific training options that are most appealing to you are very likely to be those that work best for you physiologically, because that feeling of preference is a product of your body's unconscious intelligence and self-knowledge. What's more, simply believing in your approach to training is probably as important as a good fit between your training methods and your individual physiology, especially when you are choosing specific methods from among a general pool of methods that are proved to work generally for runners. If you start your training journey by trying out the methods that best match your personal preferences, you are likely to train with a greater sense of belief in the effectiveness of your approach than you would if you started your training journey by blindly aping the training practices of a certain coach, runner, or other authority, and that belief will be self-fulfilling.

> ## MIND-BODY RUNNING
>
> *To determine which training methods work well for you, pay attention to two types of feedback: performance (workout split times, race times, etc.) and affective (fluctuations in your training enjoyment and confidence levels).*

Step 2. Pay attention to both performance and affective results. Use them to adjust (or, if need be, overhaul) your approach throughout your development as a runner. As important as I believe affective training results to be, they are no more important than performance results and should never be used apart from performance results, unless you decide you no longer care about your running performance. Just as research by exercise psychologists has shown that some exercisers self-select exercise intensities that are too low (we've all seen those folks who are barely moving as they read magazines on fitness club elliptical trainers) or too high to produce optimal results, competitive runners may fall into comfortable training habits that do not yield optimal results if they rely too much on affect and not enough on the stopwatch in shaping their training approach.

TRAINING VARIABLES

The two-step process for finding your magic formula applies to all three of the major training variables that define a runner's magic formula within the parameters of the proven methods of what works for all runners. You will first rely on a sense of preference and then on a combination of affective and performance results to determine whether you are a high-volume or moderate-volume runner, a runner who uses high-intensity work heavily or sparingly, and a runner who uses the Lydiard method or the nonlinear method of periodization.

It is beyond the scope of this chapter to define the general parameters of proven training methods. Instead, my focus here is on helping you choose how best to manipulate the three most important training variables toward the end of developing your personal, optimal training formula. I will have much more to say about the broader, inviolable laws of effective training in Chapter 6, where I will show you how to train effectively without planning ahead—something you can do only if you understand the key principles of training.

Overall Volume

There are two general philosophies of training volume, which we might call minimalism and maximalism. The minimalist philosophy is summed up in celebrated triathlon coach Joe Friel's injunction, "Do the minimum amount of training necessary to achieve your goals." By contrast, the maximalist philosophy says, "Do as much volume as your body can handle" or, alternatively, "Keep increasing your volume until you stop improving."

Both philosophies sound reasonable. But they are contradictory. So which one is better? I think you can guess my answer to that question: It depends on the individual. Minimalism works best for some athletes and maximalism for others, while still others find an ideal spot somewhere in between. Start the process of determining the approach to volume selection that works best for you by embracing the philosophy that is most appealing to you. If you like the efficiency and risk avoidance promised by minimalism, start there. If you like the promise of ongoing improvement and freedom from self-imposed limits that may come with the maximalist approach, start there. Minimalism and maximalism are personality types as much as they are training approaches. Start with the approach that matches your personality.

From that point onward, it's all about experimentation. You must experiment to find out how little training suffices to take you to your goals. You must experiment to find out how much training your body can handle. It is very likely that the experimental process will move you toward minimalism from maximalism and vice versa. For example, suppose you achieve an initial goal using a minimalist approach. Will you not then set a more ambitious goal? And will you not have to at least consider increasing your training volume to achieve it? Likewise, many an experiment with high volume ends in injury and overtraining and encourages the wise athlete to be more conservative in the future.

Because of such realities, a runner who trains by the maximalist philosophy is not always a high-mileage runner, and a runner who trains by the minimalist philosophy is not always a low-mileage runner. The minimalist and maximalist philosophies define an approach to mileage selection but do not determine the results of the experiment. If you train by the maximalist philosophy, you purposely run the most miles your body can benefit from, but your individual physiology may ultimately determine that this ceiling is relatively low. Likewise, if you train by the minimalist philosophy, you run only enough miles to attain your goals, but if you are ambitious in your goals and your body is durable, you may nevertheless end up running quite a lot. What's more important than the volume of running you do is simply knowing the running mileage that works best for you because you have paid attention to the performance and affective results you get from various running volumes. Also, consciously embracing a minimalist or maximalist philosophy will improve your results by strengthening your belief in your training.

Whether minimalists or maximalists, all beginning runners are necessarily low-mileage runners, because the body is not initially able to tolerate high running mileage. It is important for the novice runner with a maximalist bent to understand not only that it takes many years for the body to develop its ultimate mileage absorption capacity, but also that the first 20 or 40 miles per week yield far greater results than any additional mileage. Meb Keflezighi won several California state high school titles in the early 1990s on 25 to 35 miles per week. Not until he was in his mid-30s did he reach his lifetime peak volume of 130 miles per week, because he could not have handled such volume earlier in his career. He knows this because he tried a few times and always got injured.

MIND-BODY RUNNING

To find your magic formula, determine your optimal average weekly running mileage, the best use of high-intensity training for you, and whether you prefer a traditional or nonlinear approach to periodizing your training.

Some runners can increase their mileage faster than others, but even the most determined maximalist must be prepared to work many years toward reaching a lifetime maximum. On the flip side, minimalists sometimes need to be cautioned against feeling obligated to run more than they feel comfortable doing because they assume that a certain volume level is required to attain a certain level of performance in running. Grete Waitz won the 1978 New York City Marathon, setting a world record in the process, having never previously run farther than 12 miles. Steve Jones broke the marathon world record and set a personal-best time of 2:07:13 in the mid-1980s on fewer than 100 miles per week.

While these examples should give confidence to the minimalist-minded runner who feels most comfortable on a moderate-mileage program, they should not be taken as evidence that any runner can realize his full potential on relatively low mileage. There are countless examples of runners who report having experienced major performance breakthroughs after taking their running volume beyond a certain threshold—sometimes a very high threshold. My former high school running rival Kevin Beck, who much later coached me for a while, built his running mileage to an average level of 140 miles per week—something very few subelite runners even contemplate doing. But his maximalist approach yielded personal-best times of 1:08:29

for the half marathon and 2:24:17 for the marathon—significant improvements on the times he had achieved on lower mileage.

Finally, it must be noted, however obvious the point, that optimal running volume varies by race distance. Collective trial and error have demonstrated that runners get better results in shorter races when they do a fairly large amount of high-intensity running, and because high-intensity running is exponentially more stressful than slower running, it limits the total volume of running that can be absorbed. While relatively few elite marathon runners run fewer than 100 miles per week, plenty of elite 5,000 m runners do. Thus, even as a volume maximalist, if you never race farther than 10K, you should take advantage of collective learning and not waste your time really pushing to maximize your running volume at the expense of high-intensity training. You may choose to run more than most 5K and 10K runners do, but you will never run your best 5Ks and 10Ks on what amounts to marathon training.

In practice, the training mileage of most runners is determined by personal preference as much as by physiological factors. Most runners run less than they could and would run better if they ran more, but they prefer not to run more, generally because they deem the small performance boost they might get from additional running to be not worth the additional time and suffering. Thus, in the real world, a runner's habitual mileage says as much about his or her level of "seriousness" as it does about whether that training load is optimal. In fact, this practice of self-limiting is so common that it never crosses the minds of many runners to train more than they do.

In Chapter 9, which deals with injuries, Table 9.1 (page 192) presents typical running mileages for runners of different levels of seriousness. Its purpose is to show you the minimum amount of running you should expect to be able to do without an unacceptable frequency of injury. The table is relevant to the present context too, but I chose not to place it here because I want to encourage you not to place an artificially low ceiling on your running mileage, as I believe many runners do, because of the existing norms. There is nothing wrong with deciding you are not serious enough about running to really push the limit of your mileage tolerance, but I don't want to see you run less just because nobody ever suggested, explicitly or implicitly, that you could run more.

Doubling in Running

Most elite runners double, or run twice a day most days, whereas few amateur runners do. Should you? There's a simple rule to use for deciding whether to double: If you plan to consistently run more than 70 miles per week, double at least once or twice a week. The rationale behind this rule is that your training schedule must include some easy runs, and if you try to pack more than 70 miles into just six or seven runs each week, none of those runs can be very easy. If you wish, you can double on a schedule of fewer than 70 miles per week, but it only really becomes necessary when you run more.

As you continue to add mileage to your weekly schedule, continue to add doubles as necessary to keep your average run distance from creeping above 10 miles. So, for example, if you run 100 miles a week, you should run at least 10 times.

Ease into doubling by inserting one or two very short, easy runs into your schedule. Gradually increase the distance of these runs, and add more doubles until you reach your weekly mileage target, but keep the pace easy in all of these extra runs. As a rule, try to avoid performing two hard runs in a single day. Some runners do an easy run in the morning and a longer and/or faster run in the evening. Others do the opposite. It's a matter of personal preference.

High-Intensity Training

There is great individual variation in how runners respond to high-intensity training and in the amount of high-intensity running that individual runners are able to absorb before burning out. There are four major factors that influence these capacities: age, running experience, total training volume, and individual physiology. Independent of running experience, young runners respond more quickly to high-intensity training and are able to absorb more such training than older runners are. My Running .Competitor.com colleague Sean McKeon, a 14:50 5,000 m runner in college, recalls running two interval workouts and two races every week in high school and handling that load just fine. Elite running coach Brad Hudson believes that youth runners not only can handle high-intensity running better than older runners but also should place the greatest emphasis on speed training because it establishes a foundation of neuromuscular fitness that becomes increasingly difficult to establish as a runner ages. Hudson says teenage runners may feel free to run at least moderately hard as often as they please.

However, independently of age, accumulated running experience increases a runner's capacity to absorb high-intensity running but not responsiveness to it. For this reason, beginning runners of all ages should exercise some restraint in their exposure to high-intensity training. Riverbank (California) High School cross-country coach Bruce Edwards had this idea in mind when he strictly limited the amount of high-intensity training that he allowed his star athlete German Fernandez (who set a national high school 2-mile record of 8:34.23) to do. Edwards was probably more conservative than necessary, as most young runners, because of their youth, are able to train at high intensities frequently without ill consequence. They must be restrained only from trying to perform the epic high-intensity workouts that more seasoned runners are able to handle and benefit from. (One example of a workout that is not fit for the inexperienced is legendary University of Oregon coach Bill Dellinger's famous 30-40 workout, in which the runner completes alternating 30-second and 40-second 200 m segments on a track to failure: that is, until he can no longer run a 30-second 200.)

Beyond a certain point, the more total mileage you run, the less high-intensity training your body can handle. This is the case because the body can absorb only so much training stress, and both volume and intensity contribute to training stress. It is for this reason that those successful elite runners who most emphasize high-intensity work in their training maintain less total volume than the majority of their peers. For example, Maggie Vessey, one of the fastest American female 800 m runners in history, runs only 45 miles in a typical week but does high-intensity running as often as five times per week. Because longer races demand greater total volume, runners specializing in shorter events can and should do more high-intensity training than those training for longer events, and likewise any individual runner should adjust her high-intensity workload downward when moving from shorter to longer races and vice versa.

The most interesting and important factor affecting individual responses to high-intensity training is physiology. The specific physiological variables that account for such responses include muscle fiber type distribution, testosterone levels, and so forth, but it is not important for the runner to know these elements of his physiology. All runners need to know is how their bodies actually respond to high-intensity training. There are four basic types of runners in this regard.

Type 1: Responds to high-intensity training quickly but burns out quickly. An example of this type of runner is 2008 Olympian Jorge Torres, who, when he was coached by Brad Hudson (before moving over to Steve Jones), waited until he was just a few weeks out from important races to take on hard speed work.

Type 2: Responds to high-intensity training quickly and can handle a lot. An example of this type of runner is steeplechaser Anthony Famiglietti, the title of whose self-produced DVD *Run like Hell* captures the essence of his attitude toward training. Famiglietti is perhaps a good example of how personality may determine the optimal approach to high-intensity training as much as physiology does.

Type 3: Responds to high-intensity training slowly but burns out quickly. Brad Hudson himself—who was a 2:13 marathoner before he became a coach—was this type of runner. "High intensity did nothing for me," he told me. "I didn't respond to it, and it just destroyed me."

Type 4: Responds to high-intensity training slowly and can handle a lot. Former 5,000 m American record holder Bob Kennedy exemplifies this type. Kennedy was a "slow-twitch" guy who lacked the raw speed of other 5,000 m specialists, but he thrived in the intensity-focused Kenyan training system under the late coach Kim McDonald.

It doesn't take a lot of experience to determine how quickly you respond to high-intensity training, but it may take some time to determine how much you can effectively absorb, partly because experience increases the amount of high-intensity running you can absorb.

All four types of runners can be successful. What's important is developing a clear sense of your type so that you can train appropriately. You must avoid at all costs feeling obligated to incorporate high-intensity work into your training in a certain way just because your favorite coach recommends it and does so without a thought as to whether this approach is right for you.

High-intensity training tends to be unpleasant, though, so avoid the trap of too quickly deciding that you cannot handle much of it. This is a case where the affective response to training can lead a runner astray. Enjoyment of high-intensity training is an acquired taste. Many runners have trouble overcoming the initial bitterness of that taste and consequently never do as much high-intensity training as would be optimal for them. This phenomenon is not an exception to the enjoyment principle discussed in Chapter 2 but is rather a case of immediate versus deferred enjoyment. The more mature runner recognizes that, while unpleasant at times, high-intensity training stimulates greater improvement than its avoidance does, and in the long run greater improvement yields greater overall enjoyment of running. Therefore, in the process of figuring out the high-intensity training component of your optimal training formula, it is especially important that you pay attention to the performance results you get from high-intensity training and be willing to work as hard at it as the results justify.

There are three specific factors that define a runner's approach to high-intensity training: the frequency of high-intensity work within the typical training week, the challenge level of individual high-intensity workouts, and when high-intensity work is phased into and out of the training program. You can manipulate each of these factors based on what you learn about how your body responds to this type of training. A vast majority of road racers (5K to marathon) find that a schedule of two to three high-intensity workouts per week works best for them, and I suggest that every runner start there. Table 3.1 shows a typical training week in Deena Kastor's preparation for the 2004 Olympic Marathon, where she won a bronze medal. The three high-intensity sessions are bold.

More than frequency of high-intensity training, what distinguishes the optimal training formulas of runners who can handle a lot of high-intensity work from those of runners who cannot is the challenge level of those work-

Table 3.1 A Typical Elite Runner's Training Week with Three High-Intensity Workouts

	First Workout	Second Workout	Third Workout
Monday	12 miles easy	30-60 minutes easy	
Tuesday	6-8 × 1 mile ca. 4:42-4:50	30-60 minutes easy	Strength training & plyometrics
Wednesday	2-hour run	30-60 minutes easy	Strength training & plyometrics
Thursday	12 × 600 m intervals	30-60 minutes easy	Strength training & plyometrics
Friday	Easy run	30-60 minutes easy	
Saturday	Tempo run 8-10 miles	30-60 minutes easy	
Sunday	Long run 2-2.75 hours		

outs. An appropriate speed workout for a runner who is easily overwhelmed by high-intensity training might be 8 × 400 m at 3,000 m race pace with 2:00 jogging recoveries, whereas a runner who can handle a lot of high-intensity work may run 20 × 400 m.

Periodization of high-intensity training—that is, deciding when to introduce it into the training process, how quickly to increase the challenge level, and how long to continue doing it—is the trickiest aspect of manipulating this variable to accommodate your body's response to it. If you respond to high-intensity training quickly but cannot handle a lot of it (type 1), you should do minimal high-intensity training until you're within several weeks of an important race and then immerse yourself in it, as Brad Hudson did with Jorge Torres while coaching him. If you respond to high-intensity training quickly and can handle a lot of it (type 2), you can maintain a moderate commitment to this type of training throughout the training cycle but wait until you're several weeks out from an important race to truly challenge your limits. If you respond to high-intensity training slowly but cannot handle a lot of it (type 3), you should take the same approach as type 2 runners, but for you a "moderate" commitment to high-intensity training will be lighter. If you respond slowly to high-intensity training but can handle a lot (type 4), you should introduce it early in the training process and increase the challenge level of workouts very gradually.

There are other factors besides the sheer amount of high-intensity training to consider. Individual runners also respond better or worse than others to specific high intensities and require different amounts of relative rest before and after high-intensity workouts. Kara Goucher and her coach, Alberto Salazar, studied these factors in her training and modified it accordingly. "I actually train a bit differently than my training partners, just because of the fact that I am more of a workhorse," she told me. "Some people need to feel fresh and rested. But I handle a heavier load better than some of my teammates. I actually feel better after I come off sessions like 9 by 1 mile or a 15-mile tempo run than I do after running quarters [400 m repeats] and stuff like that. Sure, maybe it's not as hard physically, but I don't come off of it well. I feel sore, I get beat up, and I don't feel good. I'd rather go hammer out the miles. So we've adjusted to that."

When Goucher first joined the Nike Oregon Project in 2004, Salazar trained her very similarly to the other athletes on the team, using his generally preferred methods. But as he learned more about her strengths, weaknesses, and needs, he modified her training accordingly, and as her training became more customized, her racing improved.

Take a cue from Kara Goucher, and make the effort to learn the nuances of your body's responses to high-intensity training, and modify your training appropriately.

Periodization System

There is more than one effective way to sequence workouts for the purpose of cultivating peak race fitness, but there is an optimal way for each individual runner. The best-known way was developed by the man regarded as the most influential theorist in the history of run training, Arthur Lydiard. A New Zealand–born coach who reached his prime in the late 1950s, Lydiard developed the first major periodized training system for runners. Periodization refers to the practice of sequencing training stimuli in such a way as to produce a single peak race performance at the end of that sequence or cycle. Before Lydiard came along, runners periodized their training primarily by increasing their overall workload as their fitness and their capacity to absorb training gradually increased. But Lydiard was the first to divide the training cycle into distinct phases and establish a proper order for the different types of training emphasized within them.

You are probably familiar with this order, because Lydiard-style periodization is still practiced by most competitive runners today. The Lydiard training cycle begins with a base phase, in which runners perform an increasing volume of mostly moderate-pace running. This phase is followed by a four-week strength phase, in which aerobic running is supplemented with hill training and other strength work. Next comes a short "anaerobic" phase in which short, fast intervals are prioritized. The final phase is a racing phase in which the volume and intensity of training are reduced to promote freshness, and fitness is sharpened through tune-up races culminating in a final, peak race.

MIND-BODY RUNNING

Don't blindly train the way you are taught to train as a runner. Develop your own optimal training formula. Each runner is genetically unique, and the only way to find optimal training is through mindful, ongoing experimentation.

Lydiard-style periodization is known as "linear periodization" because the various major training stimuli (aerobic, anaerobic, strength, speed, etc.) are largely segregated from each other in the training process and arranged in a line in which each gives way to the next. This approach is distinct from "nonlinear periodization," in which the various major training stimuli are mixed together throughout the entire cycle and only the emphasis changes from period to period.

Most of the newer periodization systems—those introduced since 1980— are nonlinear. One example is the so-called multipace training method developed by David Martin and Peter Coe. In their book *Better Training for Distance Runners*, Martin and Coe write: "One sensible method for injury-free performance progress over the course of a macrocycle involves harmonious interdevelopment of strength, speed, stamina, and endurance all during the year, never eliminating any of these from the overall training plan. . . . We tend to disagree with coaches who prescribe large volumes of solely longer-distance running over an initial period of weeks, followed by a similarly concentrated bolus of solely higher-intensity speed sessions over succeeding weeks."

There are three major criticisms of linear periodization systems, two of which are alluded to in this quotation. First, many coaches and athletes with experience of such systems believe that the sudden introduction of high-intensity running after a strictly low-intensity base phase carries a high risk of injury. Second, the various important aspects of running fitness are not developed "harmoniously." Why devote several weeks to developing strength only to let this attribute slide again by replacing strength work-outs with speed work? Third, linear periodization systems require months of buildup for a rather brief opportunity to race at the very end.

Nonlinear periodization attempts to address all of these shortcomings by mixing together the various major training stimuli throughout the train-ing cycle. The presence of strength and speed training at all times keeps the muscles and joints well adapted to the stress of hard running, thus mini-mizing injury risk. It also gives runners more flexibility to race when it suits them. Because their running fitness is always "well rounded," they can peak for races fairly quickly by increasing the training load and emphasizing race-pace training. There is no need to wait for layer upon layer of fitness components to be added one by one.

Linear periodization still has its defenders, though. The proof of the pudding is in the tasting, they say, and indeed it is hard to argue against the tremendous success that runners all around the world have achieved through Lydiard-style training. Perhaps the greatest virtues of Lydiard's system are that it limits the risk of overtraining and enables runners to peak right when they want to. When I asked former mile American record holder Steve Scott, now the cross-country and track coach at California State University San Marcos, and a dyed-in-the-wool Lydiardite, how he ensures that his runners peak for their biggest races, he replied: "My be-lief is that, when you've started track-specific training, you've started the peaking process. So I have my athletes do the same thing I did with my own training. I would do mostly threshold-type runs, hill repeats, keep my mileage up, and stay focused on strength and endurance as long as possible, and then introduce event-specific training maybe six weeks out from when I wanted to peak. One of the problems we see today is that people are run-ning race-pace intervals almost all year long, and it does not provide you with a chance to peak."

In my experience it is true that in nonlinear periodization, because there is not much distinction between training phases, it can be difficult to time a peak accurately. Also, because high-intensity training never ceases, there is greater risk of overtraining. For example, Brad Hudson, who favors nonlinear periodization, blames Dathan Ritzenhein's disappointing debut marathon (11th at New York City in 2006) partly on a mistimed peak; Ritz was killing his workouts three weeks out, but turned stale between that time and race day.

I believe that perhaps the most influential factor in determining the degree of effectiveness of linear versus nonlinear periodization for the individual runner is psychological. On a purely physiological level, either method can be customized to suit the needs of any given runner. But individual runners tend to have strong preferences for one or the other system. Generally, the Lydiard approach works best for runners who like to ease into their training and put off until late in the training cycle the great suffering needed to achieve peak fitness. A nonlinear approach works best for those who like to see and feel steady improvement throughout the training cycle. Think about which approach better suits your psychology in this regard, and start there.

If you are interested in Lydiard's approach, you will find the best presentation of it in his book *Running to the Top*. However, even the most ardent Lydiard disciples among today's top coaches concede that his method was not perfect and has been improved in small ways by his disciples (mainly through the incorporation of nonlinear elements such as base-phase speed work). Therefore, I suggest that you start your journey into Lydiardian periodization through one of his more noteworthy followers, such as Jack Daniels, author of *Daniels' Running Formula*. And if you do start with a fairly traditional Lydiardian approach to periodization, be open to mixing in more nonlinear elements based on how your body responds to it.

If you are more attracted to nonlinear periodization, you have many reliable guides to choose from. Among my favorite resources on nonlinear periodization are Pete Pfitzinger's *Road Racing for Serious Runners* and Brad Hudson's *Run Faster*. Again, use such resources as initial way-pointers, not final solutions, and modify your approach to periodization based on what you learn in applying the approach you favor. For that matter, recognize that the likes of Pfitzinger and Hudson are also influenced by Lydiard, so their programs and those of traditionalists like Daniels are not as different as night and day. They have many common features. In both, the overall load increases and key workouts become more race specific as the training cycle unfolds. The real difference is how high-intensity training is integrated. It is possible to blend the Lydiard and nonlinear approaches to high-intensity running in all kinds of ways, and there is no wrong way to blend them. All that matters is that you periodize your training in the way that works best for you, and if you start with an approach that suits your preferences, learn from its results, and apply what you learn, you will get there eventually.

Sammy Wanjiru, the half-marathon world record holder and 2008 Olympic Marathon gold medalist, is living proof that it is possible for a single runner to excel under different periodization systems. Wanjiru is Kenyan by birth, but he spent his teenage years in Japan, where he took up running, before returning to Kenya as an adult. The standard Japanese and Kenyan periodization systems are very different. The Lydiardian system is deeply entrenched in Japan (in fact, the president of the Lydiard Foundation is Japanese). Kenyan periodization is based on the camp system and is different from both Lydiardian and Western nonlinear periodization. It is perhaps best summarized as a "boot camp" approach, where runners are subjected to brutally intense, high-volume training for a concentrated period of time and then sent off to recover and race. Wanjiru performed equally well under both systems, setting his world record at age 18 under the Japanese system and earning his gold medal under Kenyan training. I once asked Wanjiru which system he preferred.

"In Kenya we run very hard," he said. "The best place for training is in my country, Kenya." In the context of our conversation, I took this remark to mean that Wanjiru preferred training in Kenya because there he had lots of other very fast runners to push him. So his preference for the Kenyan training system really had nothing to do with the system itself. His concrete answer to my airy question was yet another reminder from a great African runner that it's the simple things that matter most. For all I've said here about developing your own optimal training formula, I believe that most runners can excel equally on somewhat different training formulas as long as they are running hard and having fun.

PART II

MASTERING THE PRACTICE OF MIND-BODY RUNNING

FOUR

COMFORT ZONES

> When it's going your way, it's going your way.
>
> —Brent Musberger

THE MEN'S FINAL OF THE 2009 AUSTRALIAN OPEN was an epic, five-set, four-and-a-half-hour war between the two greatest tennis players of this generation: Rafael Nadal of Spain and Roger Federer of Switzerland. Down two sets to one, Federer took control of the third set, playing aggressively, hitting brilliant winners, and forcing Nadal to be reactive. Federer won the set 6-3 and seemed poised to wrap up his record-breaking 15th Grand Slam victory in the fifth and final set. But Federer turned tentative in that set, and Nadal seized the advantage. Serving down one game to two, Federer made several unforced errors and lost the game. The commentators covering the match on television described that moment as a decisive momentum shift in favor of Nadal, who went on to win the set 6–2, and the match.

Momentum is talked about a lot in tennis, basketball, and other sports that pit opponents, whether teams or individuals, against each other. When used in sporting contexts, the word "momentum" does not have quite the same meaning as "physical momentum," which is defined as a force equal to the mass of a moving body multiplied by its speed. The product of this calculation also represents the amount of force required to stop a moving body. In colloquial usage, momentum conveys the idea that a thing is hard to stop. A runaway tractor-trailer barreling down a mountain highway has momentum—it is hard to stop in the most literal sense. But a writer who has worked his way into a rhythm with his current book project, such that those halting, hair-pulling early days are behind him and he now sits down in front of the computer each morning feeling assured that he will make good progress, might also be said to have momentum—a kind of psychological momentum. It was hard for him initially to get up to speed with his composition of the work, but now that he has, he feels that his progress will continue in a way that is almost beyond his control. There is a certain force, almost some kind of natural law, working in his favor.

Momentum in sports is psychological momentum. But does it exist in running? I think so, but it is a little different in running than in sports that pit pairs of opponents against each other. In these sports, momentum is essentially one side exerting control over the other. In running, momentum occurs primarily in training and takes the form of a period of improving fitness that seems to have its own force. The circumstances are right, things are clicking, and the runner feels assured that her improvement will continue.

Momentum is different from confidence as I defined it in Chapter 1. Confidence is a positive feeling about your capabilities. You can, of course, have confidence in your ability to continue improving through proper training, but even this form of confidence is different from psychological momentum in training. Confidence in any form is self-focused. It says, "I know I can do this." Psychological momentum is outwardly focused. It is a feeling that a force is operating on your behalf toward your desired outcome in a situation. Confidence includes a sense of control; the feeling of psychological momentum does not. Instead, it includes a sense of trust—trust in the overall situation. Perhaps the simplest way to describe psychological momentum is as the feeling that things are going your way and are likely to continue doing so.

Even the most confident athletes know that they do not have complete control over their situation and are aware that their success depends on the situation shaping itself to their benefit. This is why so many athletes are superstitious. Silly rituals like wearing lucky socks are ways in which athletes try to control the uncontrollable—that is, to keep momentum going.

Since momentum is an outside force, there is often a little anxiety mixed in with the sense of trust or assurance at the heart of psychological momentum. Every basketball player has hot and cold shooting streaks. In advanced players, most such streaks have no discernible cause. The player is not aware of doing anything differently with his technique or in his shot selection while he's enjoying a hot shooting streak than he did during his last cold streak. Because he knows that he is not entirely responsible for his hot streak, he feels an anxious dependency on whatever outside force is currently working in his favor, and he knows that the hot streak could therefore end anytime, and will end sooner or later, as it always does.

Some psychologists have proposed that psychological momentum in sports is the effect of better-than-expected outcomes—which are often the result of lucky breaks—on expectations for future outcomes.[1] A lucky break increases the athlete's confidence or optimism or sense of control or attentional focus or some other brain-based factor, and this effect in turn elevates the athlete's performance and allows the streak to continue. The basketball example just given fits this conceptualization well. Every good shooter is bound to hit three or four tough shots in a row with the aid of a little luck. Regardless, the experience of seeing three or four consecutive tough shots make it into the basket creates in the player's brain an expectation that he cannot miss, and this expectation is self-fulfilling, to a degree.

I find this explanation of psychological momentum fairly convincing, not least of all because it is consistent with the brain-centered model of exercise performance. Indeed, advanced brain-imaging techniques might one day be able to trace the causal chain of psychological momentum—that is, to show precisely how better-than-expected outcomes stimulate areas of the brain whose heightened activity during the performance of sports actions is associated with better performance.

To date, however, there has been little research on how psychological momentum works in endurance sports or even if it works—that is, that psychological momentum is performance enhancing. But there is one interesting study involving cycling that was performed by Stephane Perreault at the University of Montreal.[2] Perreault had subjects perform a simulated bike race on stationary bikes outfitted with graphical displays showing representations of the racers and their opponents. Unbeknown to the test subjects, the races were rigged so that the subjects' actual power output, which was measured throughout the race, had no bearing on whether they passed other riders or other riders passed them. Perreault found that the subjects' power output tended to increase both in moments when they passed other riders (by sheer luck) and in moments when other riders passed them. The power-increasing effect of passing other riders appears to be a performance-enhancing result of psychological momentum mediated through increased motivation. In Chapter 5 we will explore how motivation operates on the neurological level to enhance exercise performance.

But what is so special about psychological momentum if the subjects of this study also performed better when momentum turned against them—that is, when they were passed by other cyclists? In the real world, when a cyclist (or runner) is passed by a competitor in a race, the athlete being passed is usually struggling and feeling lousy. And when that is the case, being passed tends to have a deflating effect. The circumstances of this study differed from real-world racing crucially in that the subjects were passed randomly, not when they were struggling. Consequently, being passed was more likely to have a rallying effect. In any case, this study demonstrated that competition in general enhances performance. Whether it is a matter of getting ahead or of not falling behind, the motivation to defeat rival athletes encourages a competitor to try harder. That said, Perreault's study also provided evidence that, independent of competition, good luck, or having things go an athlete's way for whatever reason, psychological momentum also boosts motivation and increases effort, which is what's so special about it.

MAKING YOUR OWN LUCK

If it's true that having things go your way by sheer luck enhances performance by boosting motivation, then it is not good luck itself but feeling lucky that matters. This is good news, because it suggests that athletes are not entirely at the mercy of luck in generating psychological momentum. They can also generate it by cultivating a lucky feeling or making their own luck. Superstitious rituals such as lucky socks are one commonly used method of feeling lucky, but they are not the only, or the most effective, way to generate momentum in sports. Athletes can also nurture the feeling that things are going their way by putting themselves in especially comfortable environments or by manipulating their environments for maximum comfort.

For example, some baseball pitchers try to maintain a slow, deliberate rhythm in their setup routine between pitches, reminding themselves to slow down when they find themselves rushing in their eagerness to deliver the next perfect pitch, and they do so simply because they find that, for reasons they could only wildly guess at, they pitch better when they slow the game down. As far as they can tell, there is absolutely no difference whatsoever in the mechanics of their pitching when they are more deliberate versus hastier in their setup between pitches. They are merely doing something to control their situation in a way that somehow increases their trust that the results of their invariant pitching mechanics will be better.

Athletes perform best when they are comfortable in their situation. This is one reason that a quantifiable "home-field advantage" exists in team sports. Perhaps the baseball pitcher who throws better when he slows down his setup routine does so, not because it makes him consciously throw differently, but because he feels more comfortable in that rhythm, and/or because he derives comfort from exercising his power to slow the entire game (after all, *he has the ball*), and this sense of comfort enhances his capacity to locate pitches on a subconscious level.

If it is true that athletes can create psychological momentum, which is performance enhancing, by maximizing control of their environment, then athletes should do everything in their power to make the situations in which they train and compete as comfortable as possible. As a runner, you will race better if you create the optimal personal comfort zone in training. This notion may strike you as being as touchy-feely as it is radical, but it is not. The most successful elite runners are adept in this skill, whose benefits are conceptually validated by current exercise physiology and sport psychology. Remember, no less a runner than Joan Benoit Samuelson, after more than three decades of running at the highest level, said, "Becoming a champion requires that you are comfortable when and where you are training."

As with the feelings of enjoyment and confidence, allowing your perception of psychological momentum to guide your training decisions is a more certain way to gain fitness and elevate your running performance than is relying on reason, the science of lactate and VO_2max, and outside authority. The feeling of psychological momentum is your unconscious brain's way of telling you that there is synergy between your body and its training environment, which encompasses not only your workouts but also every element of your lifestyle that affects your running. This feeling indicates a good fit—a comfortable fit—between your body and the overall system that you are using to pursue race goals. Each runner is unique, and it is impossible to predict which specific training methods and what sort of general lifestyle will most benefit any single runner's performance. A good match can be detected only once it exists, and the most sensitive instruments for this sort of detection are emotions, including enjoyment, confidence, and comfort, or physical momentum.

As primitive as superstitious rituals may be, they reflect an understanding that familiarity is a key aspect of the situational comfort that sustains psychological momentum. You wear your lucky socks over and over because they are familiar. The baseball pitcher initially makes a habit of slowing his setup because it seems to work, but as this habit becomes familiar, he continues to do it also *because* it is familiar. Maximizing psychological momentum in running is a two-step process. Step one is to discover what works for you; step two is to make your personal comfort zone as familiar as possible by repeating its elements again and again and by defending your comfort zone against threats to its integrity. The entire notion of mind-body running supports this first step: tapping into your intuitive nature, finding more enjoyment in your training, and honing a personalized approach to training (or magic formula) based on what brings results and what keeps you healthy and injury free. In the remainder of this chapter, I will talk about how to use *repetition* in your training and lifestyle to become a better runner.

THE BENEFITS OF REPETITION IN TRAINING

Coaches and experts often talk about the need for variation in training. I myself have often written about this need. But I have come to believe that the importance of variation is overstated and that the value of variation's antipode, repetition, is underappreciated.

Coaches and experts harp excessively on variation for two reasons. First, beginning runners almost never make the mistake of varying their training too much. When I started running at age 11, I ran the same distance at the same pace on the same route every time I ran, and I think this is typical. Such a repetitive approach works just fine for a while, but eventually it leads to a results plateau that the runner can move beyond only by mixing things up a bit. The trouble is that many runners are as mentally lazy as they are physically driven. They resist doing the work of learning a wide variety of workout formats and figuring out how to change the way these workouts are mixed together to create a progressive training cycle. They cling to the familiar basics and yet wonder why they have ceased to improve. So the coaches and experts who advise runners have to constantly chide them to vary their training more.

Second, harping on variation is a form of job security. If simple, repetitive training is effective, then who needs a coach? While the best coaches know that their greatest service to runners is not at all related to their knowledge of more workouts and more training plans, the mediocre coaches who make up the vast center of the coaching ranks are more insecure about their value to runners, so they push the idea that training must be complexly varied—too complexly varied for most runners to manage on their own—to be effective. (This phenomenon exists in an even more extreme form outside of running in the personal training realm and is perhaps apotheosized by the "muscle confusion" concept of P90X creator Tony Horton. According to Horton, workouts should be so drastically varied that in a sense they "confuse" muscles.)

Competitive runners with more than a year or two of experience are the runners most likely to be excessively influenced by the variation message. Runners like me. For many years I put so much mental energy into ensuring that I "never did the same workout twice" in the training process (to overstate the reality slightly) that this effort was a continual low-grade psychological stressor. Meanwhile, in my work as a writer I noticed that, while many elite runners also lived by the principle of variation, some of those who enjoyed the greatest success over the longest periods of time trained very repetitively (to say nothing of the East Africans, who as a group train far more repetitively than runners from other parts of the world). I was actually arrogant enough to think that these champion athletes would have accomplished all the more if they had not allowed themselves to get caught in a rut. Only when I learned about psychological momentum in sports and realized that the psychological and neuromuscular benefits of training in a personal comfort zone trump any extra physiological benefits of training more variously did I see that these great competitors had been successful in the long term largely because they had discovered what worked for them and thereafter did what worked again and again.

Now, I want to be careful not to speak in absolutes. Imagine a 0–10 scale of training variation, where a program scores "0" if it is totally repetitive (the same, single workout is repeated every day indefinitely) and a program scores "10" if it is maximally varied (the same workout is never exactly repeated). Among legitimate coaches and experts, even the fiercest advocates of variation call for only, say, level 7 variation—that is, a lot of variation but hardly an absurd amount. In questioning this standard, I do not contend that runners should aim for level 0 variation. Instead, I mean to argue in favor of something more like level 4 variation.

I don't want to advocate less variation generally but rather to focus on more repetition in two of the three tiers. There are three distinct tiers of training repetition: repetition within weekly workout cycles, repetition within individual training cycles, and repetition between training cycles. When you practice repetition within a weekly workout cycle, each run looks more or less the same. When you practice repetition within a training cycle, each week looks more or less the same, although there may be quite a bit of variation within each week. And when you practice repetition between training cycles, each training cycle culminating in a peak race of a given distance takes more or less the same form as the last, although there may be variation at the two lower tiers. Coaches and experts who urge runners to vary their training are mainly talking about variation within weekly workout cycles and full training cycles. It is generally understood that runners cannot completely revamp their approach to training from one training cycle to the next for the sake of maximizing variation (the way Madonna used to come up with a completely new image for each new album release). Week-to-week variation within the training cycle is a lot more achievable, and many coaches and experts consider it an outright necessity for good results.

However, as I have suggested, some of the most successful runners are noteworthy for a relatively monotonous approach to training. While their training is certainly more varied than that of the majority of beginners who run at the same pace every day, successful runners do not mix things up nearly as much as I used to force myself to do. They practice level 4 variation. These runners demonstrate that the truly necessary variation in training is what occurs within the weekly cycle. All championship-caliber runners pack a fair amount of variety into their weekly training. But some vary their week-to-week training less than others and seem to derive a specific benefit from doing so: namely, a sense of comfort in their training that generates psychological momentum, which in turn yields steady improvement. So the level 4 variation that I am talking up here is an approach to training where training is highly varied within the weekly workout cycle, only moderately varied within complete training cycles, and only very slightly varied between cycles, at least for the runner who has already developed a mature personal training formula.

Consider the example of 2008 Olympic Women's Marathon gold medalist Constantina Dita-Tomescu of Romania. According to an article in *Running Times*: "Constantina Dita-Tomescu's marathon training is based on a one-week block of workouts that has remained constant for years, with only slight variations for the season and distance from a goal race. Not only are the distances and intensity of each day consistent, but also the location, even the course." Could this be true? I contacted Dita-Tomescu's coach (and ex-husband), Valeriu Tomescu, to confirm it, and he told me that the *Running Times* article was indeed accurate.

The benefit of repeating certain key workouts throughout the training process is that it allows for apples-to-apples comparisons of performance and thus encourages the athlete to compete against herself, trying to best her previous benchmark each time she repeats a given session. The athlete doesn't necessarily have to become fitter and fitter for this process to work.

She just has to try harder and harder. As some of the recent science on the brain's regulation of exercise performance suggests, one of the most important outcomes of an effective training program is the ability to do more with the same resources. Engaging in a training program in which certain bread-and-butter key workouts are frequently repeated is a great way to enhance this underappreciated outcome of training.

My advocacy here of repetitive training does show a bias toward nonlinear periodization and against Lydiardian periodization (as discussed in the last chapter). With its distinct phases, the Lydiardian approach is inherently less repetitive than the nonlinear approach. Or, more accurately, nonlinear periodization tends to put more variation into the training week and to have less week-to-week variation than Lydiard-style periodization does. I am not, however, suggesting that every competitive runner ought to use a more repetitive training program than those that most coaches and experts prescribe. I am merely presenting it as an option to consider. Switching from a highly varied training system to a more repetitive system has been beneficial for me and might be for others.

That said, here's the general approach I recommend: Early in a training cycle, when you perform the first session of each of your bread-and-butter workouts, don't kill yourself. Just go hard but controlled to establish a benchmark. The next time you perform the same session, don't try to demolish that standard; just shave it down a tick or two by trying a little harder. Continue in this manner until in the peak period of your training, you really have to turn yourself inside out to improve your key workout times. Among the noteworthy elite runners who use this approach is Deena Kastor, who has said that she holds back a little bit in her key workouts in the early part of a training cycle and then pushes harder and harder as she feels ready.

It's not all about trying harder, of course. Training should make you fitter, too. But the very process I just described will itself make you fitter and give you the resources to progressively improve your key workout performances. Pushing hard but not too hard in your early key sessions will stimulate physiological adaptations that give your body the physiological wherewithal to reach higher the next time.

You should also manipulate the context in which your go-to workouts occur to stimulate fitness gains that you can then exploit in subsequent iterations of these workouts. Specifically, as the training cycle unfolds, there should be an overall gradual increase in your training load that is punctuated by short recovery periods. Also, your key workouts should become progressively race specific. You will make the biggest improvements in your key workout performances when you perform them within recovery periods.

So what exactly are the bread-and-butter key workouts that you might want to consider doing repeatedly in your training? There is no single right answer to this question. However, in general these workouts should collectively test and provide an opportunity to assess the various major components of your overall fitness: strength, speed, aerobic capacity, lactate threshold, and endurance. Examples of workouts that might be used to test each of these components in running are as follows:

Strength	10 × 2 minute hill intervals with 3-minute jog recoveries
Speed	10 × 300 m with 400 m jog recoveries
Aerobic capacity	5 × 1 km with 400 m jog recoveries
Lactate threshold	10 km relaxed time trial
Endurance	20–30 km relaxed time trial (90–95 percent effort)

Each of these sessions could be performed as often as once every other week, in a staggered arrangement such that you never perform more than three hard workouts in a single week. The variety would come from sensible variations on these formats, from other key sessions sprinkled into the mix, and from fluctuations in overall training volume.

Let's take a look at how level 4 variation looks in the context of a real training program. As I mentioned previously, East African runners typically train more repetitively than do elite runners from other parts of the world. In his invaluable resource of information on Kenyan training methods, *More Fire*, Toby Tanser presented the training that Moses Tanui did in the five weeks leading up to the 1996 Boston Marathon. Tanser kindly granted me permission to reprint the material here (see Table 4.1).

As you can see, the foundation of Tanui's training throughout this period was two runs per day of roughly one hour each. Tanser reported that one of these two runs was usually performed at a moderate pace, the other at an

Table 4.1 Moses Tanui's 1996 Boston Marathon Training

Date	Training Session	Description
February 21	A.M.	70 min.
	P.M.	60 min.
February 22	A.M.	110 min.
	P.M.	
February 23	A.M.	70 min.
	P.M.	60 min.
February 24	A.M.	25-min. warm-up, 10 × 1 km with 2-min. recoveries
	P.M.	60 min.
February 25	A.M.	22 km uphill
	P.M.	
February 26	A.M.	70 min.
	P.M.	60 min.
February 27	A.M.	120 min.
	P.M.	
February 28	A.M.	30-min. warm-up, 20 × 1 min. fast/1 min. slow
	P.M.	60 min.
February 29	A.M.	60 min.
	P.M.	60 min.
March 1	A.M.	30-min. warm-up, 4 × 3 km with 3-min. recoveries
	P.M.	60 min.
March 2	A.M.	60 min.
	P.M.	60 min.
March 3	A.M.	38 km run in 2:15
	P.M.	
March 4	A.M.	70 min.
	P.M.	50 min.
March 5	A.M.	25-min. warm-up, 25 × 1 min. fast/1 min. slow
	P.M.	
March 6	A.M.	22 km uphill in 1:28
	P.M.	
March 7	A.M.	70 min.
	P.M.	70 min.
March 8	A.M.	25-min. warm-up, 4 × 3 km with 3-min. recoveries
	P.M.	60 min.
March 9	A.M.	70 min.
	P.M.	60 min.
March 10	A.M.	38 km in 2:15
	P.M.	

March 11	A.M.	60 min.
	P.M.	50 min.
March 12	A.M.	25-min. warm-up, 12 × 3 km with 2-min. recoveries
	P.M.	50 min.
March 13	A.M.	70 min.
	P.M.	60 min.
March 14	A.M.	Half-marathon, fast
	P.M.	
March 15	A.M.	60 min.
	P.M.	60 min.
March 16	A.M.	30 km in 2:00
	P.M.	
March 17	A.M.	70 min.
	P.M.	
March 18	A.M.	25-min. warm-up, 6 × 2 km with 2-min. recoveries
	P.M.	50 min.
March 19	A.M.	70 min.
	P.M.	60 min.
March 20	A.M.	100 min.
	P.M.	
March 21	A.M.	70 min.
	P.M.	60 min.
March 22	A.M.	25-min. warm-up, 5 × 3 km with 2-min. recoveries
	P.M.	50 min.
March 23	A.M.	70 min.
	P.M.	60 min.
March 24	A.M.	38 km in 2:15
	P.M.	
March 25	A.M.	70 min.
	P.M.	
March 26	A.M.	25-min. warm-up, 25 × 1 min. fast/1 min. slow
	P.M.	60 min.

Source: Toby Tanser, *More Fire: How to Run the Kenyan Way* (Yardley, PA: Westholme Publishing, 2008). Reprinted with permission.

easy pace. So there's a little variety in the pacing right there. But the program contained only a handful of other types of workouts besides these aerobic base sessions. There were sessions of intervals ranging from 1 km to 3 km, but the total amount of fast running in these was held constant at 10–12 km, and the differences in pace probably were not all that great either (perhaps

5 seconds per 400 m) if Tanui executed these workout formats the way most runners do. The program also contained a long run, which was always about two hours in duration; a moderately long uphill run, which appeared to be always the same; and a long fartlek run. And that's it.

These workouts were arranged such that there was a good variety of training stimuli within each week, but every week was more or less the same. Even the total volume appeared to be fairly constant. The variations that made this program progressive were small things, such as a slight lengthening of the fartlek workout between the first time and the last time it was done and a shortening of the recovery periods from 3 minutes to 2 minutes in Tanui's 3 km intervals workout. And probably Tanui gradually increased his effort and suffering level in his key workouts as the Boston Marathon drew closer. By the way, he won the race in 2:09:16.

It is rightly said that you can't improve by doing the same workouts over and over. But as this example shows, when you try progressively harder in each iteration of a standard key workout format and manipulate the context in which these sessions are performed, you're really not doing the same workouts over and over.

REPETITION BETWEEN TRAINING CYCLES

One of the questions I like to ask endurance athletes when I interview them is this: "Are you trying anything new in your training this year?" I started asking this question years ago, long before I ever questioned the doctrine of maximum variation. Understanding that most elite endurance athletes are successful because they use effective training methods and are not, thanks to inordinate talent, successful despite using ineffective training methods, I valued this question as a good way to learn how top performers in running and triathlon pursued improvement by modifying their training programs from one cycle to the next. But more often than not, I was disappointed by the answers I received. Most champion endurance athletes, it seemed, modified their training little between training cycles.

By the time I interviewed Spanish triathlete Eneko Llanos in 2009, I had long since ceased to be surprised to hear athletes tell me they were not trying anything new in their current training, and I had embraced greater repetition in my own training. But I still asked Llanos whether he had modified his training at all in pursuit of winning the Hawaii Ironman, in which he had been the runner-up in 2008. "Basically we are doing the same training we did last year," he said. "It worked very well last year, and I think this year it is still working well. We are making some little adjustments but no big changes from last year. I think I'm improving year after year, and I'm improving with my races. Every time I do an Ironman, I am a little bit better because my body's still adapting."

Here was a man who understood psychological momentum. Having found a training recipe that worked for him, he chose to stick with it. But what is different about the consistency of Llanos's training and that of a majority of lesser triathletes is that earlier in his career he experimented with different training approaches and evolved a customized approach. Only when his system was fully mature did he settle into repetition. In fact, after the 2004 Olympics, frustrated by a lack of improvement, Llanos left his first coach and hired a new coach whose methods seemed a better fit. He did not make the mistake of trying to train the way everyone else was training and sticking with that approach through sheer laziness. And his training is indeed a little different from that of most elite athletes. Specifically, he maintains significantly less volume and performs more high-intensity training than many of his rivals do. A particularly interesting wrinkle in his training is that he does most of his long bike rides at a very leisurely pace—so leisurely that I was able to accompany him for a five-and-a-half-hour ride without slowing him down. This approach is not the norm, but it works for him, so he keeps doing it.

In conversing with Llanos, I discovered that he not only appreciated the value of psychological momentum but that he also understood something about the purely physiological benefits of repetition in training that few coaches and experts knew. "I feel that if I train right, the rest will come," he told me. "I will improve just because I have been training and competing for one more year." On its face, this statement contradicts the notion that new training stimuli are required to stimulate new physiological adaptations, without which improved performance is impossible. But the concept of repetition, as it applies to endurance training, is not so simple, which Llanos knew intuitively. Suppose you start a 20-week training cycle at a relatively low fitness level. After completing your peak race, you rest for two weeks and then repeat the entire 20-week cycle. When you start the second cycle, you are no longer the same athlete you were when you started the first. Your body has changed, becoming stronger and more efficient. Thus, when you repeat your second 20-week training cycle at a greater level of fitness and experience than during the first, you are not really repeating exactly the same program. You will be able to perform the workouts at a higher level and absorb the physiological stress more easily, and as a result you will continue to improve despite the repetition.

The primary manner in which runners pursue long-term improvement through cycle-to-cycle training variations is by training harder, of course. They add more volume or more high-intensity work or both. Increasing the training load is a very effective way to stimulate improvement. However, it is not the only way, as most coaches and experts once believed and many still believe. According to the old, energy-based model of exercise performance, runners can improve only by increasing energy-related capacities such as VO_2max and lactate threshold, and these capacities can be increased only by doing more. But the newer science fueling the development of the brain-centered model of exercise performance has shown that there is greater potential for long-term improvement in neuromuscular adaptations than in metabolic adaptations, and that runners can stimulate ongoing neuromuscular adaptations without necessarily increasing their training workload. Repetition of the stride—or practicing the act of running—stimulates neuromuscular adaptations, which amount to nothing more than improving the stride (which will be covered in more detail in Chapter 8). A certain amount of variation within repetition is required, but level 7 variation is not necessary. Level 4 variation will do, and that variation need not always take the form of increasing workload.

Many elite runners make small adjustments to their training from one year to the next in pursuit of the small improvements in performance they need to win races, and more often than not these changes do not involve volume increases. Consider the example of Matt Tegenkamp, who worked out a customized training formula under the guidance of coach Jerry Schumacher during and after college. This recipe led Tegenkamp to a sizzling 5,000 m PR of 13:04.90 in 2006 and a 2-mile American record of 8:07.07 the next year. But Tegenkamp wanted more, so in 2008 he and Schumacher decided to make some adjustments. As most smart coach-athlete teams do, they did not make any drastic changes. Instead, they identified a couple of training patterns that worked especially well for Tegenkamp and expanded their place in his regimen. They did not increase his mileage; instead, they kept his mileage more consistently elevated toward the high end through the base training period and into the racing season. Tegenkamp also increased his reliance on longer tempo runs and longer interval sessions, as he had responded well to these types of training in the past but had never done a lot of them, so it seemed reasonable to him and his coach that he had untapped potential to benefit from them. And they were right: In 2009, Tegenkamp lowered his 5,000 m PR to 12:58.56.

Among the adherents to the philosophy of pursuing year-to-year improvement by means other than increasing volume is triathlon and running coach Alan Couzens, who has coined the term "sweet spot mileage." Couzens contends that each runner has an optimal training volume for long-term improvement, and that this volume is not necessarily equal to the highest mileage level the runner can handle without becoming seriously overtrained or injured. He coaches runners to gradually build up to their sweet spot mileage over their first several years as runners and then hold their volume at that level essentially for the remainder of their careers, without worrying about ceasing to improve, but instead relying on repetition to stimulate neuromuscular adaptations that yield continuing improvement.

One specific example of such an adaptation is myelination. In an excellent article on Kenyan training methods published in the newspaper the *East African*, Jackie Lebo wrote about this process as it related to the repetitive nature of training in the Kenyan running camps in the town of Iten:

Myelin is the substance that insulates neurons; for many years, it was thought to be a passive actor, but is now known to interact with the neurons it protects. Neurons transmit impulses that control everything we do—breathing, walking, running. But neurons transmit in fractions of a second, which doesn't explain how long it takes to learn a complex skill.

It has now been discovered that deliberate practice, in the same way that it builds muscle, also builds myelin by thickening and strengthening it. The myelin controls the speed and accuracy with which neurons transmit signals, and the thicker and stronger the myelin, the faster and more precisely the neuron transmits the signal. So a person with hours of practice has the advantage of both muscle and myelin, and motions become hardwired in the brain.

The running camps in Iten have training schedules that can seem mind-numbingly repetitive to the outsider. But repeated over weeks, months, years, each session ensures the motions get hardwired into the runners' brain circuits and become as much part of their existence as breathing.

The last paragraph of this quotation clearly implies that, while the training schedules in the running camps may seem mind-numbingly repetitive to the outsider, they are comfortably repetitive for the insider—that is, the runner. Indeed, the running camp is the ideal comfort zone for the typical Kenyan runner, perfectly designed to generate psychological momentum for athletes raised in Kenyan culture.

A COMFORTABLE LIFESTYLE

The act of running is just one part of being a runner. Every single aspect of your life influences your running, from the amount and quality of your sleep to your diet to the fulfillment and stressfulness of your job. For this reason, a familiar, personalized training formula is not the most encompassing comfort zone that you can create to benefit your running. Your entire lifestyle can be a comfort zone that benefits your running by fostering psychological momentum.

Imagine that running was the most important priority in your life and that you were thus determined to do absolutely everything in your power to maximize your running performance. Every lifestyle decision you made would be made primarily to benefit your running. You might have to replace your full-time job with a part-time job or even live off savings (supposing you were fortunate to have enough savings) to make time for two workouts every day and ensure that you were able to recover optimally. You might have to move to a new location with easy access to lots of great running trails, a track, a state-of-the-art gym, and good sports medicine specialists, sports massage therapists, and so forth.

In short, if you were smart, you would think everything through and create the perfect environment and lifestyle to support your running, and then you would sustain them. And beyond the concrete benefits you would derive from each element of your lifestyle, you would also enjoy the overarching benefit of being extremely comfortable in your situation: psychological momentum.

> **MIND-BODY RUNNING**
>
> Do everything you can to create a lifestyle to support your training, which will facilitate a feeling that things are going your way and will continue to go your way in training.

The Kenyan running camp is the result of choices made by an entire national subculture that rates running as more important than everything else. As such, it represents the ideal comfort zone for the typical Kenyan runner. In these camps each runner is surrounded by other runners, and only by other runners, with whom he not only trains twice a day but also eats, sleeps, and socializes. He is coached by an experienced coach whom the entire group trusts. His daily schedule is organized with monastic regularity and simplicity and is centered on running. There are zero distractions from running. I think you can see how athletes who participate in these camps not only get very fit but also develop a feeling of total trust in their perfect situation that makes improvement seem inevitable.

There are no such camps in most other countries, nor could there be because of cultural differences. That's not a problem. What is a problem is that runners in countries such as the United States are generally left on their own to create their own comfort zone lifestyles but never learn that having such a comfort zone would be beneficial to them. A few intuitive runners do figure this out and are determined enough to create the optimal personal comfort zone lifestyle by their own wits.

The best example I know of is American marathon record holder (2:19:36) Deena Kastor. When Kastor, then Deena Drossin, graduated from the University of Arkansas in 1995, she had never won a national title and she was a little burned out on running, so she took a break and used it to decide whether to continue in the sport. In the end, she told me, "I didn't feel that I had done everything for my running. I felt I had much more potential and I didn't want to walk away from it. I could open up a bakery or write a book at any time in my life, but I wanted to make sure that I got that running fever out while I was still young and energetic enough to do it."

Kastor realized that to "do everything" for her running, she needed to work with a great coach. Her subsequent search led her fatefully to Joe Vigil, legendary winner of 20 NCAA (National Collegiate Athletic Association) national championship titles at Adams State College in Colorado and widely considered the greatest motivator in the sport.

A powerful first impression by telephone was enough to motivate Kastor to make the huge commitment of relocating to Alamosa, Colorado, to begin training with Vigil. "We clicked from the start," said Kastor. "He instills in all of his runners a passionate belief in what they're doing. Anybody who's worked with him will attest that he's a very special person who brings out the best in people." Vigil continued to coach Kastor through the 2004 Olympics, in which she won a bronze medal in the marathon. When Vigil retired, he turned Kastor over to his handpicked successor, Terrence Mahon, who has coached her ever since. Kastor feels that she has benefited not only from having had two great coaches, but also from having had great continuity in her coaching. Knowing her coaches well, knowing that her coaches know her well, and knowing that she has always been successful with her coaches (it was Mahon who coached her to her American marathon record) are a big piece of her comfort zone.

Another big piece is where she lives: Mammoth Lakes, California, population 7,500, elevation 7,500 feet above sea level. It is a plain but often overlooked fact that successful athletes often come from traditions of success rooted in particular places. It is often said that Kenyans are dominant in running because of genetic advantages. Really? And I suppose that Canadians are dominant in hockey because of their good hockey genes, Cubans are dominant in boxing because of their favorable boxing genes, and Kansas has a great basketball tradition because Kansans are born taller and with better hand-eye coordination. Obviously not. Cultures of sporting dominance begin in particular places because of fortunate accidents (an abundance of frozen ponds in the case of Canada and hockey; perhaps high altitude, among other things, in the case of Kenya and running; the fact that basketball inventor James Naismith was a University of Kansas man in the case of Kansas and basketball) and are then perpetuated primarily because people care more about that sport in that particular place than they do elsewhere. Mammoth Lakes works for Deena Kastor because it lies at high altitude, it has extensive running trails, it is the home of a tightly knit elite running team whose other members include fellow American record smashers Ryan Hall and Meb Keflezighi, and, as Kastor told me, "everyone who lives there is an athlete of some sort. We have skiers, mountain bikers, climbers. We're just the runners who fit into this extraordinarily fit community, and it definitely shows in the support that we get from everyone outside of our training group. It's fun to be connected to the community in that way." The Mammoth Track Club in Mammoth Lakes is perhaps the nearest parallel to a Kenyan running camp in the United States, and its production of seven Olympians so far is an indication of the strength of the comfort zones it creates for its members.

Another key element of Kastor's comfort zone is her daily routine, which I asked her to describe for me. "I wake up at about six o'clock and then eat breakfast and then take the dog for a walk," she said. "As soon as I get back, my husband will stretch me out and get me ready for practice. At 8:30 everybody meets for practice. Whether it's a hard day or an easy day, I'm usually back at around 11:00 or 11:30. I'll eat a snack and then take an ice bath and then eat lunch right afterwards. Then I lay down to take a nap. When I wake up, I eat another snack, walk the dog again, and do my second run. At 4:30 I meet my trainer at the athletic club for a gym session. Then I come home and prepare dinner for my husband and myself. It's usually early to bed."

Kastor took pleasure in describing her daily routine to me, because she loves her daily routine—as well she should, because she created it one deliberate choice at a time. Kastor chose each element of her daily routine because it helped her running in a specific way, but years later the whole routine benefits her running through its very familiarity. It puts her in the zone and gives her an expectation of success, which is self-fulfilling, much as hitting three shots in a row puts the basketball player in the zone and increases the chances that his next shot will hit the mark, and much as the roar of the home crowd after back-to-back big plays puts the football team in the zone and increases the chances that a third big play will follow.

Now Deena Kastor makes a good living as a runner and has no children, both of which enable her to arrange her life around her running more than you may be able to. But that's not the point. You can still go out of your way to live close to the best, most beautiful running roads or trails in your area so that you enjoy each run a little more and thus get a little more out of each. There are plenty of anonymous runners with children and demanding jobs who, like Kastor, intuitively understand the value of creating the best routine they can to support their running and then ritualizing that routine—sticking with it for weeks, months, and years on end because its individual elements work for them and because eventually its very familiarity will make it an asset to their running. This routine becomes a comfort zone that promotes psychological momentum—a warm feeling of trust in the way they do things, which creates an expectation of success that then breeds success. There is no reason you cannot do the same—but differently, of course.

FIVE

TRYING HARDER

> Pain is good because it teaches your
> body and your soul to improve.
>
> —Lance Armstrong

In October 2007 I received an e-mail from a stranger named Andy Petranek, the owner of a business called Petranek Fitness, located in Santa Monica, California. Petranek had seen an article about my book *Brain Training for Runners* in the *New York Times,* and he was intrigued by what he had read. He invited me to visit his facility and present a seminar on brain training for his members. I gladly accepted.

Petranek Fitness is a CrossFit facility. CrossFit is a fitness movement based on extremely intense and highly varied group workouts and characterized by a marine-like, no-pain-no-gain, give-110-percent-every-time ethos that is well summed up in the t-shirt slogan "Pain is weakness leaving the body." Knowing a little bit about CrossFit, I understood why Petranek was attracted to my book, in which I explained the brain-based limits of exercise performance and how to train the brain to enable the body to perform better. While I shared the CrossFit belief that mental toughness is critical to success in sport, my understanding of what mental toughness is and how best to go about developing it was based on the new, brain-centered model of exercise performance that few athletes had heard of when my book was published. So I was hopeful that Petranek's clients would appreciate what I had to offer in, and learn something from, my presentation.

At the beginning of the seminar, I called for a volunteer to join me up front. I asked him to grab a dumbbell in his right hand and extend his arm straight forward from his shoulder and hold that position absolutely as long as he could. (You may recognize this test as an old military punishment, where a rifle is used instead of a dumbbell.) I told my volunteer that I would time his effort, but I would not give him any time feedback information until after he failed. He lasted 15 seconds.

I then asked the man to repeat the test with the dumbbell in his left hand. This time, however, I informed him that he had lasted 15 seconds with the right arm and that I wanted him to try his best to beat that mark with the left. Also, this time I gave him constant time information feedback (that is, I counted the seconds elapsed). And as it happened, the other seminar attendees spontaneously shouted encouragement at my volunteer as he held the dumbbell aloft. This time he kept his arm raised for 22 seconds.

My volunteer was right-handed. His left shoulder was no stronger than his right. "So," I asked my audience, "how was he able to hold the dumbbell longer in his left hand?" The remainder of my presentation was essentially devoted to answering this question.

You probably have an intuitive sense of why my volunteer made it longer on his second try: He had the advantages of a goal, feedback, and encouragement. But what's interesting is that until very recently the theories and models of exercise science were utterly incapable of explaining this phenomenon, which regular exercisers are able to decipher intuitively. That's because exercise science almost completely excluded the brain from its explanations of exercise performance and muscle fatigue.

Traditionally, the body's performance limits have been defined strictly in terms of physiological limits within the muscles themselves or within other systems, such as the cardiovascular system. But within the past 15 years or so sports scientists have learned that performance is really governed by the brain. When fatigue occurs, it is not because the muscles or cardiovascular system have run up against a hard functional limit. It is because the brain has essentially voluntarily shut down the muscles before they hit a limit in order to prevent the body from suffering serious harm.

That the true limits of exercise performance exist in the brain does not make these limits any less real. You cannot increase the maximum duration you can sustain a running pace of, say, 5:25 per mile by simply recognizing that your muscles could do more than your brain wants them to do and over-riding those brain-based limits through "mind over matter" any more than you can jump off a building and fly by using mind over matter to override the force of gravity. The mechanisms that cause your brain to impose fatigue in response to warning signals from your body are designed so that it is almost impossible to endanger your health in exercise by sheer force of will.

Essentially, what this means is that you can never truly exercise as hard as you can. There is always reserve capacity in your muscles at the point of fatigue. Runners hate this idea. We want to believe we are running abso-lutely as hard as we can in our toughest workouts and races. But a true, 100 percent effort is actually unattainable. The brain won't allow it.

But here's the good news: That you can never exercise as hard as you can means you can always exercise harder. That's a concept that runners will get on board with. Because the brain imposes fatigue before failure oc-curs elsewhere in the body, the threshold of fatigue is movable. Indeed, the very phrase is misleading, as the threshold of fatigue is more a zone than a line. This means that an athlete may be able to push closer to the point of true physiological failure in some circumstances. Thus, the athlete who val-ues maximum performance can learn the factors that enable him or her to push closer to "muscle catastrophe" and then ensure that all of those factors are in place when maximum performance is desired.

Much of the evidence in support of this concept comes from studies in which fatigue is imposed through some sort of exercise protocol and dif-ferent types of electrical sensors are used to determine whether fatigue oc-curred because the muscles quit or because the brain quit or because some combination of muscle quitting and brain quitting occurred. One study of this sort involved trained competitive cyclists. Eleven subjects rode for 2 hours at roughly 66 percent of VO_2peak (which is more or less the same thing as VO_2max) and performed 1-minute sprints at evenly spaced inter-vals throughout the ride. The purpose of the sprints was to determine the point at which fatigue began and the progression of fatigue within the work-out, which is almost impossible to do in a steady, submaximal effort. Before and after this test, researchers measured the maximum contraction force of the quadriceps muscles through direct magnetic stimulation. Normally, the muscles contract as a result of electrical stimulation from the brain. But because its job is to prevent harm to the body resulting from overexertion, the brain cannot stimulate the muscles to contract as forcefully as an outside force can. So outside forces such as magnetic energy can be used to determine the true internal functional capacity of the muscles. In this study, the subjects were also asked to contract their quadriceps muscles as forcefully as they could on their own before and after the cycling test.

By comparing the decrease in magnetically stimulated contraction force to the decrease in maximum voluntary contraction force between the rested (pre-exercise) state and the fatigued (postexercise) state, the designers of this study were able to determine the contributions of "central fatigue" (or brain-induced fatigue) and "peripheral fatigue" (or actual internal muscle fatigue) to the overall fatigue that occurred during the cycling bout. They found that before the cycling test the force generated by magnetic stimulation was 17 percent greater than the force generated voluntarily in the quadriceps muscles. This means that even in a fresh, nonfatigued state, the cyclists were unable to use 17 percent of the full capacity of their muscles. After the cycling test, that gap increased to 29 percent. So even though magnetically stimulated contraction force itself decreased, indicating that there was some loss of capacity within the muscles themselves, the major contributor to overall fatigue was a reduction in the brain's capacity—or willingness—to drive the muscles.

As I have suggested, however, while we can never use sheer willpower to completely override the brain's protective fatigue mechanisms, there are some things we can do to delay the activation of these mechanisms and use a little more of that reserve capacity to perform better. Following are brief descriptions of some of seven proven ways to make the brain let the body try harder.

TRAINING TO SUFFER

The CrossFit ethos is based in part on the belief that effort is related to the capacity to suffer. Those athletes who are willing or able to suffer more are able to perform at a level closer to their true physical limits. Likewise, increasing the individual capacity to suffer is one of the most effective ways to try harder and perform better.

This tenet of the CrossFit philosophy is squarely supported by the latest science on the role of the brain in exercise performance. And I think it is also supported by every competitive runner's experience. The capacity to tolerate suffering is as critical to success in running as are the various components of physical fitness. And like those physical adaptations, the capacity to tolerate suffering can and must be trained. The runner who is serious about realizing his full potential in competition must suffer for the sake of suffering in training.

One of the leading researchers on anticipatory regulation (the mechanism by which the subconscious brain controls exercise pacing, as described in Chapter 1), Carl Foster of the University of Wisconsin–La Crosse, has proven that the capacity to suffer is trainable and that as the capacity to suffer increases, performance improves. In a 2009 study, Foster and his colleagues recruited a group of highly fit individuals with little or no racing experience and required them to perform a sequence of time trials (which are effectively solo races, of course). In all, they performed six 3 km time trials on indoor bikes, three 2 km time trials on rowing ergometers, a separate set of four 2 km rowing time trials with a training period between the second and third of these, and three 10 km time trials on indoor bikes.[1] Performance in all of these tests was measured in terms of time and power output. Additional measurements, including blood lactate levels and ratings of perceived exertion, were also recorded.

A clear learning pattern was demonstrated in all of the tests. In the first time trial of each type, the subjects started at a relatively low power output level and sustained that level throughout most of the task, then drastically increased their power at the end of the task, indicating a conservative initial approach to pacing. The subjects appeared to deal with the unfamiliarity of the tasks and their uncertainty regarding the maximum pace they could sustain in them by erring on the side of caution. Only when the subjects

> **MIND-BODY RUNNING**
>
> Purposely train your capacity to suffer over each training cycle, as doing so will reduce the amount of reserve muscle capacity your brain protects in races and will thereby enhance your performance.

were close to completing the tasks and certain that they had enough reserve capacity to complete them at a higher effort level without bad consequences did they open up the throttle and sprint to the finish. But having learned from these experiences, in each subsequent time trial of each type the subjects started at incrementally higher initial effort levels, and thus their overall performance improved. On average, their performance improved by 6 percent over three time trials and by 10 percent over six trials. Foster was able to determine that these improvements were due entirely to better pacing and not to any training effect or to improved fitness.

The RPE data demonstrated that the subjects were learning specifically to feel their way toward their physiological performance limits. In the early time trials, ratings of perceived exertion (or how hard exercise feels) started low, increased slowly, and peaked at a moderate level compared to later time trials. The subjects allowed themselves to suffer more as they gained familiarity with the tasks and figured out how to maximize their performance by guiding their work output level by perceived exertion.

Prior to this study, Foster had done a lot of work on pacing in competitive athletes. In this 2009 study involving nonathletes, he noted that their pacing patterns were clearly evolving in the direction of those exhibited by trained athletes. However, the former patterns never matched the latter, and so Foster concluded that it takes more than six tries to learn optimal pacing by feel.

Whereas Carl Foster is interested mainly in the general patterns that people exhibit as they learn optimal pacing, another leading researcher in this area, Bertrand Baron, an exercise physiologist at Université de la Reunion in France, has focused his work specifically on the role of suffering tolerance in this learning process. In a 2009 paper on the part emotions play in pacing strategies and performance in sport events, which makes a scientific case for training to increase mental toughness, Baron wrote:

> The pacing strategy may be defined as the process in which the total energy expenditure during exercise is regulated on a moment-to-moment basis in order to insure that the exercise bout can be completed in a minimum time and without a catastrophic biological failure. Experienced athletes develop a stable template of the power

outputs they are able to sustain for different durations of exercise but it is not known how they originally develop this template or how that template changes with training and experience. Whilst it is understood that the athlete's physiological state makes an important contribution to this process, there has been much less interest in the contribution that the athlete's emotional status makes. . . . We suggest that training sessions teach the athlete to select optimal pacing strategies, by associating a level of emotion with the ability to maintain that pace for exercise of different durations. That pacing strategy is then adopted in future events.[2]

The term "emotion" is a little misleading here. Baron was really referring to a continuum of comfort and discomfort. Through training and racing experiences, endurance athletes learn how much discomfort they ought to feel at any given point in a maximum effort of a certain distance or duration. Thereafter, they can feel their way to the optimal pace in each specific effort. But the maximum amount of suffering that an athlete is able to tolerate before slowing down is not fixed. It is influenced by a variety of factors, including experience and motivation.

Baron used the term "affective load" (AL) to refer to the quantity of discomfort an athlete experiences during individual training and racing efforts. He wrote: "If the object of training is to improve the physiological responses in order that a greater physiological stress can be sustained during exercise, in the same way training could also be designed to insure that a more demanding emotional loading could also be accepted by the athlete. Hence, it might be proposed that the athlete should be trained also to accept high levels of AL during training and competition."

In other words, exposing yourself to intense suffering—in a controlled and sensible way, of course—will increase the amount of suffering you can tolerate in races and thereby increase your sustainable speed. That's right: no pain, no gain. In his memoir *Every Second Counts*, Lance Armstrong described this phenomenon brilliantly in lay terms: "Pain is good because it teaches your body and your soul to improve. It's almost as though your unconscious says, 'I'm going to remember this, remember how it hurt, and I'll increase my capacities so the next time, it doesn't hurt so much.' The body literally builds on your experiences, and a physique and a temperament that have gone through a Tour de France one year will be better the next year, because it has the memory to build on."

Very few runners think of themselves as avoiding suffering in their training, but in my experience most do. They embrace a certain kind of suffering, which is the grind of high volume, but they shy away from exposing themselves to much of the acute suffering of burning lungs and legs that is experienced in challenging high-intensity workouts.

In fact, lately I have noticed a trend among runners of trying to put a positive spin on their suffering avoidance by couching it in terms of a Lydiardian training philosophy. High-intensity training is risky, even dangerous, they say, and therefore its place in the training process must be minimized to prevent injury and overtraining. It's not that these athletes are afraid of the misery of high-intensity training. They're just being smart.

Yeah, right. Having been an endurance athlete since 1983, I am experienced enough to see this philosophy for the excuse-making it really is. Now I must confess that I fear and loath lactate interval workouts as much as the next runner. But I do a lot more of this type of training than most runners because I have simply been around the block too many times to live in denial of its effectiveness.

Even elite runners fall victim to the tyranny of the comfort zone.[3] In an interview, Charles Pedlar, an exercise physiologist employed by the English Institute of Sport to provide physiological support to elite British endurance athletes, told me, "As athletes tend to improve rapidly over the first few weeks of training, they then find a comfort zone and sit there, so we use intensity targets to push them on." Specifically, Pedlar and the coaches he works with will challenge athletes who appear to be coasting a bit in their training to hit faster pace times, higher heart rates, and so forth in workouts. And mind you, these are some of the best athletes in the world we're talking about, including 2009 London Marathon runner-up Mara Yamauchi and 2009 European indoor 3,000 m champion Mo Farah.

Think about the level of discomfort you experience in races, and then ask yourself how often you approach this level of discomfort in workouts, if ever. If you're like most runners I know, and you are honest with yourself, the answer is not very often. Once or twice every week you should expose yourself to near-race-level suffering in high-intensity workouts such as speed intervals, threshold runs, and hill repetitions, if only briefly in those periods of the training process when you wish to train well within your limits. And this discomfort should be an explicit objective of the workout, along with the specific physiological adaptations you seek from it. In my experience, actively seeking the misery of high-intensity fatigue in workouts actually makes it more bearable. And like anything else, you get used to it. Indeed, stepping outside your comfort zone can almost paradoxically become a part of a bigger, braver comfort zone. It's worth doing.

Scientific and real-world evidence suggests that athletes increase their tolerance for suffering by developing "mental coping" skills that make the misery of fatigue more tolerable during repeated exposure to suffering. For example, in a 2003 study researchers from the University of Stirling, Scotland, experimentally induced pain (by cutting off blood flow to specific limbs) in 20 male competitive rowers in training and a control group of 20 nonathlete men. Pain tolerances were measured and found to be significantly higher in competitive rowers. The authors of the study noted: "The rowers also reported using a range of self-generated pain-coping strategies during testing which, they claimed, they also used during training. Pain tolerances were correlated with the number and quality of coping strategies used during testing."[4]

Here you might expect me to give you a laundry list of pain-coping strategies to use in training and racing, but I will not. The only way such techniques can work is if you come up with them on your own in the heat of battle, and I can assure you that you will. That's why you have to keep "going there" in your workouts. But while I cannot tell you which specific pain-coping strategies will work for you, I can give you a couple of examples of different pain-coping skills that work for different runners.

Example 1: When I asked Kara Goucher how she copes with suffering, she told me: "For me it's about being able to focus on all the positive things. When I'm running a marathon or another race or even a hard training session and I'm hurting, I pick out all the good things. When you're running, there are a million things telling you you can't do it. Your foot hurts, it's windy, someone else looks great. I try to find those few positive things that tell me I really can and focus on those. 'It hurts, but I am running a great pace.' 'Maybe I am tired, but I still have control over my body.'"

Example 2: During hard workouts I frequently call upon the mantra "This is where you want to be." I came up with this mantra after thinking about how a big part of the experience of suffering in hard running is the desire for the effort to be over with. I want to press a magical fast-forward button that transports me past the pain. Yet when I go to bed at night, I think about running hard before sleep washes over me. My life largely revolves around creating opportunities to run hard. Running hard is one of my most treasured experiences in life—especially when I'm not doing it!

So when I am running hard, I like to remind myself that I am exactly where I—the real me, if not the coward in me who sometimes caves in to pain—really want to be. "You've been waiting all week for this workout," I'll think, "and tonight when you go to bed, you're going to remember it fondly. So let's not wish it over with while we're actually here experiencing it." This is perhaps a bit metaphysical as performance self-talk goes, but it works very well for me, except on the days when I am especially struggling. Then I go to my old stand-by: "Man up, Matt."

MAKING IT MATTER

The degree of suffering that a runner is willing to tolerate is largely dependent on the perceived importance of the effort. This is why runners are usually able to run faster in races than in workouts. Because performance in races generally matters more to us than performance in workouts, we are able to tolerate more suffering and run faster.

If we set aside for the moment the phenomenon of choking (performing poorly because of the psychological pressure that attends efforts of extreme importance), as a general rule the more important we can make individual workouts, the training process as a whole, and our races, the harder we will try in them and the better our results will be. Such meaningfulness can come from all kinds of sources. For some it comes primarily from innate competitiveness. Great runners often talk about hating to lose. It physically sickens them. So they would rather suffer all kinds of pain in the effort to win than lose and feel ill for days or weeks. The social environment can also give importance to running. Many observers believe that one reason Kenyans train so hard is that running is seen as one of the few viable paths to wealth and fame in that society. And closer to home, I believe one of the reasons I underachieved as a high school runner was that running well was not valued in my school or hometown. I never had any mentor who made me feel that my running mattered.

The most important factors affecting the meaningfulness of running are those that can be manipulated to fit the individual runner's psychology and circumstances. Virtually every decision you make as a runner has implications for the meaning of your workouts and races, and you should consider these implications in your

MIND-BODY RUNNING

Make your individual workouts, overall training process, and key races as personally meaningful as possible. The more personal a race is, the closer your brain will allow your body to come to its physiological limits.

decision-making process. For example, in choosing peak races to compete in, try to rank the various options in order of importance and commit to the one that feels most important. This is something that Kara Goucher does. She feels that she races harder and better when she races for her supporters, and for this reason she chose to race her first two marathons in the United States (New York and Boston) instead of taking lucrative opportunities to race abroad.

Another example of a decision with implications for the meaningfulness of training and racing is whether to work with a coach or to self-coach. In 2008, I hired a coach for the first time to prepare me for the 2009 Boston Marathon. In performing the workouts he prescribed for me, I discovered that I did so with a sense of accountability that I had never experienced in coaching myself. I wanted to nail the target times and distances he gave me partly to please him and make him proud, and in the effort to do so I turned myself inside out in some workouts, accepting a level of suffering that I seldom had previously.

Before you make any decision as a runner, whether it is to train in a group or solo, to race often or seldom, to specialize in longer or shorter events, consider how your choice will affect your motivation to try hard. Always bear in mind: There is no bad source of motivation.

SETTING GOALS

In the example given at the beginning of the chapter of the volunteer holding a raised dumbbell as long as he could, the primary reason he held it longer in his left hand than in his right was that he had a goal to shoot for when holding the dumbbell in his left hand. Numerous studies by sports psychologists have shown that setting goals enhances athletic performance. New insights into how the brain works suggest why. As we have seen, there is really no such thing as "exercising as hard as you can." One of the major factors that determine your performance limit in any given circumstance is your maximum tolerance for suffering, which is influenced in turn by a number of other changeable factors, so that your tolerance for suffering—and thus also your performance capacity—changes from workout to workout and race to race even when your fitness level does not. In exercise science, the results of experiments in which subjects are asked to perform at a fixed exercise intensity (for example, pedaling a stationary bike at 200 watts) until they are completely exhausted are notoriously variable. If subjects are asked to pedal a stationary bike at 200 watts as long as they can on three separate occasions, there will probably be three very different results. But when subjects are asked to complete well-defined tasks with specific goals, the results are typically much more consistent, and the performance level is higher.

MIND-BODY RUNNING

Set goals not only for races but also for all workouts. Goals provide anchor points for your subconscious, allowing it to make better calculations of what your body can really do.

For example, suppose you are asked to run at 8:00 per mile as long as you can, and you quit after 1 hour, 13 minutes, and 30 seconds, or 11.68 miles. If you are then asked to run 11.68 miles as fast as you can on another occasion, you will likely be able to sustain a slightly faster pace than 8:00 per mile. This is so because your brain's anticipatory regulation mechanism requires external anchor points—that is, well-defined tasks shaped by specific goals—to make the best calculations regarding how hard you can work without seriously harming yourself. Without such anchor points, your brain will almost always be more conservative. The brain appears to use anticipated end points to various tasks to determine how much effort and suffering is tolerable in the performance of those tasks. Concrete goals tend to increase the amount of effort and suffering the mind is willing to tolerate. Also, goals tend to enhance the perceived meaningfulness of a task, further increasing the acceptable level of suffering.

Every runner has goals in racing, but it's important also to have specific performance goals for important workouts. Perhaps the most effective way to set goals is to simply aim to beat your own best-performance standards. In Chapter 7 I will present a system of workout performance goal-setting based on training pace targets that you can use to consistently try a little harder in training and thus get fitter and race faster.

GATHERING FEEDBACK

Many years ago, in the race in which I set my 5K PR, I thought I had gone out too fast. I ran the first mile in 4:56—about 20 seconds faster than I meant to. When I reached the 2-mile mark at 10:10, I assumed that my inevitable unraveling had only just begun. Sure enough, shortly thereafter I started to feel terrible. My suffering took on cosmic proportions. But when the finish clock became visible in the distance and I realized I still had a chance to break 16 minutes for the first time, all of that disappeared. I caught an instantaneous, powerful second wind and kicked strong to the finish line.

This is a clear example of how fatigue is essentially a choice, which the brain has a certain amount of leeway to reverse under the right circumstances. The motivation derived from monitoring performance feedback is one circumstance that can push back the wall of fatigue. Performance feedback is information that tells you exactly how you are doing in pursuit of a specific performance goal. It is another source of information that your brain's anticipatory regulation mechanism can use to make more accurate and aggressive calculations about what your body can really do. When I counted off the seconds aloud as my CrossFit volunteer held the dumbbell aloft for the second time, I was giving him performance feedback that helped him beat the mark of 15 seconds he had achieved the first time. He would probably not have destroyed that mark if I had not given him performance feedback and instead had left him to guess how he was doing.

The most important form of performance feedback in running is time. How long did it take me to cover that distance? How fast am I running? Constantly asking and answering such questions in your training will stimulate your brain to tolerate a greater affective load in pursuit of workout goals, enabling you to run faster and derive greater benefit from the run.

> ## MIND-BODY RUNNING
>
> Constantly monitor pace and time in pursuit of workout goals. Doing so will also enable your brain to tolerate a greater affective load.

In an e-mail interview I asked Tirunesh Dibaba, who holds world records for 5,000 m on the track (14:11.15) and 15K on the road (46:28), where she gets the confidence to attempt a world record. The answer was, in two words, performance feedback. "When I attempt a world record it is not something I decide when I enter the track on the race day," she replied. "I see how my shape is and confirm as much as possible beforehand how fit I am in my training and see my times, and I believe that is where my confidence comes from."

I must warn you (as if you don't already know) that it works both ways: On your bad days, performance feedback will make things worse. But it will also make your best days better, and on balance, if you train smart and have more good days than bad, performance feedback will make your training better. I will say more about the importance of performance feedback in training and how best to use it in Chapter 7.

GRADING MENTAL TOUGHNESS

In the traditional, "brainless" scientific explanations of exercise performance and fatigue, the mental suffering of hard exercise serves no purpose. But in the brain-centered model of exercise performance and fatigue, suf-

fering serves the essential function of anticipatory regulation. Specifically, suffering encourages you to slow down, or at least avoid speeding up, when necessary to avoid both self-harm and performance-destroying involuntary bonking. But it's clear that some athletes can tolerate more suffering than others and that those who can tolerate more suffering often perform at a level that is closer to their true physiological limits. And again, fortunately, the capacity to tolerate suffering is trainable. As stated previously, one way to train that capacity is by repeatedly exposing yourself to the suffering of running hard.

MIND-BODY RUNNING

After each key workout and race, ask yourself whether you held back at any point to spare yourself from suffering. If you did, vow to do better next time.

Another, compatible way is to rate your mental toughness in key workouts and races. That is, after completing each race and key workout, review it mentally, and decide whether you ran slower than you could and should have at any point to spare yourself some suffering. Naturally, in races the idea is to run absolutely as hard as you can over the full distance, so any seconds added to your finish time unnecessarily by intolerance of suffering are unacceptable. In workouts you seldom want to run as hard as you do in races, but often you want to run hard enough to experience intense suffering, meaning hard enough that, as in races, you must guard against running slower than intended to spare yourself a bit of that suffering.

There is an expression in business that applies to training and racing: What gets measured gets managed. When you make the effort to measure an important variable, you naturally act to affect that variable in positive ways. For example, research has shown that dieters lose more weight when they simply journal what they eat. I believe the same thing happens when a runner grades her mental toughness in workouts and races. The very act of paying attention to her tolerance of suffering, coupled with caring about it, will almost automatically cause her to bear more suffering.

I used to feel that I often failed to "leave it all out on the racecourse," and I hated myself for that. So I decided to programmatically increase my mental toughness by grading my effort level after each race. I am not talking about school-type letter grades (A, A-, B+, etc.). I simply asked myself whether I had held back unnecessarily at any point to spare myself additional suffering. If I was able to conclude that I had not, I was satisfied, regardless of how fast or slow I had actually run. If I concluded that I had held back more than necessary, even in one of six intervals in a given workout, I was dissatisfied, regardless of my actual time(s), and I vowed to try harder next time. In races this grade became more important to me than my actual finish time and placing, and it had the intended effect. I am now much more mentally tough in races than I was several years ago. And I think what worked for me can work for you, too.

COMPETING AND PERFORMING

In a fascinating study by Arizona State University researchers, student volunteers were asked to bench-press as much weight as they could on three separate occasions: once in a group environment but without competitive comparisons; again in an actual competition against the other volunteers; and once more individually in front of an audience of passive onlookers. The subjects were able to lift significantly more weight when performing alone before seated watchers than they were in competition, and they lifted least in the noncompetitive group environment. In fact, the numbers were not even close. On average, the students benched 231 pounds before an audience, 226 pounds in competition, and only 204 pounds in a noncompetitive group.[5] Same people!

These results suggest that competing and being watched trigger social instincts that allow us to push closer to our true performance limits than we can otherwise. You can use this instinct to your advantage by actively involving yourself in your age-group competition and by inviting everyone you know to watch you compete in your next marathon.

You can also take advantage of your social instincts to try harder in training by training with a group—at least in some of your key workouts—

> **MIND-BODY RUNNING**
>
> Take advantage of the scientifically proven fact that you run faster when people are watching you and when competing against others than you can alone. Train with a partner and run in larger marathons.

instead of alone. While you don't want to get carried away with competition in training, many runners report a beneficial effect of being "pushed" by well-matched athletes in training. Research suggests that training in a group may increase the release of brain neurotransmitters that dull pain, enabling athletes to work harder. For example, a study by scientists at Oxford University found that rowers were able to tolerate pain induced by a blood pressure cuff twice as long after a group training session than after an otherwise identical solo training session.[6]

Group training is not for every runner, and training in the wrong group (such as a group of runners who are a lot faster or slower than you, whose workouts are not appropriate for you, or whom you don't "click" with on a personal level) is certainly worse than training without a group. But group training is something to consider in your efforts to try harder.

ENJOYING YOURSELF

The major shortcoming of the CrossFit ethos is its failure to recognize that, as we saw in Chapter 2, enjoyment motivates effort. There is a lot of talking about suffering at CrossFit facilities, but not a lot of talk about having fun. In the CrossFit ethos, the desire for enjoyment is derided as a fear of suffering. Perhaps this is one reason that CrossFit itself suffers from a notoriously high attrition rate. Club members might stick with CrossFit longer and get more out of the program if it recognized that the more they enjoy exercise, the harder they will work in their workouts.

Nonexercisers and those who have never been able to enjoy exercise view this notion as paradoxical, but it is not. Enjoyment and suffering are not mutually exclusive. It is possible to enjoy and suffer in exercise (and a variety of other activities, for that matter) simultaneously. In fact, enjoyment of exercise increases the capacity to suffer because it makes suffering seem worth being borne.

A study by a pair of neurobiologists at the University of Illinois found that mice reacted more slowly to heat pain that was applied when they were eating or drinking than was applied at other times. The pleasure the mice took in tasting chocolate or slaking their thirst made them less aware of the discomfort in the foot that stood atop a heating element—a foot they were free to move at any time, but took their time in moving while enjoying food or drink. Exercise enjoyment works in a similar way. It does not do away with the suffering of working hard; it makes that suffering more tolerable and thus increases the capacity to work and the capacity to suffer.[7]

Bertrand Baron recognized this fact. In his paper on emotions and pacing, he presented a 21-point scale of affective load in which an athlete's current AL was calculated as the difference between his positive (pleasure) and negative (pain) affect levels. In other words, enjoyment and suffering were understood to coexist in varying degrees of intensity in different exercise circumstances. If you are experiencing maximum enjoyment and minimum suffering during a run, your AL score will be -10. If you are experiencing minimum enjoyment and maximum suffering, your score will be +10. And if you are experiencing equal amounts of suffering and enjoyment—either a little or a lot of each—your AL will be 0.

Besides a high fitness level, the other major factor that allows a runner to enjoy individual workouts and races is general enjoyment of the training process. This, too, is something that Baron recognized. In a discussion of the need for training to tolerate greater affective loads, he stated: "However, training at lower levels of AL must also be performed in order to restore and to maximize not only the physiological capacities, but also the optimal AL level. If this is ignored, overload of both the physiological and cognitive mechanisms will occur, leading to underperformance. This analysis predicts that underperformance can be due to physiological but also to emotional disorders as it is often suggested by elite athletes."

In this passage, Baron wrote as if taking it easy sometimes in training were the only way to keep the training process enjoyable. But as you know from reading Chapter 2, there are other ways, among them developing a customized training system that appeals to your preferences. Contrary to the CrossFit ethos, following your bliss in this manner does not constitute wimping out. In fact, it is one of the best ways to try harder and race tougher.

MIND-BODY RUNNING

Don't ever train so hard that running is no longer fun. Give yourself enough easy days to balance out the very hard ones, increasing your capacity for both work and suffering.

SIX

WINGING IT

It's done on the fly based on how
I'm feeling and responding.

—Kara Goucher

I BEGAN LEARNING THE ART AND SCIENCE of training the way many runners do: by soaking up the wisdom (such as it was) of the coaches who led my high school cross-country and track teams. Oyster River High School in Durham, New Hampshire, had a revolving door of coaches during my years there—I remember five men whom I addressed as "Coach" at one time or another, and I may have forgotten one or two—and only one of them was an active teacher of the sport. From him I learned a few scattered training principles, such as the idea that the training process should be broken down into a sequence of phases and that the whole point of training was to build toward a performance peak at the end of the process. And that's about all I learned, except how to do the various types of workouts I did with the team—that is, how to do the sport.

Having quit running in the middle of my senior year and not seriously taken it up again until eight years later, I did not know much more about the art and science of training when I set about training for my first marathon in my mid-20s. The only "new" idea I applied then was the idea of gradually increasing mileage, which I had learned from watching my dad train for three marathons when I was a kid and from having been a distant observer of my older brother's training for a marathon during his freshman year of college. I was entirely ignorant, however, of the concept of training work-load modulation and, more specifically, of the practice of scattering short recovery periods throughout the training process. Consequently, I tried to increase my overall running mileage and my long run distance every single week throughout the entire training process, which must have lasted at least 12 weeks and probably closer to 16.

Needless to say, I was overcooked by the time race day rolled around. I felt good, and indeed better and better, throughout the first several weeks of training, but I started to feel lousy around the time I made a cross-country trip to New York City to attend my friend Mike's wedding a few weeks before the marathon. I went for a run in Central Park with the groom and just felt lousy. As it happened, I had chosen to take Joe Friel's seminal triathlon training book, *The Triathlete's Training Bible*, on the plane. This was the first real training book I had ever read. I learned many things from it, including the importance of training workload modulation. I clearly recall looking up from the book at one point and staring at the back of the seat in front of me, thinking, *"I'm doomed."*

I was reading Friel's book at this time because I had been contracted to write a triathlon book of my own. Aware that I was wholly unqualified for this task, I embarked upon a crazily ambitious crash self-education process that entailed reading Friel's book; every other triathlon book ever written; cycling, triathlon, sports nutrition, and exercise science books; and the entire 18-year archives of *Triathlete* magazine. Among all this literature, no resource had a more profound effect on me than *Daniels' Running Formula* by the great coach and exercise physiologist Jack Daniels. Every true training authority develops a system, but he or she usually begins the process of becoming a training authority by buying into someone else's system. That's what I did with Daniels's formula.

At the back of that book is a selection of very logically structured training plans. I followed one of the marathon plans in training for my next marathon, and things went much better. Before long I was creating original training plans based on the Daniels system, both for myself and for the rapidly increasing number of other athletes who came to me for coaching as I prematurely developed my own little reputation as an endurance sports expert. I came to really enjoy writing training plans. It appealed to me as an intellectual challenge—a game, really, where the object was to produce a particular output (a peak race performance) by selecting just the right inputs (workouts) and arranging them in just the right order. In the case of my own training, no matter how well or poorly the actual training process went, I always derived great intellectual stimulation from comparing the results of my plan's execution with the predictions encoded in the plan. Invariably, I learned lessons that challenged me to create a better plan the next time.

I also discovered that there was a robust market for training plans. The common complaint I received from readers of my first triathlon book was that it contained no training plans, so I wrote a second triathlon book that contained nothing but training plans: 42 in all, for every race distance and all ability and experience levels. That book sold quite well, as did the interactive versions of the plans that I posted at trainingpeaks.com. In 2004, TrainingPeaks invited me to create online run training plans that could be downloaded in their entirety onto speed and distance devices, which runners could then use to guide their training day by day for as long as 24 weeks. The result was 40 more training plans for the 5K, 10K, half marathon, and marathon. These plans proved to be quite popular as well.

THE LIMITATIONS OF TRAINING PLANS

Yet even as I made a cottage industry of training plan design, I became increasingly frustrated by the limitations of training plans. The major limitation I discovered was neatly summarized in that classic Robert Burns line: "The best laid schemes o' mice an' men / Gang aft agley" (which is sometimes translated from the Scots dialect as "The best laid plans of mice and men / Often go awry"). Nothing ever went as planned in my training or in the training of any other endurance athlete I knew. Sooner or later in the process of executing a training plan, aches and pains, illness, outright injuries, fatigue, bad days, fitness plateaus, and other factors force the athlete to miss or modify or put aside planned workouts and in the process discover that many, if not most, of the remaining planned workouts are no longer appropriate. In other words, sooner or later, unless the athlete stubbornly sticks to the plan all the way through, with inevitably disastrous results, he has to keep scrambling to steer the best daily course toward the original goal. The plan essentially goes out the window—or at least it should.

I laughed out loud sometimes when I compared my training plans to the training I actually did. They shared almost no resemblance, not because I lacked the discipline to adhere to a plan, but because setbacks and surprises always steered me off course and required me to improvise if I were to have any chance of achieving the goal for which I had designed the plan. I began to wonder why I even bothered creating plans.

TRAINING BY FEEL INSTEAD OF BY PLAN

Coincidentally, as I set about experimenting with a more improvisational approach to training, the name of a rising new elite running coach was suddenly everywhere on the running Web sites and in the running publications I read. A former elite runner, Brad Hudson graduated from competition to coaching after the 2000 Olympic Trials Marathon and quickly made a name for himself as an innovative student of the sport. And it appeared from what I read that Hudson's approach to training was highly improvisational, relying more on immediate adaptive responses than on advanced planning to guide the fitness-building process.

What intrigued me about this approach was that it validated the course I had recently taken in my own training and a conclusion I had drawn from my recent immersion in the new brain-related research in exercise science. The novel brain-centered model of exercise performance that emerged from this research suggested to me that the training process should be guided by feel, for reasons I have explained in preceding chapters. To me this cutting-edge science made sparklingly clear sense of important experiences familiar to every competitive runner. It explained why we feel we can go faster or farther when we are in fact capable of going faster or farther—our bodies communicate this ability to our brains through chemical and electrical messages. It explained why there will never be a better indicator that we are fatigued and need to rest than that of simply feeling lousy—because dozens of different physiological factors contribute to fatigue and only the brain can effect a synthesized assessment of all of them. It explained why when we get a sudden hunch about what we ought to do next in our training, it's probably correct—again, because our bodies know. So, I reasoned, if our consciously experienced feelings are such accurate sources of information about our physiological state and such reliable pre-dictors of how our bodies will respond to various types of training stimuli, then it should be possible to train very effectively by feel. And since train-ing plans never work out, I further reasoned, then perhaps runners really *should* train by feel.

In the hope of learning more about how to train by feel, I contacted Brad Hudson. He was graciously willing to mentor me, and we quickly developed a friendly relationship. Eventually, we agreed to collaborate on a book, entitled *Run Faster*, that explained his improvisational train-ing philosophy, which we named "adaptive running." If you read that book, you will find a few training plans in it, and Brad Hudson does write train-ing plans for the elite runners he coaches. But these plans are much more flexible than conventional training plans. "I plan every workout in pencil (literally and figuratively)," Brad explained in the introduction to *Run Faster*, "and make a final decision about the workout at the last minute." You might think that training by feel and working with a coach are incompatible, but Brad plans his athletes' training largely by observing and asking how his runners feel, and he is often more willing to heed the messages of their bod-ies than they are. "My runners often grumble about replacing planned hard workouts with lighter ones when I determine it's necessary," he wrote. "And I am certain that in most cases they would go ahead and do the planned workout—usually with bad consequences—if I were not around. That's just how runners are."

Since the time I mixed Brad Hudson's adaptive training philosophy with my understanding of the practical implications of the new brain-centered model of exercise performance, I have not created a single training plan for myself. In each successive training cycle, I have worked to further refine my own method of improvisational training, which I cheekily like to call

MIND-BODY RUNNING

Never train in strict obedience to a prefabricated training plan. Con-sider every scheduled workout tentative, and be ready to change or substitute it based on what your body tells you it needs.

"winging it." But while I have not created a single training plan for myself in the last few years, I did have one training plan created for me. As I mentioned in an earlier chapter, in the late autumn of 2008 I hired a coach to train me for the 2009 Boston Marathon. My rationale for hiring a coach was that I wanted to take my running performance to a new level and felt that doing so might require that I try a new approach—one I might never think of myself. My coach created a detailed 23-week training plan that I followed as closely as possible. I was able to adhere to it almost to the letter for more than 12 weeks, and I got great results, even setting a new half-marathon personal best in a tune-up race. But then I began to experience signs of overtraining, and by persisting in training by plan despite these signs, I dug a hole for myself that I was never able to climb out of. Eventually, I had no choice but to abandon the plan completely.

It wasn't really my coach's fault, and I knew better myself. In retrospect, I think that unconsciously I treated my plan as gospel partly as one final test of whether creating training plans is worth the bother. The final conclusion I drew from this experience was that conventional training plans—that is, written schedules consisting of many weeks of workouts articulated in detail—are totally unnecessary for the experienced competitive runner. They are not inherently useless, though. Creating a formal training plan will do no harm as long as the runner treats each scheduled workout as provisional and is willing and able to depart from the plan whenever necessary, as it is sooner or later bound to be. Planning out the next training cycle is for many runners an exercise that generates confidence and motivation. It enables them to get their heads around what it will take to achieve their race goals and gives comfort in presenting a visible path forward. I would never try to convince a runner who draws such benefits from planning that she should abandon the practice. However, even the best training plans offer nothing close to a guarantee of successful fitness development and racing. Execution is half the battle, and successful training execution depends on the runner's ability to improvise based on information her mind receives from her body regarding its status (e.g., fatigue level) and its needs (e.g., recovery). Effective training execution can be done only by feel, and even most competitive runners are not very good at training by feel, largely because they are never encouraged to do so. For every 10 runners who devise great training plans, there is perhaps one who demonstrates a highly developed capacity to improvise. So I will devote the remainder of this chapter to describing my method of winging it in training.

TRAINING WITHOUT A PLAN

Beginners need training plans because effective improvisational training requires experience. Only by drawing upon a substantial body of running experience can you consistently make accurate interpretations of your body's messages and develop good hunches about what you should do next. Experience also teaches you what works and what does not work for you. Training without a plan, as I define it, is not exactly training without planning. It merely replaces a detailed written schedule with a minimal set of definite parameters that are carried inside your head. These parameters include a typical weekly workout schedule, a peak workload, and a definite duration for the training cycle.

Improvisational training is therefore not truly winging it. The improvisation occurs within a specific framework, and that framework is defined through experience. For example, you will train more effectively if, instead of having no idea what kind of run you will do later in a day, you decide, for example, that in the next training cycle you will run six times in a typical week, with high-intensity workouts on Tuesdays and Fridays and a long run on Sundays, and then wait for your body to give you reliable hunches about what is best to do in successive weeks. Only past experience can tell you that a typical weekly schedule of six runs per week with high-intensity work on Tuesdays and Fridays and a long run on Sundays is the best weekly schedule for you. And for that matter only experience can give you good hunches about the specific form each run should take as you come upon it. Therefore, as a beginner you must rely on conventional training plans initially and then gradually wean

MIND-BODY RUNNING

Consider training improvisationally within these three parameters: a standard weekly workout schedule, peak workouts and a peak week, and a training cycle duration.

yourself off them as you gather experience about what works and what does not and you develop a mind-body connection as it relates to running.

Improvisational training can be likened to jazz, an improvisational musical genre. Most jazz is not completely free-form. It has some structure. Improvisation takes place within a few basic parameters, such as a tempo, a key, and a refrain (or a core melody that the song returns to repeatedly between solos). Without such parameters, the music is so chaotic that it is not even music. Improvisational training requires a similar minimal structure. The key parameters that establish the framework of a training cycle are a standard weekly workout schedule, a peak workout and workload, and training cycle duration.

A Standard Weekly Workout Cycle

The seven-day, or weekly, training cycle is as arbitrary as the seven-day week itself. Or is either really arbitrary? Have you ever wondered why the week is seven days long? Four weeks fit neatly in the 28-day lunar cycle, and that is not arbitrary. Human calendars in all societies are organized around terrestrial and celestial cycles. The Christian Bible says that God worked six days to create the universe and then rested one day, and that's where the seven-day week comes from, and like many things in the Bible, this story may have a truth that is deeper than literal. Perhaps six days are about as long as the average person can work hard without rest. If this is true, then the seven-day training cycle is needful for the same reason that the seven-day week is.

Creating a standard weekly workout schedule is not an absolute necessity, and there are a few noteworthy examples of runners who do not use them, including marathon world record holder Paula Radcliffe, who settled upon an eight-day cycle early in her career. But seven-day cycles work well for almost every runner, and in any case what is far more important than the exact number of days in the cycle is the repetitive, customized routine of the cycle itself. When you commit to doing certain types of workouts in a certain sequence over and over, you soon begin to observe predictable patterns in your body's responses to training. You may notice that you almost always feel less fatigued and more ready to run the day after Sunday's long run than you do after Tuesday's intervals. Or you may notice that you typically perform better in Tuesday's intervals when you do an easy run on Monday instead of not running at all. Such observations present valuable information that you can use to further customize your weekly routine. Even if the weekly routine you start out with is somewhat arbitrary (as mine was in high school), the emerging predictability of your body's responses to it enables you to modify this schedule bit by bit to make it ever more productive for you. Undoubtedly, this is how Paula Radcliffe came to her eight-day cycle.

A standard weekly training cycle is a simple thing. There is no need to write it down; you can easily remember it. But it alone goes a very long way toward making the outcome of your training predictable. Once you have established a weekly schedule that works for you, all you really have to do to ensure that the predictable outcome of your training is the desired outcome is to correctly guess how hard you should train in pursuit of that outcome and for how long.

Naturally, the weekly workout schedule itself plays a role in determining how hard you train. If your weekly schedule includes 12 runs per week, you will probably train harder than you would if your weekly schedule included only 6 runs per week. If you wish to realize your full potential as a runner, you will need to evolve your weekly schedule in response to what it teaches you about your body and gradually make the schedule harder (by adding easy runs, hard runs, or both) as your body makes long-term adaptations to training that enable it to handle harder training. Few runners can handle twice-daily runs as beginners, but most will eventually have to run twice daily to fulfill 100 percent of their genetic potential for running performance.

If you have no idea where to begin, start here: This is the standard weekly workout template that works reasonably well for all runners, if not quite perfectly for many.

Monday	Rest or easy run
Tuesday	Intervals or tempo
Wednesday	Easy/moderate run
Thursday	Easy/moderate run
Friday	Tempo or intervals
Saturday	Easy/moderate run
Sunday	Long run

The template looks more or less the same for advanced runners, with the addition of a second run—almost always easy—on most days. The devil is in the details, though, and on the level of details the optimal weekly workout schedule you use after starting with this template and slowly evolving it is likely to look a little different from that of most other runners starting the same way.

Peak Workouts and Peak Workload

In addition to giving runners knowledge about how their bodies respond to various training patterns, experience bestows on them a sense of "what it takes" in their training to meet certain performance standards in races. In Chapter 1, I discussed the concept of physical confidence, which I defined as your subconscious brain's informed prediction of your body's current performance capabilities. This prediction is fundamentally self-fulfilling, because your brain will not allow you to run harder than it predicts you safely can run. Remember, the name of the mechanism that performs these calculations is anticipatory regulation, and indeed this mechanism not only anticipates your body's performance limits but also enforces, or regulates, them. In consideration of this fact, the goal of training becomes to teach your anticipatory regulation mechanism that your body can do what you want it to do—that is, to establish physical confidence that you can achieve your race goals. Because mental confidence largely follows from physical confidence, a reliable way to develop physical confidence is to put yourself through training experiences that maximize your mental confidence in your ability to achieve your race goals.

Before you begin to train for your next big race, try to imagine some realistic training performances that would leave you feeling very good about your chances of success in that race. Also imagine how hard your hardest week of training would have to be to maximize your confidence. Establish these peak workouts and this peak training week as the terminal point of the training cycle. It does not matter if the workouts you come up with are a little unusual or if the peak training week you envision is unlike anything you have seen in a book or on a Web site. If you have enough experience to have a strong sense of what it takes for you to achieve certain race performance standards, trust your subconscious brain's suggestions.

Nothing can give you greater confidence in being able to achieve a certain performance in a race than achieving exactly the same performance in a workout. That's why I suggested that you imagine "realistic" training performances. Unless there is something very wrong with your training or race execution, you cannot perform at the same level in any workout as you do in races. This is so for two reasons. First, as discussed in Chapter 5, a runner's immediate performance capacity is determined in part by his immediate tolerance for suffering, which in turn is influenced by factors such as the perceived importance of the present effort and the presence of competition. Second, performance is also affected by both fitness level (positively) and fatigue (negatively), and the wise runner always does his important races at a fitness level that is at least as high as at any point in training and at a fatigue level that is at least as low as at any point in training.

In other words, runners race in a high-fitness/low-fatigue body state that is not manifest at any other time. Thus, there is an inherent unpredictability in racing. Australian elite running coach Nic Bideau told me: "You should know from your training what is generally reasonable, but there's a black box between the training and the performance. In other words, you put what you do in your training into this black box and then in the race it comes out as a great performance—or not." Exactly so. This limitation of the subconscious brain's performance foreknowledge is one of those things that make running a mentally stimulating sport. Anticipatory regulation cannot exactly calculate the body's performance limits when the body is in a state it has never or seldom before been in, if only very slightly so; but *slightly* is everything in such calculations. (If you overestimate the speed you can sustain for a marathon by just a few seconds per mile, you might not even finish the race.) For this reason, deciding upon the peak workouts and the peak workload that are most likely to best teach the anticipatory regulation mechanism that your body is capable of achieving your goal is a creative challenge. It is not obvious what you should do. It may seem obvious to two different runners that each should do three very hard marathon-specific workouts in the final 10 days before tapering for a marathon, and one may run a great marathon because she was right and the other may run a lousy marathon because she was wrong. Perhaps the second runner would have been better off performing several slightly less challenging peak workouts over a slightly longer period of time, and performing well and feeling great in each, than in slightly overwhelming herself with those three superworkouts and consequently performing below expectations in two of them.

Every runner is destined to make some mistakes in choosing peak workouts and workloads. But these mistakes are learning moments. A runner who pays attention gains self-knowledge that enables him to choose better next time and still better the time after that. And the more expert that runner becomes in the practice of this skill, the less necessary training plans are. A few planned peak workouts and one peak training week are easy to remember. As with the standard weekly training schedule, there is no need to write them down.

Training for a Peak Race

To run faster on race day than you can run today, you must be fitter then than you are now. Fitness gains accrue at a generally predictable rate (although they accrue for some faster than others, of course). Thus, the less fit you are today, the more time you need to prepare for the race. Deciding how long to train for a peak performance is one of the most basic decisions in running, and yet it does not get a lot of attention. The training plans that runners find in magazines and books and online have certain typical durations that vary by race distance, but the rationales for these durations are seldom explained. Thus, it is unclear to the curious runner whether these typical durations are optimal (and if so, are they optimal for everyone?) or if their lengths merely represent conformity to convention.

If I asked you to run your best possible 5K race, how much time would you request to train? What if I asked you to run your best 10K? How much time would you need for that? And your best half marathon? Marathon? You need to be good at answering such questions if you are to have success with any training approach, including the improvisational approach I'm preaching here. As with creating the optimal weekly workout schedule and choosing the optimal peak workouts and workload, establishing the optimal training cycle duration is an aptitude that improves with experience. But what works for one runner is generally within the zone of what works for most runners, so it makes sense for beginners who lack experience they can draw from—and even veteran runners who just have not paid much mind to the matter—to begin by trying what works for most runners.

Among the few running experts who have explicitly addressed the matter of optimal training cycle duration is Jack Daniels. In *Daniels' Running Formula*, he identified 24 weeks as the ideal training duration for every race distance and for runners of every level, with some exceptions. All of the training plans in the book, for races ranging in length from 1,500 meters to the marathon, were 24 weeks in length.

Although Daniels did not explicitly explain why he considered the 24-week duration ideal, we can deduce from his overall explanation of his training system that it simply takes 24 weeks to work through all four phases of his periodization method, but no longer. It follows that if you have already completed the first part of this training process, or something resembling it when you set your sights on a specific race, then you don't need a full 24 weeks to prepare for peak performance at a given race distance. For example, each of Daniels's plans begins with a 6-week aerobic base-building phase. If you already have a solid aerobic base when you decide to train for a specific race, then presumably you can skip this phase and devote only 18 weeks or thereabouts to building toward peak fitness.

Not only are 24 weeks enough time to cultivate peak fitness for any race, but they are also approximately the maximum amount of time a runner can train progressively without burning out. Reaching lifetime peak fitness takes years, and this multiyear process must be broken into individual cycles separated by brief periods of regeneration in which some fitness is intentionally lost. A runner who attempts to continue improving his or her fitness indefinitely, even from a low starting level, is likely to find that burnout (or injury) occurs after 24 weeks or so.

Daniels's approach is not the only approach to determining how long runners train for specific events. For example, Brad Hudson uses a nonlinear periodization approach that mixes the various types of training together more than the Daniels system does. Hudson believes in maintaining a high level of aerobic fitness and speed year-round in his runners, so that they require little time at all to sharpen up for peak performance. His marathoners typically devote only 12 weeks to focused preparation for their big races.

The higher your starting fitness level is—in other words, the closer you are to peak fitness when you begin focused training for a peak race—the more you risk burning out before your race if you plan a longer training cycle. Hudson's runners would likely become overtrained if they trained longer than 12 weeks for a marathon, so fit are they at all times. Indeed, Hudson blames an overlong training cycle for his former star client Dathan Ritzenhein's poor performance in his debut marathon.

You can intentionally delay a peak when necessary to avoid overtraining, however, by holding yourself back in your workouts until you reach a point where you can ramp up steadily without a high risk of burnout. Suppose, for example, that you are 15 weeks away from peak marathon fitness when you decide to run a marathon that's 20 weeks away. In this case you could train relatively lightly for the next 5 weeks and perhaps focus on types of training that will make your body more resilient when you begin ramping up 15 weeks out from race day.

Naturally, this sort of calculation works best when you are able to accurately judge how close you are to peak fitness in terms of training time. This ability comes with experience, but nobody ever perfects it. There are simply wild guesses and informed guesses. In the end the best you can do is commit to a schedule that seems sensible and make adjustments as you go. It's always easier to slow the pace of your ramp-up to prevent burnout than to accelerate it to hasten a peak that seems too slow in coming.

We might assume that it does not take as long to develop peak fitness for shorter running events as it does for longer running events. This is true to some degree for runners who are beginning the training process at a low level of running mileage. A runner who currently trains just 12 miles a week can achieve peak fitness for a 5K sooner than she can for a marathon, because her endurance is very far away from the level needed for optimal marathon performance. But it takes almost as much time for the relatively untrained runner to hone the speed and aerobic capacity needed for optimal performance in the 5K as it takes to develop the endurance needed for optimal performance in a marathon. Runners usually allow enough time to train for marathons because they simply can't finish otherwise, whereas they just as often do not allow enough time to train optimally for shorter races because merely covering the distance is no problem and it's harder to appreciate how long it takes to fully develop speed and aerobic capacity.

Training Seasonally

There is an alternative approach to developing peak fitness for races that may in some cases obviate the need to decide upon training cycle durations or at least reduce their necessary scope. Every day I receive e-mails from runners (and triathletes) who are following or have followed training plans that I created for one of my books or for a magazine article or for Training-Peaks. Many of these questions are versions of one question, which is essentially this: What do I do if I want to peak for more than one race within a span of time that is shorter than the duration of your training plans?

This question cuts to the heart of the greatest limitation of the prefabricated training plans that I have created in such abundance. Whereas my training plans treat individual peak races in isolation, in the real world most competitive runners take a seasonal approach to the sport, giving more or less equal importance to several races taking place between spring and fall. There's nothing wrong with this approach. In fact, it is the racing approach that most elite runners (except marathon specialists) practice, too. Taking a seasonal approach to training almost demands a nonlinear approach to periodization, like Brad Hudson's adaptive running system. Here are three guidelines for seasonal training that I learned from Brad.

1. Maintain a high level of general running fitness at all times. The designer of prefabricated training plans is more or less obligated to assume that the runners using them are beginning at a relatively low fitness level relative to their own individual peak levels. Essentially, these plans assume you're coming off a nice off-season break and are just beginning the process of establishing a fresh fitness base. This assumption makes the plans more inclusive than they might otherwise be. A plan that assumed you already had a solid foundation of general running fitness would not work for you if you lacked that foundation, even if the peak training load prescribed in the final pretaper weeks was appropriate for you given adequate time, because you'd be in over your head from the very start.

Every runner needs a nice off-season break, and every runner needs to take time to build a fresh fitness base after that off-season break. But if you want to successfully execute a seasonal approach to racing that allows you to race at peak level several times between spring and fall, you need to maintain a fairly high fitness level at all other times. Doing so will enable you to return to peak form fairly quickly after each important race.

It's important that you avoid training too hard for too long, however. If you try to sustain truly peak training loads throughout the racing season, you will get injured or burn out. Except during the short periods when you are actively working to stimulate a fitness peak for an important race, your training should be "manageably hard." In other words, the volume and intensity of training should be close to—but one solid step below—the maximum that you could sustain indefinitely without getting injured or burning out.

Give yourself a full week to relax and recuperate after major races, of course, but after that, get back after it. The exception, again, is marathons. After each marathon you need to treat yourself to a true off-season.

2. Always move in a definite direction in training. Restated, the first step in successful seasonal training is to train for high-level fitness maintenance at all times except when you are taking a short break after a race, taking an off-season break, or peaking for an upcoming race. This does not mean you should do exactly the same workouts week after week and intentionally go nowhere with your fitness during maintenance periods, however. Your training should always have some kind of direction, even when you are not actively pursuing an immediate fitness peak.

So what sort of direction should your training have during maintenance periods? Focus on addressing a weakness or working on one or more foundational aspects of your running fitness that will necessarily take a back seat during peak training. Specific things to work on include running technique, raw endurance, sprint speed, and muscle strength, power, and balance. The idea is to develop one or two of these qualities during maintenance periods without pushing against the overall limits of the training load your body can handle. With this approach your body will be truly ready for peak training when its time comes.

3. Peak for races with short periods of heavy training. If you are successful in maintaining a high level of general running fitness at all times, you can peak for any race in a short period of time by increasing your training load to your maximum limit and prioritizing challenging, race-specific workouts. This gives you the flexibility to race well on the schedule that suits you (provided you avoid making fundamental mistakes such as overracing). You can peak for a 5K with as few as 4 weeks of maximal specific training and for a marathon with as few as 12 weeks of such training.

As always, you will need to experiment a bit to find the maintenance training regimen and the peak training format that work best for you, but even in the trial-and-error stage, you will probably find that this seasonal approach works better than using separate, whole training plans for every race.

SUCCESSFUL EXECUTION

Whether you employ the seasonal method or the single-race method of improvisational training—that is, whether your planning is limited to choosing a standard weekly workout format, peak workouts, and a peak load or it also includes a training cycle duration—limited planning is only half the battle. Execution is the other half. When you wing it in training, your approach to execution is necessarily quite different than it is if you train with a conventional plan. When you train by plan, you always do the workout you planned unless your immediate circumstances give you cause to change it. But when you wing it, you wait for a specific idea for each workout to come to you. Most times you know in advance generally what kind of run you will perform, thanks to your standard weekly workout schedule. You're just waiting to fill in the details, except when intuition tells you another kind of workout would be better on that day.

Waiting for specific workout ideas to come to you does not necessarily mean waiting until the very last minute to decide on a workout format each day, and in fact in my practice of improvisational training, it seldom means that. These ideas can come at any time. Usually, I think about next week's workouts while performing this week's workouts. Affective and performance feedback from my most recent workouts tells me where I am in my training. My conscious knowledge of my race goals, my planned peak training, and how much time remains before that peak training and my peak race allow me to contextualize my assessment of where I am in my training. Through this process I naturally come up with ideas for the next step or two in my training. Seldom do I have to put much thought into the matter or even consciously set aside time for such short-term planning. It is something that I let happen instead of something I do. It's more like growing a beard than chopping wood.

On occasion I do wait until I am a day or two or even hours out from a key workout before settling on its format. Other times I get ideas a few weeks early. For example, at a relatively early point in a training cycle I might get an itch to do one of my favorite workouts, a 10 km "relaxed" (or 95 percent effort) time trial, but knowing that I am not quite ready for it, I mentally plan to do it three Tuesdays from now.

The dimness of my path forward in training is never stressful to me. Seeing miles ahead is of little value if you have little reason to believe that you will actually be able to stay on the path you see. While relying on the mind-body connection to light my way does not allow me to see far ahead, it usually leads me a short way in the direction. Thus, I usually feel more confident in performing workouts that I made up mere days or hours earlier than in performing workouts from a schedule I wrote many weeks before. This confidence is based on trust in my experience and my knowledge of the sport.

There is no substitute for such experience and knowledge, which only time (and attention) can supply, but there are a few basic principles of training execution that can help you choose appropriate workouts on the fly. The first is the principle of *progression*. The goal of the training process is to become fitter. To become fitter you must train harder. To avoid injury and overtraining in your efforts to become fitter, you must train incrementally harder. Your workload should increase slowly and steadily throughout the training cycle. Next week's training load should be a bit greater than this week's, and so forth. You can also work backward. The workouts you do in the week preceding your peak training week should be slightly less challenging, and so forth.

The second guiding principle of effective training execution is *specificity*. Your training should become increasingly specific to the demands of your most important race. For example, if your peak race is a marathon, your long runs should move closer and closer to marathon distance and you should do more and more running in the range of your goal marathon pace, while de-emphasizing less marathon-specific types of training (e.g., speed intervals) as race day draws nearer.

The third and last principle of effective training execution is that of *recovery*. As I learned the hard way when training for my first marathon, you cannot train harder every single week for the full 12 to 24 weeks you devote to preparing for a big race. Your body needs regular, small opportunities (easy runs, days off) and somewhat less frequent medium-sized opportunities (recovery weeks) to regenerate throughout the training process. Prefabricated training plans always include rest days, easy days, and recovery weeks. You can duplicate the effect without planning by including easier days in your standard weekly workout schedule and by regularly reducing your workload every third or fourth week as you go.

The thing about recovery, though, is that you inevitably end up needing it when you did not expect to need it. Your body tells you loudly and clearly when it needs a rest. While planned rest days and recovery weeks will often anticipate this need, they will not always do so, and consequently if you are unable to recognize your body's need for recovery or unwilling to address it properly, your training will always go disastrously off course. Because it is relatively easy to recognize fatigue and critically important to address it, training yourself to pay attention and respond to the need for recovery is one of the best possible places to start developing your mind-body connection as a runner. If you can master that, the rest will follow.

EFFECTIVE WORKOUTS

In the first paragraph of this rather long chapter, I said something that perhaps seemed enigmatic. I implied that my high school coaches, in teaching me little more than how to do various standard workouts, really taught me everything I needed to know about the sport. Workouts are indeed the fundamental components of training for running races. To be a runner is to run, and all running is done in the context of workouts. That is all there is to it. There truly is nothing else a runner needs to know besides how to do effective workouts except which workouts to do when. In this chapter I have taken workout format knowledge as given and focused on teaching you how to choose the right workouts by establishing a few basic parameters and listening to your body. But your body can only suggest a specific workout to do if you have previously internalized knowledge of the sundry options. This is one of the reasons experience is required for successful improvisational training. Prior experience in executing various types of workouts will teach your body how each affects it and enable your body to pair these effects with its needs at any given time.

If you had all the time in the world, you could train completely by feel and never bother to learn the standard workout formats. If you are very good at listening to your body, after 80 or 90 years of blind trial and error you would re-create the standard workout types that all competitive runners use: speed intervals, recovery runs, tempo runs, long runs, and so forth. You may never have wondered where these workout formats came from, but I can assure you that they were developed by blind trial and error over a very long period of time—not by a single runner, of course, but by millions of runners and thousands of coaches all around the world.

Consider the specific example of the standard recovery durations used in speed interval workouts. Exercise scientists like to blather about the physiological rationale for the work/rest ratios of 1:2–1:3 that are typically used in such workouts (e.g., 12 × 400 m in 75 seconds with 2:30 jog recoveries), but this rationale was unknown at the time this standard was established. Runners discovered it by feel, as the minimum amount of rest time needed to enable them to complete an appropriate total number of speed intervals (this appropriate number also being established by feel) without a decline in performance. A very interesting study demonstrating how this process worked was performed by researchers at St. Mary's University College in England and at East Stroudsburg University in Pennsylvania.[1] Twenty student volunteers were asked to complete a workout consisting of 12 × 30 second sprints on four separate occasions. They were instructed to rest just long enough after each sprint to perform at the same level in the next. This had to be done entirely by feel, as the subjects were not given access to external timepieces.

In general, the students succeeded very well in maintaining their performance through all 12 sprints in each of the four trials. That is, in most cases the subjects ran just as fast in sprint number 12 as they did in sprint number 1. The researchers were able to gather additional information that provided some insight into how the students were able to use body awareness to accurately determine how long they needed to rest between sprints to maintain performance.

First, the average amount of rest time taken between sprints was not the same in all four trials. Instead, it varied from one trial to the next. But the amount of variation between individuals within each trial steadily decreased from trial to trial. In other words, as a group the subjects moved toward resting for a similar amount of time between sprints. These patterns suggested that a learning process was at work. The students unconsciously experimented with different amounts of rest and gradually moved toward a consistent amount that represented the true minimum amount of time needed to maintain performance.

Second, the researchers observed that ratings of perceived exertion steadily increased over the course of the workout even as sprint times held steady. On average, RPE was 10 on a 20-point scale after the 3rd sprint and increased to 14 after the 12th sprint. This finding suggested that the subjects got a sense for how fatigued they should feel at any given point in the workout to avoid becoming totally exhausted before the workout was completed.

Finally, the researchers observed a negative correlation between the individual students' rest times and their VO_2max measurements. In other words, the more aerobically fit an individual student was, the less time he tended to rest between sprints. Since a higher VO_2max does enable a person to recover faster after high-intensity exercise efforts, this observation suggested that individuals of various aerobic fitness levels were able to accurately sense their capabilities and make appropriate training decisions based on these feelings.

While the subjects of this study were able to feel their way toward discovering the optimal work/rest ratio for speed intervals in less than two weeks, this was a rather small thing to discover when every other parameter of the workout was given to them. In the real world, the modern sport of distance running had existed for more than half a century before anyone even got the idea to run intervals. So while you could reinvent the most effective workouts on your own by feel, you really should not try. Recovery runs, base runs, long runs, progression runs, fartlek runs, hill repetitions, interval runs, tempo runs, and a few other types of workouts are proven to work well for every runner, and learning them is step one of becoming a runner. An overview of the basic run workout types is presented in the Appendix.

IN GOOD COMPANY

Winging it is not a radical training approach practiced by a small lunatic fringe of coaches and athletes. Many of the best coaches and runners have abandoned the use of training plans in favor of an improvisational method. I have already mentioned Brad Hudson. Another is the great Alberto Salazar, the success of whose athletes should provide all the confidence you need to determine that winging it is worth trying in your own training. One of Salazar's top runners, Kara Goucher, told me: "I usually find out the night before that I'm having a track session and then I show up to the track session and I usually find out then what the workout is. In my old situation, when I was training under coach [Mark] Wetmore, we had our workouts laid out about a month ahead of time. But now it's done on the fly based on how I'm feeling and how I'm responding and things like that." On the fly means on the fly. Salazar does not secretly plan ahead and wait until the last minute to share his plans with his runners. "It's not that he's trying to keep it from me; he still doesn't even really know which workout he's going to give me until the next morning," Goucher said. "And sometimes we'll adjust it at that point as well based on how I've warmed up."

Goucher confessed that she found Salazar's approach somewhat harrowing in her early days under his guidance, but as it yielded results, she put more and more trust in this method, and now she is not bothered by not knowing what next week's runs will be. While you will not be so fortunate as to have Alberto Salazar as a coach, you can learn to trust yourself as much as Kara Goucher trusts him.

SEVEN

HOW RECORDS ARE BROKEN

> Most of us make the mistake of
> going medium-hard all the time.
>
> —Michael Sandrock

WE DO NOT KNOW WHEN the first timed running race occurred, but whenever, wherever, and however it happened, this race was a seminal event. While there is surviving evidence of formal running races taking place as early as the eighth century B.C., the first footrace timed in the way we are accustomed to—in hours, minutes, and seconds—probably did not happen until sometime in the sixteenth century in Europe. Clocks capable of keeping time in such small increments did not exist until then, but human nature being what it is, it was likely not long before someone thought of using these new clocks to time footraces. Running became a popular betting sport in England in the seventeenth century, and there are abundant surviving records from that era of winning times and of record times for races of various distances. For example, we know that by the 1690s, runners challenged themselves to run as far as they could in one hour. Times for the mile run began to appear in the 1700s.

The reason I say that the first timed footrace was a seminal event is that runners run differently when they are timed than they do when they are competing against others or running as hard as they can alone without timekeeping. So the advent of timed races created a whole new way of running. Specifically, it made runners run faster. How so? Well, before the advent of timekeeping, a runner could do no better than run faster than everyone else in a given race. After the advent of timekeeping, runners could aim higher: They could try to cover a given course or distance faster than anyone had ever done before. And while only the fastest of the fast could aim so high, runners of all ability levels could now try to run faster than each individually had ever done before. Indeed, before timekeeping there was not much point in racing if a runner was not capable of winning (which is probably why most races in eighteenth-century England were one-on-one matches staged for betting purposes). But with timekeeping, anyone interested in running had a motive to run hard.

The reason that runners are generally able to run faster in timed than in untimed races has to do with how the brain regulates running performance. As we have seen, in events in which a runner wishes to complete a defined running task in the shortest time possible, the brain's job is to ensure that the runner completes the task in the shortest time possible without any serious harm. Through communication with the rest of the body, the unconscious brain has a sense of the absolute physiological limits of the muscles and other organs and tissues. During hard running it monitors the proximity of the various physiological systems to their ultimate limits. As necessary, the brain acts to prevent these limits from being reached by reducing muscle activation and by making the runner feel miserable. This mechanism is not robotically exact and consistent. While the brain never allows the body to reach its true performance limits, exactly how close it allows the body to get depends on the details of the situation. The presence of competition is one situational detail that typically enables runners to come closer to running themselves to death, hence to run faster. Timing is another, and it works in basically the same way: Running against time is a competition against a device or against yourself or against nature or against other runners indirectly—depending on how you look at it.

This may be a book about running by feel, but I will be the first person to tell you that you will run better if you run by feel against others or against time than you will if you run by feel alone. It is easy to see why this is the case. The capabilities and limitations of every species are always linked to survival. Humans exhibit a tendency to fatigue more quickly during running (or any other form of exercise) when there is no particular urgency to the running task. How does this tendency help us survive? That's obvious: It helps us survive by limiting unnecessary exposure to the health risks of extreme fatigue. On the flip side, it is easy to see how our capacity to run harder when there *is* an urgent need to run harder also helps us survive. Before there were footraces of any kind, there were humans hunting prey by running and humans fleeing predators by running. In the good old days we ran frequently to satisfy urgent needs, and it was a blessing that we could run faster and longer when chasing an antelope or being chased by a lion. Human-versus-human competitive running undoubtedly began as a form of serious play, where men established an order of rank with respect to this critical survival skill. While there is nothing so great at stake in training and racing in the twenty-first century, our genes don't really know that. Through evolution, our species developed an instinctual tendency to run harder when chasing or fleeing something outside ourselves, a tendency that remains with us, because while our environment has changed significantly since the birth of humankind, our DNA has changed little. So today we can, if we choose, manipulate this instinct to make a game of running faster by consciously trying to run faster against the clock.

WHY WE KEEP GETTING FASTER

Widely recognized world records for events ranging from the mile to the marathon existed by the late nineteenth century (although the marathon distance was not formalized at 26 miles, 385 yards until well into the twentieth century). In 1886, the mile world record was 4:12.75. In 1908, the marathon world record was 2:55:18. The world records at these distances and every distance in between have dropped dramatically over the past century. At the time of this writing, the men's mile world record stood at 3:43.13 and the men's marathon world record at 2:03:59. The rate at which world records are broken has slackened in recent decades compared to when the events were new, but they continue to fall, as do major national records and age-group records. Experts have forecasted the imminent end of running record progressions for generations, and while we are certainly closer to the end now than ever before, it is amazing how long we have been able to sustain the march.

Explaining this phenomenon has become a fun parlor game for running fanatics with a scientific mind-set. Many have pointed to a growing talent pool as part of the explanation. For example, until the 1960s East Africans did not compete internationally in running. When they began doing so, the rate of record-breaking increased. Now that people in most parts of the world have the opportunity to run, it is the growth of the world's population that increases the talent pool. Everyone knows that a runner must first "win the genetic lottery" to have any hope of breaking records later through proper training and long-term development. Researchers have already isolated a number of genes that support endurance performance, each of which exists in only a minority of the population. For example, a gene variant called R577X, which exists in just 18 percent of the population, alters metabolism in fast-twitch muscle fibers in a way that enhances their endurance capacity.

> **MIND-BODY RUNNING**
>
> Pursue personal records as single-mindedly as great runners pursue world records. Chasing personal bests encourages your mind and body to conspire to allow you to run faster than you ever have before.

As of 2007, scientists had found 23 such genetic variants that tend to favor endurance performance. The odds of any single person having all of them are 0.0005 percent, according to Alun Williams of Manchester Metropolitan University in England, who published a paper on this topic.[1] And it is widely agreed that other performance genes are yet to be discovered, bringing the chances of the perfect runner being born even lower. "However," Williams noted in his paper, "with population turnover, the chance of such genetically gifted individuals existing increases." In other words, as the world population grows, genetic lottery winners with increasing numbers of endurance performance genes are born. "Consequently," Williams concluded, "with population turnover world and Olympic records should improve even without further enhancement of environmental factors," such as better training and nutrition.

Environmental factors undoubtedly were major contributors to the first several decades of record progressions. The advent of interval training brought records down in the 1950s, the advent of altitude training brought records down in the 1960s, the advent of sports drinks may have brought records down at the marathon distance specifically in the 1970s, and the use of pacers (or "rabbits") probably aided record-breaking in the 1980s. However, it is hard to think of any major environmental innovation within the last 20 years that can be tied to the trend of record progression. The specter of drugs and blood doping hangs over the last 50 years, and more, of course, but while I am not such a Pollyanna as to believe that no world records have ever been tainted by drugs, I do think that most of the current records are legitimate—that, in fact, our latest improvements have actually surpassed the bump that the record progression got from cheating.

I believe that the single most influential factor in the progression of running records is what might be called the "attractor factor." In a 2006 paper, a Spanish researcher named Juan García-Manso explained the progression of running world records through complexity theory—the same theory that is used to mathematically explain the behavior of large, dynamic systems such as market economies and climate systems.[2] In complexity theory, each system is understood to have one or more "attractors" that pull the elements of the system toward it, thereby serving to create a dynamic order and stability. García-Manso argued that world records function as attractors in the sport of running.

"The sporadic appearance of [runners] able to deliver times that are clearly better than those existing would define new goals or targets that would act as attractors or reference points for other athletes," he wrote. In other words, records beget records. Record-setting runners themselves understand this force very well. Former mile world record holder John Walker of New Zealand shared his take on it with Nic Bideau in a conversation that took place in 1986, when Steve Cram held the mile world record at 3:46.42 and Walker was still running subfour miles at age 34. "I remarked that it was amazing he was still running so well at that age," Bideau told me. "He said, 'Well, back in 1975, when I was 22 years old, if the world record had been 3:47, I would have run 3:46. But the world record was 3:51, so I just ran 3:49.'"

Records exert their attractive force through the mind-body connection. The process begins when a runner consciously embraces the goal of breaking a particular record. This commitment changes the way the runner subsequently trains and prepares. For example, the runner may choose workout target times differently. But the majority of changes may occur on a subconscious level. Once the goal of breaking a world record has been internalized, it suffuses the runner's workouts, thoughts, and other behaviors in ways that she may be largely unaware of but that serve to align her completely with this goal.

Such goals may also help runners find their optimal individual training formula. Genes not only give certain lucky men and women the talent required to break records, but they also determine how their bodies respond to various training practices. It is only a small exaggeration to say that a runner's magic formula is encoded in his DNA. Actually discovering that formula requires experimentation (and a bit of luck). Setting a challenging goal creates a pressure that impels experimentation. Not every record attempt meets with success, of course, but record pursuers generally perform better for having pursued records than they would have done otherwise. If this is true, then the progression of running records has continued as long as it has because the faster the records become, the more forcefully they act to match up the runners who have the requisite genes with the optimal individual training methods for each runner in that select cohort.

BEATING YOUR BEST PAST SELF

You probably do not have the requisite genes for record-breaking, and you will likely never try to break a major running record. But setting goals to break personal records can do for you more or less the same thing that the pursuit of world records does for the genetic lottery winners. When you go after a personal record, you essentially set up a race against yourself—specifically, against your former best self. Such a goal awakens those ancient survival instincts that enable you to run faster in pursuit or flight than you ever can without a specific purpose. Indeed, by definition, chasing personal bests encourages your mind and body to conspire to allow you to run faster than you ever have before. And in most cases, I think it also sets you up to run faster than you could in pursuit of any other goal, even a more challenging one, as goals overwhelm when they are too challenging. The subconscious brain never allows the body to venture too far into unknown territory. That's why no runner sets a goal to break a world record unless he or she has already come close. For example, Haile Gebrselassie had run a 2:05:56 marathon before he set his first marathon world record of 2:04:26 in a deliberate record attempt. Exactly one year later he ran 2:03:59. Did he run faster then because he was fitter or more experienced? No. He ran faster because he tried to run faster.

Well, perhaps he was fitter. But if he was, then he was probably also fitter because he was trying to run faster. As I suggested, setting a goal to break a world record influences the pace at which a runner starts the race and how hard she tries to sustain that pace, but it also influences how she trains. Having already developed his personal magic training formula, Gebrselassie probably trained very similarly for his second marathon world record as he had for his first, but in preparing for the second, he undoubtedly consciously strove to match or beat his times in certain benchmark workouts. That is the sort of thing that makes sense to Gebrselassie. Heart rates and blood lactate levels and rates of oxygen consumption mean nothing to him. But if he wants to race faster over a given distance, he knows he ought to be able to run faster in training.

MIND-BODY RUNNING

Consciously try to beat your recent times in key workouts throughout the training process, and include plenty of repetition within your key workout progressions to facilitate this self-competitive approach to training.

In this way, as in so many other ways, Haile Gebrselassie's simple approach to training is a model for the rest of us. As I have said often in this book, if you want to run your best, you must fully harness the power of your brain, which is the seat of your performance capacities and limitations. Racing in pursuit of personal-best times is a powerful tool to harness the power of your brain. And extending the pursuit of faster times into the training process is an effective means toward the end of breaking personal records. Clearly stated, one of your primary tactical objectives in training should be to run faster and faster in your workouts.

It sounds like such an obvious thing, but very few coaches and experts encourage runners to look at the training process in this way. Instead of telling runners to just try to run faster, most coaches and experts advise runners to target the appropriate physiological intensity level for each workout (whether determined by heart rate or by pace as a proxy for VO_2), and the importance of not training too intensely (fast) is stressed as much as that of training intensely enough.

This point is illustrated by an e-mail exchange I had with Rick, a triathlete who was following one of my online triathlon training plans. Rick e-mailed me to express his confusion about how to do workouts such as one described in the plan as a 45-minute ride at "moderate aerobic intensity" (which is essentially a default cycling intensity when a runner is just logging miles by feel and not consciously trying to hold back or push hard). He noted that when he started such a workout, it took his heart rate 10 or 12 minutes to rise to the level associated with moderate aerobic intensity. So, Rick asked, should he add 10 or 12 minutes to the workout to ensure he got a full 45 minutes at moderate aerobic intensity, or was the workout really designed to consist of a 10–12-minute warm-up and 33–35 minutes at moderate aerobic intensity?

In my reply, I explained to Rick that exercise intensity is not defined by heart rate. Thus, even though it might take his heart rate 10 or 12 minutes to reach a plateau at the beginning of a workout performed at the effort associated with moderate aerobic intensity, if his actual work output level (wattage) is consistent, then he's already working at that intensity from the very first pedal stroke.

Rick's confusion about the relationship between heart rate and exercise intensity is representative of a general bias among triathletes, cyclists, and runners—caused largely by the popularization of heart rate monitors—to view their training in terms of physiology instead of performance. I believe this bias reduces the effectiveness of many athletes' training by discouraging them from pushing themselves as hard as they would push if they kept their focus on performance. When your main concern in workouts is to stay within a target heart rate zone, you place a somewhat artificial ceiling on your performance. But when you focus instead on performance variables such as speed, distance, and power output, you naturally push to beat the standards set in previous workouts—that is, you work harder, and as a result you get a bigger fitness stimulus from the session.

Now, I know what all of the heart-rate junkies reading this are saying: "It's not good to treat workouts like races! It's just as important to avoid working too hard as it is too avoid going too easy, and heart-rate monitors help with that!"

Fair enough. But I'm not talking about treating workouts as races, where the goal is to hold nothing back and finish with nothing left. I'm talking about aiming to perform just a little better in each workout of a given type than in the last workout of the same type. This sort of performance mind-set encourages a runner to work slightly harder than she might do otherwise but still involves a measure of healthy restraint.

TRAINING AT YOUR NATURAL PACE

Maintaining a performance mind-set in training requires that you give close and consistent attention to the performance-relevant metrics of time and pace and push performance-irrelevant metrics such as heart rate into the background. This guideline even applies to the easier runs that should predominate in your training, as they do for nearly all serious competitive runners. You don't need a heart-rate monitor to keep from running too hard when you're supposed to run easy. You can simply go by feel and run at your natural pace, or the pace you fall into automatically when you go for a typical moderate, steady run of a certain predetermined distance or duration (5 miles, 45 minutes, or whatever)—a format that probably accounts for 90 percent of all runs performed daily by the worldwide population of runners. Yet while the intensity of these runs is best controlled by feel, it is still helpful to monitor pace in them. Each runner's natural pace changes over time as fitness is gained or lost, and it even changes from day to day based on how the runner feels—a factor influenced by fatigue from preceding training, above all. Therefore, monitoring the pace of runs performed by feel at natural pace provides valuable information about fitness and fatigue levels.

What determines a runner's natural running pace? Exercise scientists have made few efforts to answer this question, and the answers that have been proposed are unsatisfactory. In a 2001 study, researchers from the University of Udine, Italy, tested the hypothesis that natural running pace is determined by blood lactate level.[3] They expected to find that natural running pace would correspond to the maximal lactate steady state, or the fastest pace a runner could sustain without lactate accumulating to a concentration that would cause fatigue. Eight recreational runners were first tested for their lactate threshold speed and heart rate and were then asked to run for 1 hour at their natural pace. On average, the runners did complete the 1-hour run at approximately their maximal lactate steady state; however, while there was a lot of variation in the individual lactate steady state speeds among the eight subjects (some were much faster than others), there was significantly less variation in pace levels maintained in the 1-hour run, a finding that led the study's authors to conclude that "besides the need of avoiding lactate accumulation in blood, other factors must be involved in the choice of speed in running."

There were two problems with the University of Udine researchers' lactate-based hypothesis. First, there is no evidence that running pace is strictly limited by blood lactate levels. In short races, for example, runners routinely achieve blood lactate levels that exceed the lactate threshold value. If such high lactate concentrations are "allowed" in short races, how could they impose an immovable ceiling on running pace in other circumstances? Second, there is no mechanism whereby blood lactate could regulate running pace even if it did cause muscle fatigue. If blood lactate did regulate running pace throughout exercise prior to fatigue, then each runner would run the same pace in every run—the pace corresponding to the "right" blood lactate level.

What the University of Udine researchers were forgetting, and what almost all exercise physiologists forgot in all of their work until sometime after 2001, was the role of the brain in exercise regulation. It is the brain that tells the muscles how hard to work—in this case, how fast to run—during all exercise situations. Therefore, the true explanation of the natural running pace phenomenon must be seated in the brain. This truth was suggested by another 2001 study—this one performed by researchers at Wayne State University in Wayne, Nebraska.[4] Eighteen men and women were asked to complete 20-minute workouts at their individual preferred intensity level in three separate modalities: treadmill running, stationary cycling, and stair stepping. The physiological variables were all over the place in the three workouts. On average, the subjects completed the cycling workout at a much higher percentage of VO_2max than the treadmill and stair stepper workouts and completed the stair stepper workout at a much higher percentage of their maximal heart rate than the cycling and treadmill workouts. However, their ratings of perceived exertion were almost exactly the same in all three workouts. Clearly, then, natural running pace and preferred intensity in other forms of exercise are not totally determined by physiology but are instead selected by feel. And where does feeling happen? In the brain.

Other studies have produced similar results. When given the freedom to go by feel, exercisers consistently choose an exercise intensity that is toward the high end of the comfortable range in relation to the duration of the workout they are trying to complete. Why this particular level of exertion? I believe it represents a compromise between two competing desires that the brain manifests in every exercise session: the desire to complete the task as quickly as possible (in other words, to get the workout over with) and the desire to feel comfortable. So a natural running pace—whether it's 9:00 per mile, 7:30 per mile, or 6:15 per mile—represents the running-specific version of this compromise relative to individual running ability.

But is your natural running pace a good thing or a bad thing with respect to your goal of increasing your running performance level? After all, the mere fact that it is natural does not necessarily make it an effective means to the competitive ends you seek as a runner. Well, it so happens that natural running pace corresponds closely to the running intensity associated with the maximal rate of fat burning, making this pace ideal for longer runs designed to increase fat-burning capacity and raw endurance. And because natural running pace does not tax the body as much as faster paces, it is possible to maintain a greater overall volume of running when most of your running is done at this pace, and the more you run, the more your running economy improves.

So your natural pace does have a place in your training. However, natural pace becomes a limiting comfort zone for many runners. Specifically, as a consequence of focusing too much on numbers and not enough on how their bodies feel, competitive runners often refuse to run any slower than their accustomed pace, even on days when they feel flat and their planned run is not supposed to be challenging. Consequently, these runs leave them feeling flat the next time they are actually supposed to run hard, and they are unable to run hard enough. So they fall into a rut of training without any healthy extremes of easy and hard.

Smart runners teach themselves to instinctively weigh how their bodies feel more than the pace clock in determining their pace for basic aerobic runs and recovery sessions. Kenya's runners are famous for the dawdling pace of many of their easy runs. But many Western elites get it, too. Frank Shorter, the 1972 Olympic Marathon gold medalist, ran many of his easy runs so slowly that runners with a fraction of his ability could keep up with him. In the late 1970s, Michael Sandrock was a student at the University of Colorado and Frank Shorter was a two-time Olympic medalist living and training in Boulder. In his book *Running Tough*, Sandrock wrote of a day when Shorter invited Sandrock, whose cousin was Shorter's roommate, to join him for an easy run. They started slow—much slower than Sandrock expected—but what surprised him even more was that Shorter never picked up the pace. They ran 10 miles so slowly that Sandrock considered running again later the same day.

Before they parted, Shorter invited Sandrock to join him for a track workout the following day. Sandrock accepted, and 24 hours later Shorter tore him limb from limb. "That was one of Shorter's secrets," Sandrock wrote, "running his easy days very easy, and his hard days extremely hard. A simple concept, but so hard to implement for some reason. Most of us make the mistake of going medium-hard all the time."

As long as you do know when and when not to use your natural running pace, it is helpful to monitor it. Indeed, tracking changes in your natural running pace is one of the simplest and most motivating ways to monitor your running fitness level. As the training cycle progresses, you should see this pace gradually come down. That is, you will run faster and faster at the same, high-end-of-comfortable exertion level. But this is not something you should force—just go by feel, and let it happen in the appropriate workouts. For the other workouts, target pace training is more effective.

MIND-BODY RUNNING

Consider using a target pace system to aid the process of setting appropriate pace targets for key workouts.

TARGET PACE TRAINING

As I have said previously, the most important knowledge that any runner can gain is what many young runners acquire in their first year of high school: how to do the workouts. Decades of worldwide collective trial and error have produced a set of standard workout formats that represent the best practices of running. Sure, there are all kinds of wrinkles that can be applied to make common workouts seem unusual, but that's window dressing. Every runner can fulfill his potential by performing the same base, long, progression, fartlek, hill, tempo, threshold, and interval runs that a million other runners have done. The challenge lies in figuring out the best ways to combine, arrange, and execute them to unlock the full potential encoded in his DNA.

The most important element in workout execution is appropriate pacing. If you run a given base run too fast, you may be too fatigued to perform well in an interval run the next day. If you run the intervals in a given workout too slow, neither your body nor your mind will get as much out of it as possible. Experience is an invaluable tool in effective workout pacing. Through experience you learn, for example, the consequences of running too hard on your easy days and hence the appropriate perceived exertion level for easy runs. Through experience you also accrue a record of performances in various types of workouts and hence the standards to use.

I think it is helpful, though, to complement experience with a set of objective standards that are based on, and thus allow individual runners to take advantage of, collective experience. There are many target pace systems that coaches and experts have come up with over the years. I have even come up with a couple of my own (or, more accurately, modified a couple created by others). But my favorite is the McMillan Running Calculator, developed by coach Greg McMillan. (You can find this terrific tool on McMillan's Web site: www.mcmillanrunning.com.) A former regional-caliber competitive runner who now coaches a stable of elite runners in Flagstaff, Arizona, McMillan was mentored by the great Italian coach Gabriele Rosa, who has coached a long list of top African runners. While studying for a master's degree in exercise physiology, McMillan became interested in the correlation of blood lactate levels to running performance. He was especially curious about three things: (1) how blood lactate levels and other physiological markers of running intensity correlated to pace at different race distances for runners of various ability levels; (2) the physiological adaptations associated with running at the full range of intensities used in training, as measured by these same physiological markers; and (3) how these markers correlated with pace at the full range of intensities used in training. In the mid-1990s, McMillan began using his knowledge about physiology-pace relationships to develop a calculator that would allow runners to predict their finishing time at any given race distance based on their time at another distance and target appropriate paces in all types of workouts given their current fitness level as represented by a recent race performance or estimated current race performance capacity. When these two functions are put together, the result is a tool that runners can use to set and pursue immediate and intermediate training performance targets on the path toward a peak race performance goal.

Greg McMillan is wise enough to know that practice trumps theory as a standard for effective training, so he did not rely on physiology-pace relationships exclusively in designing his calculator. Instead, he used these relationships to establish provisional pace targets and then modified them based on the results of real-world application with runners of widely varying ability levels whom he coached. I believe that McMillan could have ignored physiology altogether and created a calculator based entirely on data from real-world racing and training and on mathematical formulas extrapolated from patterns found in those data. But while he may have taken an unnecessary extra step, McMillan eventually got where he wanted to go. His calculator is the best tool I know to facilitate effective training execution by giving runners appropriate performance targets to shoot for throughout the training process.

To use the tool, first set a specific race time goal for your next peak race. Enter that time in the calculator, and study the recommended pace targets for the various types of training, which range from recovery runs on the slow end to sprint intervals on the fast end. The pace target for each workout type is not a single number but rather a pace range. For example, if your goal is to run a 32:50 10K, your recommended target pace range for 1,000 m intervals is 3:05.7–3:12.9. (Figure 7.1 presents the McMillan Running Calculator's estimated race time equivalencies and recommended training pace targets for a 32:50 10K.) The reason for the use of such ranges is that runners begin the training process at a significantly lower fitness level than they hope to attain by the end of the process. Thus, at the beginning of the training process, they cannot achieve workout performances that are truly equivalent to their peak race goal time. So the idea is that at the beginning of the training process, you aim for the pace at the slow end of each range, and then you try to run incrementally faster in subsequent workouts of the same type. In the final weeks of training before your peak race, you will want to hit the fast end of each target range in workouts.

I make a distinction between key workouts and other workouts, however. Key workouts are challenging sessions performed at faster paces. It is only in these workouts that you should compete against yourself by trying to improve upon the standard you set in the last workout of the same type. A key workout may be loosely defined as any workout in which you run at marathon pace or faster if you're a serious runner or at half-marathon pace or faster if you're a more casual runner. Key workouts are supposed to be hard, so it is appropriate to use target paces to push harder in them. But recovery runs, base runs, and some long runs are not meant to be hard, so you should not try to run faster in them every time. Use McMillan's recommended pace targets for these workouts more to prevent yourself from running too fast than to ensure that you run fast enough.

McMillan's pace target system is effective only if you perform the right workouts, of course. For example, if you are chasing a 10K PR of 32:50, you will find McMillan's recommended pace range of 3:05.7–3:12.9 rather easy if you perform a workout consisting of only 2 × 1,000 m with a 5:00 active recovery between intervals instead of the more standard 5 × 1,000 m with 3:00 active recoveries that McMillan probably had in mind when he created those pace targets. So again, you need to have some knowledge of how to do the various types of workouts before you begin to make use of the pace target system. (Again, I refer you to the Appendix for a brief overview of the basic workout types.) You also need to understand how to format your key

Event	100m	200m	400m	500m	800m	1000m	1500m	Mile	2000m	3000m	2M	4000m	3M	5000m
Time	13.4	26.9	56.2	01:13.3	02:03.4	02:41.3	04:14.2	04:33.7	05:47.1	09:03.8	09:44.2	12:23.0	15:14	15:48
Pace/Mile	–	–	–	–	–	–	–	–	04:39.2	04:51.7	04:52.1	04:58.9	5:05	5:05
Pace/K	–	–	–	–	–	–	02:49.5	02:50.1	02:53.5	03:01.3	03:01.5	03:05.7	3:09	3:10

Event	4M	8000m	5M	10K	15K	10M	20K	13.1M	15M	25K	30K	20M	25M	Marathon
Time	20:40	26:03:00	26:12:00	32:50:00	50:53:00	55:01:00	1:09:14	1:13:04	1:24:16	1:27:57	1:46:58	1:55:41	2:25:50	2:34:05
Pace/Mile	5:10	5:14	5:14	5:17	5:28	5:30	5:35	5:35	5:37	5:40	5:45	5:47	5:50	5:53
Pace/K	3:13	3:15	3:15	3:17	3:24	3:25	3:28	3:28	3:30	3:31	3:34	3:36	3:37	3:39

Endurance Workouts	Pace/Mile	Pace/K
Recovery Jogs	7:23 to 7:53	4:35 to 4:54
Long Runs	6:23 to 7:23	3:58 to 4:35
Easy Runs	6:23 to 6:53	3:58 to 4:17

Stamina Workouts	Pace/Mile	Pace/K
Steady-State Runs	5:35 to 5:45	3:28 to 3:34
Tempo Runs	5:21 to 5:35	3:19 to 3:28
Tempo Intervals	5:17 to 5:28	3:17 to 3:24

Cruise Intervals		Time/Interval
	(mile)	5:14 to 5:21
	(1200m)	3:54 to 3:59
	(1000m)	3:15 to 3:19
	(800m)	2:36 to 2:40
	(600m)	1:57 to 2:00
	(400m)	1:18 to 1:20

Speed Workouts	Middle Distance Runners	Long Distance Runners
400m	1:08.0 to 1:11.0	1:09.4 to 1:13.4
800m	2:18.8 to 2:25.2	2:25.0 to 2:31.8
1000m	3:01.3 to 3:09.7	3:05.7 to 3:12.9
1200m	3:37.8 to 3:47.6	3:42.9 to 3:54.2
1600m	4:57.2 to 5:08.6	5:03.5 to 5:14.7
2000m	6:19.4 to 6:30.3	6:25.8 to 6:33.4

Sprint Workouts	Middle Distance Runners	Long Distance Runners
100m	14.1 to 15.4	14.7 to 16.1
200m	29.3 to 32.3	30.1 to 33.1
300m	44.0 to 50.8	45.1 to 51.5
400m	1:01.7 to 1:08.6	1:04.5 to 1:09.4
600m	1:36.8 to 1:44.1	1:41.7 to 1:46.4

Race time equivalencies and recommended training pace targets in this example work toward the goal of running a 10k in 32:50. The calculator can be used for various race distances.

Figure 7.1 Example of McMillan Running Calculator Output

workouts appropriately given your current fitness level and given where you are within the training cycle. For example, if you do four sessions of 1,000 m intervals within a training cycle, perhaps the first one should be 4 × 1,000 m at the slow end of the target pace range with 3:00 recoveries and the last should be 5 × 1,000 m at the fast end of the target pace range with 2:00 active recoveries.

The more repetition there is in your key workouts, the more you will benefit from using pace targets to stimulate improvement through self-competition. If you do only one set of 1,000 m intervals in a training cycle, you have no chance to beat your performance in that session and reap the special physiological and psychological benefits that come from doing so. But if you do multiple sessions of 1,000 m intervals and all goes well, you can look back after completing the last of them and see a steady march of improvement, as in this hypothetical example:

Session 1	3:12.6 avg. per 1,000 m
Session 2	3:10.1 avg. per 1,000 m
Session 3	3:07.7 avg. per 1,000 m
Session 4	3:05.4 avg. per 1,000 m

In Chapter 4 I made the case for using more repetition in training than many competitive runners do because it creates a comfort zone that facilitates psychological momentum. But repeating workouts achieves this effect only if performance improves, and performance improves most when better performance is actively pursued through the use of pace targets and self-competition.

There is a limit to how much repetition is sensible. Trying to run set distances faster is only one way to develop race fitness. Another is to run longer at set paces. It is very important to increase the distances of your key workouts as the training process unfolds instead of focusing exclusively on running faster and faster in exactly repeated key workout formats. Runners have greater capacity to increase their range (how far they can go) at various speeds than to increase their speed over fixed distances or durations, so it is very helpful to work on developing range-at-speed in training. For example, suppose your next peak race goal is to break three hours for the marathon. Hence, your race-pace goal is 6:51 per mile. Assuming you begin the marathon training process with a decent base of endurance, developing race-specific fitness is going to be more about increasing your current range at 6:51 per mile than about increasing your current sustainable pace over 26.2 miles. This means you will want to include in your training a thread of marathon-pace workouts that require you to run farther and farther at more or less the same pace. That's a different way of stimulating and measuring progress than trying to run your third 5 × 1,000 m session faster than your second 5 × 1,000 m session and your second faster than your first.

Generally, when you introduce a new type of key workout into a training cycle, you should do a very manageable version of that workout type. In each subsequent workout of the same type, you can add an appropriate amount of distance, and sometimes also run faster, until you arrive at an appropriate maximum distance for that type of workout. From that point forward you can keep the format the same and focus entirely on going faster.

AN EXAMPLE FROM ON HIGH

In November 2009 I traveled to Mammoth Lakes, California, with a few colleagues to watch Mammoth Lakes Track Club member Josh Cox perform a big workout. We filmed it for a Running.Competitor.com video series called *Training Day*.

The workout consisted of 15 miles run at a marathon-effort level, which was not quite the same thing as marathon pace in this case because the workout took place 7,100 feet above sea level. Including warm-up and cooldown, Cox would cover a total distance of 23 miles. Cox completed the workout nine days before racing the Rock n' Roll San Antonio Half Marathon in hopes of breaking his personal record of 1:03:54 and exactly one month before competing in the California International Marathon with the goal of breaking his PR at that distance (2:13:58). It was what I call a peak workout: one of the toughest, most race-specific workouts in the training cycle, performed late in the cycle, when he was already in excellent shape and just needed to complete the process of establishing the physical confidence to achieve his race goals.

"This was one of those workouts you circle on your calendar and say, 'Okay, this is one I have to nail,'" Cox told me after completing the workout. "If I had tried to do that a month and a half ago, it would have been a nightmare," he said.

Cox's marathon-pace run was also the last in a series of such workouts that were spaced at intervals of 7 to 10 days. The first in the series was just 6 miles. The remaining seven workouts in the series were 8 miles, 10 miles, 10 miles, 12 miles, 12 miles, 15 miles, and 15 miles. In each of these runs Cox tried to match or slightly beat his pace from the previous one, even when he ran farther. His average pace in the first of the two 15-milers was 5:16 per mile. He set out to beat that pace in the session I witnessed, and he did, finishing the run in 1:17:09 (5:08 per mile), which he described with evident satisfaction as "better than expected."

MIND-BODY RUNNING

There are six guidelines for effective key workouts progressions: Make them repetitive, ease into them, build them gradually, do them frequently but not too frequently, do not overextend them, and use target times.

Indeed, Cox rated the workout as one of the best of his life. It came about as no accident. There were six key features of the marathon-pace sequence that coach Terrence Mahon prescribed for Cox that set him up for success. Make sure your key workout progressions of all types have these same features:

1. *The workout series was repetitive.* Three times within the eight-workout progression, Cox exactly repeated a workout. All of the runs were also performed on the same route: the famously nicknamed "Green Church Road," which has long been the proving grounds for other Mammoth Lakes Track Club legends such as Deena Kastor, Meb Keflezighi, and Ryan Hall. "You always know exactly where you stand," Cox told me, meaning that doing the same workouts in the same place repeatedly allowed him to measure his current self against his past self with perfect accuracy.

2. *The workout series was eased into.* The first, 6 mile marathon-pace run was run at the slower end of Cox's goal marathon-pace range. Six miles at marathon pace is a good workout, so it sufficed to stimulate fitness gains that Cox could take advantage of to run faster and farther in the next marathon-pace workout, but it was not so challenging as to overwhelm his body and mind at an early stage in the training cycle.

3. *The workout series built up gradually.* Progress never happens by leaps and bounds in training, and the results are always disastrous when a runner tries to force improvement to happen that way. Cox never increased the distance of his marathon-pace run by more than 2 miles, and he was always satisfied by any improvement in his average pace from one session to the next, even if it was just a second or two per mile.

4. *The workouts were frequent but not too frequent.* Holding back a bit in the first session enabled Cox to improve his performance from one session to the next in part by simply trying harder and suffering more. But while training the capacity to suffer is important, it is more important to actually build physical fitness between iterations of the same key workout so that you can run faster at the same effort level. Again, these adaptations take time, so it's best to separate the workouts by at least a week. On the other hand, it is important to develop and maintain a sense of momentum as the runner works through a key workout progression, so it's usually best also to separate the workouts by no more than 10 days.

5. *The workout series was not overextended.* A runner can only improve from key workout to key workout for so long before reaching a temporary adaptive limit. Therefore, it's important to carefully limit the number of workouts you include in any key workout progression. Cox's marathon-pace workout progression included eight workouts. That's about the right number for most key workout progressions.

6. *The workout series used target times.* Josh Cox clearly knew that one of the most effective ways to run faster is to try to run faster. He started the race preparation process by setting explicit goals to beat his best past self at two distances. His coach then created a

training plan that included key workout progressions incorporating target times appropriate to his race goal times. On the march toward beating his best past self in a half marathon and a marathon, Cox tried to beat the Josh Cox of the previous week or of the week before that in key workouts.

So how did those races go, anyway? Cox had a rough time on the day of his half-marathon-record attempt; the weather was warm and humid. But at the California International Marathon he had the race of his life, vying for the win all the way through and ultimately finishing a very close second to eventual victor Tesfaye Girma-Bekele of Ethiopia in 2:13:51. When asked afterward if he was disappointed to lose, Cox replied: "I'm thrilled. I set a PR!"

PART III

THE FINER POINTS OF THE MIND-BODY METHOD

EIGHT

RUN BEAUTIFULLY

> People always notice my stride.
>
> —Lucas Verzbicas

When it was announced in August 2005 that Kenenisa Bekele would attempt to break his own 10,000 m world record in Brussels, Belgium, and that video of the attempt would be streamed live on the Internet, I made sure to tune in. Not only was I interested in seeing history made; I also simply love watching Bekele run. Some people would find the monotony of a man running around a 400 m oval 25 times unbearable. Not me. Few things are more beautiful than the stride of a great runner. Each runner's stride is unique in its nuances, but in the stride of every great runner we see power and grace commingled in some fashion.

In the same way that a great song, novel, or film can resonate with the masses, I believe that everyone can recognize a beautiful stride. Suppose you are watching a couple dozen runners of widely ranging ability levels running individually at a fixed, moderate pace for 20 seconds. If you were then asked to rate the stride of each for pure aesthetics, your scoring would probably correspond closely to the results of a performance test, such as a 5,000 m time trial, of the same runners. In other words, the runner with the most beautiful stride would also be the fastest, and so on down the line.

In 2010 Lucas Verzbicas became the first sophomore to win the Foot Locker high school boys cross-country championship in the event's 31-year history. This young man, who had already set a national high school record for 5,000 m indoors (14:18.22) as a freshman, not only won the race, but also utterly destroyed the other 39 boys in the race, all older than he was. Verzbicas stood out in another way, though. His stride was beautiful—noticeably lovelier than those of the slower kids. My astounded media friends and I were all struck by it. And Verzbicas himself was not unaware of it. "That is what people always notice and acknowledge about me is my stride," Verzbicas told me after the race, answering my compliment in the aw-shucks manner of a Midwestern prom queen praised for her beauty, albeit with a slight Lithuanian accent (his family immigrated to the United States when he was 8).

Running ability is plainly visible in the form of the stride. In fact, I daresay that it is possible not only to identify the better runner in almost any pair of runners by observing their respective strides but also to accurately assess the fitness level of any single runner whose stride is well known by seeing how it looks today. American mile record holder Alan Webb has had an up-and-down career. I never know which Alan Webb is going to show up for the next race. But within the first 100 m, I always know which Alan Webb is racing, because his stride tells me. I could never put into words exactly what looks different about Webb at his worst versus Webb at his best, but it could not be more apparent to my eyes.

The stride is everything in running. Ability, fitness, fatigue, motivation, and all other factors that affect running performance are wholly mediated through the stride, mostly in visible ways. There is simply nothing else going on in running but the stride. This fact may seem too obvious to bear mentioning, and yet it has been oddly overlooked in exercise science over the last several decades. The dominant theoretical paradigm of running performance views body form and biomechanics as a transparent receptacle within which lies all the stuff that really matters—mainly, the machinery of oxygen transport. To be sure, a large aerobic capacity, or VO_2max, and all of the physiology underlying this capacity (high muscle capillary density, high muscle mitochondria concentration, and so forth) are critical to running performance, but only inasmuch as they influence the stride. While it may be neat to have your VO_2max measured in a laboratory and to learn that number, there is absolutely nothing useful you can do with this knowledge. The whole VO_2max concept has done nothing but overcomplicate the pursuit of better running performance. Looking beyond the running stride at VO_2max for the sake of running better is like looking beyond the cookie at its sugar content for the sake of finding out how it tastes.

Exercise scientists understandably got pretty excited about the relationship between oxygen consumption and exercise performance when they discovered it a century ago. But what happens so often in science is that scientists overestimate the importance of what they can measure and underestimate the importance of what they cannot measure. When exercise scientists developed the ability to measure oxygen consumption, they soon came to believe that oxygen consumption was everything to exercise performance. Even though it may be obvious that the stride action itself is no small piece of the running performance puzzle, scientists have had difficulty quantifying its characteristics, and so the stride has been marginalized as an object of study and wrongly considered a peripheral factor in running performance.

QUANTIFYING GOOD FORM

This situation has begun to change. Some clever scientists have lately developed new ways of distinguishing better strides from worse strides, and such lines of research may help create a new paradigm of running performance that correctly identifies the stride itself as the thing that really matters.

One of these researchers is Stephen McGregor, an exercise physiologist at Eastern Michigan University with whom I had the good fortune to coauthor a book entitled *The Runner's Edge*, which is largely based on his work (and which might at first reading seem a total refutation of the thesis of this book). McGregor comes from a cycling background, and in the early 2000s he became interested in developing new tools to quantify training loads in cyclists. These tools relied on data from power meters, which are a cycling-specific instrument. Thus, when McGregor set his mind to transferring these new conceptual tools to running, he needed new sources of data and hence new instruments. There are two types of devices able to capture distance, pace, and other such data in runners: GPS (global positioning system) devices and accelerometers.

McGregor saw more potential in accelerometers, because unlike GPS devices, accelerometers can capture not just speed and distance information but also much higher-resolution information about stride characteristics. In his work in cycling, McGregor was not interested in technique, because he understood that the importance of pedaling technique in cycling is small (because the fixedly rotating pedals basically force every cyclist's legs to move the same way). But he rightly recognized that stride technique is a major factor in running, so he decided to use accelerometers instead of GPS devices in his research with runners, which began in 2005.

An accelerometer is a fairly simple mechanism that essentially measures the speed and direction of its own movement. In his work with runners, McGregor used triaxial accelerometers, which measure accelerations in all three planes of movement: forward-backward, up-down, and side-to-side. He and his colleagues and students performed a few interesting studies using these devices, and they have several others planned. McGregor's first study demonstrated that data from running accelerometers could be used to accurately estimate the oxygen cost of running and thus to quantify a runner's training load over time.[1] Other studies used accelerometers to identify signature differences in the stride characteristics of trained and untrained runners and to identify changes in stride characteristics associated with fatigue.[2] Some of the findings confirmed truths about running biomechanics that had been previously discovered through other forms of measurement, whereas other findings taught us things about running biomechanics that had not been previously known.

As expected, McGregor found that trained runners accelerated less in all three planes of motion. At any given speed, the members of the nationally ranked Eastern Michigan University cross-country team whom McGregor used as subjects bounced up and down less, moved less from side to side, and lost less forward momentum between strides than did the nonrunner students in the study. But there were also differences within the pool of trained runners, with the fastest runners tending to accelerate least in all three planes. This finding suggested that some runners were gifted to be more economical than others, but McGregor's studies also produced compelling evidence that training enhanced stride efficiency in a highly specific manner. Fascinatingly, McGregor found that trained runners were rather uneconomical walkers and were even somewhat inefficient at running speeds that were slower than their habitual training speeds. One in particular, who had the highest VO_2max on the team, was among the least economical members of his team at a slow jog. McGregor speculated that this runner wasted a lot of energy at these speeds because, thanks to his huge aerobic engine, he could afford to. Because he never ran slowly to the point of exhaustion and hence never subjected his body to the crisis required to force a more efficient stride to delay exhaustion at those specific speeds, his body seemed not to have bothered adapting to the slow running.

Indeed, one of the general conclusions that can be drawn from McGregor's research is that running becomes efficient only inasmuch as it has to. Another runner on the Eastern Michigan team is a case in point. We'll call him John (as the subjects in proper scientific studies are anonymous, I will keep him anonymous here). John was the highest performer on the squad despite having one of the lowest VO_2max measurements. How did he do it? He was the most economical at faster speeds. McGregor told me he wondered if John had not become extremely efficient as a consequence of forcing himself to keep up with more aerobically powerful runners in training and races. If so, this case is evidence that training in a group environment with some slightly faster runners may be an effective way to develop a more beautiful—I mean efficient—stride.

The result may not be automatic, however. After testing John, McGregor became quite curious about him and asked the team's coach if he could account for the test results based on real-world experience in working with John as a runner. "He's not the most talented guy, but he can really suffer," said the coach. When he heard this remark, McGregor was reminded of the VO_2max testing he had done with the team members. In a VO_2max test, the subject runs on a treadmill at incrementally increasing speeds, each of which is sustained for one to two minutes, until he can go no faster, while breathing into a tube connected to a machine that calculates oxygen consumption. Most runners reach their highest level of oxygen consumption at their fastest running speed in the VO_2max test, but some are able to survive one or even two more belt speed increases after reaching VO_2max, and John was one of them. So perhaps training with naturally faster runners is a good way to develop a more economical stride—but only if such a runner is willing and able to suffer more than most other runners.

Another interesting finding of Stephen McGregor's work with accelerometers was that vertical acceleration accounted for a greater proportion of total oscillation in all three planes for trained runners than for nonrunners. In other words, when changes in forward velocity, side-to-side movement, and up-and-down movement during running at any given speed were totaled, up-and-down movement accounted for a greater portion of the total in trained runners than in nonrunners. According to McGregor, there are two possible reasons training reduces up-and-down movement less than movement in the other two planes. First, while training reduces acceleration relative to speed in all three planes of movement, vertical oscillation can be reduced only so much, because runners have to be able to take big strides to run at high speeds and they have to get airborne to take big strides, as all runners fall toward the earth at the same rate. Second, a certain amount of vertical acceleration (bouncing) is required to maximize the "free energy" that the legs can capture from impact with the ground and then send back into the ground to propel forward motion. In any case, whereas vertical oscillation tends to increase steadily with increasing speed in nonrunners, vertical oscillation increases only to a certain point with increasing speed in trained runners, then plateaus and actually begins to fall at very high submaximal running speeds. This phenomenon is undoubtedly a training adaptation that enables runners to "put everything" into moving forward as they approach their physiological speed limit.

It bears noting that all of the training adaptations that distinguish the trained from the untrained stride are almost entirely the results of unconscious, automatic operations. Not only did the runners in McGregor's studies not train consciously to minimize their side-to-side and forward-backward accelerations more than their vertical accelerations, but they were also not even aware that their strides had changed in this way through years of training. Although all of the trained runners involved in McGregor's research thus far have also been naturally gifted runners, it's safe to assume that the improvements in running performance that occur in runners of all natural ability levels through training are largely the results of automatic improvements in stride efficiency as well.

STRIDE ENTROPY

McGregor's most intriguing study so far is one in which he measured and compared entropy levels in the strides of trained and untrained runners. Entropy is essentially a measure of the predictability of the behavior of a system. In the case of the running stride, entropy has to do with how much each individual stride looks like the one before and the one after. McGregor speculated that entropy would decrease as runners approached exhaustion—that reduced entropy would prove to be a signal of fatigue. He anticipated finding that the stride would become more predictable and less varied near exhaustion because such predictability in any system would indicate that system was "constrained."

In the case of running, it stands to reason that the stride becomes constrained when some component of the stride runs up against a performance limit. To oversimplify, suppose that after sustaining a certain speed for a certain period of time, a runner's left soleus muscle begins to lose contractile force. This limit becomes a constraint on the whole system of the runner's stride, making each stride look more like every other stride than when the runner is not fatigued and his stride is not thus constrained, so that it has a little more "play." Research has shown that certain individual muscles do fatigue faster than others during running, and that the brain responds to local muscle fatigue by tweaking the entire stride to ensure that it remains properly coordinated within the limit set by that one tired muscle.[3] It's sort of like putting the most tired sled dog at the head of the team to keep the whole unit working together.

In his study, McGregor did indeed find that stride entropy decreased as runners approached the point of fatigue. Among the Division I college runners used in the study, entropy stayed high at speeds up to 20 km per hour (kph, or 4:50 per mile). But when speeds above 20 kph were sustained, entropy decreased, anticipating the moment of exhaustion. This finding suggested that decreasing stride entropy was a manifestation of fatigue. An important question raised but not answered by these results is that of the specific nature of the constraints that caused entropy and fatigue. The two main categories of constraint sources are metabolic and biomechanical. An example of a specific metabolic constraint is the inability of the cardiorespiratory system to provide enough oxygen to sustain a given running speed. An example of a biomechanical constraint is joint decoupling, which is a fancy name for a loss of the precisely coordinated rhythm of movements required for efficient running (which is a bit like juggling in that any small, localized loss of rhythm causes the whole show to fall apart). Such a slippage in coordination could be caused by local muscle fatigue, a loss of elasticity (or springiness) in certain muscles, or changes in central drive (will) from the brain. McGregor did not favor any particular hypothesis in his study, but in conversation he told me that he thought the primary constraint on the stride at exhaustion was biomechanical.

Whatever the source of fatigue may be, McGregor's work demonstrates that fatigue ultimately manifests as changes in the stride. Indeed, fatigue does not even exist except inasmuch as the stride changes. This idea stands in stark contrast to the conventional idea of running fatigue, which sees the source of fatigue as always entirely metabolic and ignores the stride per se. My most recent conversation with McGregor about his work got me to thinking: If fatigue exists only to the extent that it changes the stride, then a sort of fatigue profile for each individual runner could be created and then used to precisely assess the runner's present fatigue level at any time thereafter. For example, suppose an accelerometer was used to measure stride characteristics in a given runner as she ran at 7:00/mile, beginning in a fully rested state and ending at exhaustion. The gradual changes in stride characteristics observed during that span of time would become a fatigue spectrum for that runner (at that pace). And so, if the same runner were to show up at McGregor's lab the day after running a marathon that McGregor did not know about, strap on the accelerometer, and start running 7:00 miles, the runner could not fool the scientist. McGregor would see that after only a minute of running at this pace, the runner's stride characteristics looked like they normally did after three hours of running at that pace, and McGregor might say, "Did you by chance run a marathon yesterday?"

In support of the accelerometer data, direct visual observation would undoubtedly also reveal to McGregor, and anyone else who knew the runner, a telltale *ugliness* in the runner's stride. Indeed, because fatigue is stride deterioration, and stride deterioration is almost always visible, runners can seldom fool a good coach about their fatigue level even if that coach does not have fancy equipment with which to measure biomechanical changes.

Steve McGregor has no immediate plans to pursue my hypothesis. Instead, he has plans for even more ambitious research that could profoundly validate the stride-based philosophy of running performance. McGregor's idea is to track physiological and biomechanical changes (using accelerometers) in college runners over the course of four years—their entire collegiate running careers—and correlate these changes with changes in their competitive performances during that time. The objective will be to determine whether it is primarily physiology or biomechanics that accounts for the improvement of those runners who improve the most over four years. McGregor is far too good a scientist to prejudice the results of his work with his own expectations, but based on what he has learned from his research so far, he says he does expect to discover that, at this level, improved performance is caused mainly by changes in the stride—that is, by neuromuscular, not cardiovascular, adaptations to training.

THE WRONG WAY TO RUN "RIGHT"

The teaching of running technique has become popular lately. The top-selling running book of the last several years prior to the publication of Christopher McDougall's *Born to Run* was *Chi Running* by Danny Dreyer, which taught a quasi-yoga-based style of running purported to reduce injury.risk.[4] Dreyer has made a thriving business of Chi Running, with videos, clinics, and even a certification program that trains new instructors in the technique. The Chi Running method is very similar to the Pose running method, created by Nicholas Romanov, which has been around for many years but has really taken off only within the last decade. Once all but ignored, running technique is now the topic of countless magazine and Web site articles, is taught by a growing number of running coaches, and is intensively discussed on Internet chat forums and actual training runs. Underlying all of this discussion is a gradually spreading consensus that running technique can in fact be effectively taught—that there is an identifiably correct way to run that every runner can learn and use to run faster and with fewer injuries. (Most of the popular running technique systems, which, in addition to the Pose Method and Chi Running, include Evolution Running, are indeed similar to one another. Each is, at its core, a way of correcting the common error of overstriding. The various methods don't peddle wildly different notions of the right way to run.) This belief that there is a single right way to run represents quite a departure from the old-school view of running technique from previous decades, which held that good running technique was essentially something that a runner was either born with or not, and that the only way to improve running technique was to simply run and let the process happen naturally.

There are some running experts who still believe that this is the case. Among these experts is Ross Tucker, an exercise physiologist at the University of Cape Town, South Africa, whose work I discussed in Chapter 1. Tucker is not persuaded that there can be a single right way for every runner to run. In an article on his Web site, Tucker explained: "My personal opinion is that if there [were] a way to run faster and with fewer injuries that was guaranteed to work in all people ... then it would be discovered by default. It's difficult to fathom that millions of people, with different body shapes and sizes and leg lengths and [centers] of gravity and joint angles could fit into one single pattern or technique. Rather, the passage of time would filter out any flaws for each person." Tucker believes that individual runners naturally develop the stride pattern that works best for them in the normal course of training, but that this pattern is not transferable—in other words, past a certain point, what works for me is unlikely to work for you.

Scientific research on the teaching of running technique tends to support Tucker's view. For example, a 2005 study published in the *Journal of Sports Sciences* reported that the running economy of 16 high-level triathletes was actually reduced (meaning the athletes became less efficient) after 12 weeks of practicing the Pose running method.[5] In fact, to my knowledge no study has ever demonstrated an improvement in running economy or performance resulting from technique training.

Consciously meddling with your stride may indeed make it less efficient instead of more efficient. Research has shown that there is less activity in the brains of skilled performers of all manner of coordinated movements when performing those movements than in the brains of the unskilled. The more you think about something while you do it, the less efficiently you do it. This is as true of running as of any other activity, as shown in a recent study from the University of Münster, Germany.[6] Trained runners were asked to run for 10 minutes at a designated pace on three occasions: once while thinking about their breathing, once while thinking about their stride, and once while thinking about the environment around them. Oxygen consumption was monitored during all three runs. And guess what? The runners consumed the least amount of oxygen—that is, they were most economical—while not thinking about their bodies as they ran.

As you probably know from experience, as running speed and fatigue levels increase, it becomes increasingly difficult to concentrate on the external environment and more and more necessary to consciously will that next stride to happen. This act of willing, called "executive brain function," costs a lot of energy and thus actually hastens fatigue even as it is called upon to resist fatigue. While all runners have to concentrate on the movement of their limbs when running near the limits of their speed and endurance, it appears that better runners don't have to think as much about running while they run, and indeed the very unconsciousness of their running is a major aspect of their superior efficiency. Much as an expert knitter can carry on a conversation while knitting a sweater, seemingly paying no attention whatsoever to the workings of her fingers, whereas the beginning knitter develops a headache after 20 minutes of totally focused knitting, so ferociously must she concentrate on the needles, the highly trained runner can mentally "get out of the way" of his stride and let the brain's unconscious motor centers control it with no wasted energy, whereas the beginner must force his legs to obey the command to keep moving.

Where running differs from skills such as swinging a golf club and knitting is that golfers and knitters have to begin the learning process with conscious imitation of demonstrated techniques, but runners do not. In all skilled movements, technique becomes more unconscious as it becomes better, but the learning of running technique can be (and usually is) done through blind trial and error from the very beginning. The question that Chi Running and other running methods challenge us with is whether runners would be better off learning running the same way golfers learn golf and knitters learn knitting, even though running is clearly innate.

While there is still much more that we need to learn about how the running stride improves, a preponderance of existing evidence indicates that conscious manipulation of the stride is not the best way to run better. Conscious stride manipulation forces the runner to think about his stride, and as we have seen, thinking is the enemy of movement efficiency. Defenders of Chi Running, the Pose method, and the rest will argue that thinking is required only until the new technique becomes "second nature," but there are other problems. Chief among them is that conscious stride manipulation involves making gross motor changes in movement patterns that are usually plainly visible to the outside observer. However, the real improvements in running economy resulting from long-term training that Stephen McGregor was able to measure are fine motor adjustments that cannot be consciously controlled. In the real world, the stride improves as the unconscious brain figures out how to sustain desired speeds with less activation of fewer motor units, not by changing where the arms and legs go. Such gains in efficiency are visible only as a general increase in the beauty of the stride.

The only common running technique flaw that exists at the level of gross motor coordination is that of overstriding, which is caused by the wearing of shoes and is best corrected primarily by addressing footwear, not by learning an entirely new way to run. Indeed, I believe that if all runners ran barefoot, the various running technique systems would not exist. Yet another problem with the technique systems is that they force every runner to try running the same way, whereas it is rather obvious—as Ross Tucker pointed out—that our very different bodies do not allow us to run the same way. A glance at the lead pack of runners in any major marathon will reveal all kinds of variety even among the best of the best. Some runners have a pronounced forward lean, while others are perfectly upright. Some carry their arms high; others, low. Some runners are forefoot strikers, while others are midfoot strikers. Some have loose, loping strides, while others exhibit compact strides with very high turnover rates. Each runner, through years of practice, has "solved" the "problem" of running fast over long distances by working out the optimal stride for his or her unique body. Yes, there are many characteristics that are common to the strides of all elite runners, but the rest of us cannot become elite runners—or even measurably better runners than we are today—by consciously aping these characteristics.

For example, faster runners typically have higher natural stride rates than slower runners. If two runners of different ability levels run together at the same pace, the more gifted of the two will take smaller, more frequent strides than the other. When I ran with Haile Gebrselassie, I observed that he took approximately 9 strides for every 8 I took. The natural stride rate of the typical elite runner is 90 strides per minute. The average stride rate of the typical midpack runner is closer to 80 strides per minute. Now, you might think that consciously increasing your stride rate from 80 to 90 strides per minute would be an effective way to gain a more efficient, elitelike stride. However, research has shown that runners become less efficient, not more efficient, when they force themselves to run at any stride rate other than their natural one.[7] Indeed, I felt extremely awkward when I tried to match Geb's stride rate while running with him.

It appears that with respect to most aspects of running technique, the unconscious brain knows better than the conscious mind what is most efficient. Each runner naturally adopts the stride rate that is most efficient given the totality of his or her biomechanics and body structure. My natural stride rate is lower than Gebrselassie's because of largely unchangeable differences in the ways our bodies are put together. Trying to run more like him in this or just about any other way cannot possibly do me any good. This is not to say that my stride rate could not increase in a manner that would enhance my running economy, but if it did, it would have to do so through an unconscious evolution of my overall stride. There is, in fact, anecdotal evidence from runners who train with speed and distance devices with cadence-monitoring capability that stride rate increases naturally and unconsciously as fitness increases.

Not only is it difficult to identify stride changes that are actually helpful, but it is also extremely difficult to make most specific stride changes (whether potentially helpful or not) stick. On a visit with the Mammoth

Lakes Track Club, I watched three-time Olympian Jen Rhines work consciously to increase her knee lift while running 100 m sprints under the watchful eye of her coach and husband, Terrence Mahon. "I've always had a bit of a shuffle, so that's our goal this year, is to get rid of the shuffle," she told me. Frankly, I expect to see Rhines shuffling as always the next time I watch her race, and if I do, I am confident it will be for the best. Rhines shuffles for a reason. I think it is highly likely that her body is designed in a way that makes low knee lift and a low back kick more efficient for her than the high knee lift and high back kick seen in some other elite runners, such as Kenenisa Bekele. Forcing a change probably will not help her running, and because her unconscious brain knows this, it will cause her to revert to her efficient shuffle in the heat of competition.

Jen Rhines is not alone among elite runners in fiddling with her stride. Nowadays many elite runners in the West do the same. Alberto Salazar told me: "Biomechanics are vital. The old idea that your form really doesn't matter is so outdated. We know without a doubt that the very best runners that have the longest careers are the ones that are most biomechanically sound. So that's something I really stress with my runners. I feel it's as important as how many miles you run and the pace that you run your intervals."

Conscious stride manipulation might make more sense for elite runners than for the rest of us. Stride technique improvement methods are like nutritional supplements. A balanced, high-volume, progressive running program is like food. Nutritional supplements are not intended to provide the foundation for optimal nourishment. Health is best supported when a person uses supplements minimally to augment a nutritious diet. Elite runners have a nearly perfect "diet" in the sense that their bodies are exceptionally well designed for efficient running and they already do what is known to improve running efficiency: hard, varied, high-volume running. So there is nothing left for these athletes to do with respect to enhancing the "beauty" of their running but to supplement their training with conscious stride fiddling (which they never do in the form of learning a universal technique system like the Pose method but instead do by identifying and attacking specific limiters in their individual strides, as in the case of Jen Rhines's shuffle). But the rest of us have much more to gain from improving our "diets" by developing strength, mobility, and power to make our bodies structurally better suited to efficient running and by increasing the repetition, variation, and exposure to fatigue in our training.

The value of conscious stride manipulation is debatable even for the elites. The very best runners in the world, the East Africans, do not widely practice stride technique manipulation. (Nor do they take nutritional supplements, for that matter.) I do not, however, rule out the possibility that stride technique manipulation can sometimes yield performance gains. There are a few celebrated cases of successful stride manipulation, such as that of Derek Clayton, an Australian who had an unspectacular career as a track runner before deciding to move up to the marathon. When he made this transition, Clayton consciously replaced his bouncy track stride with a lower-impact marathon shuffle, which he credited with helping him break the marathon world record twice in three years between 1967 and 1969.

For every success story like this one, however, there are probably dozens of unknown stories of consciously made stride changes that produced negative results. So while it can work, conscious stride manipulation is the last place I would advise you to seek improvements in the beauty of your running. The first place you should seek it is in a running program that is properly designed to serve as "stride practice."

Some scientists I know (but cannot identify here because they currently wish to keep their work secret) are working to develop a tool that will enable runners to continually measure their running economy in real time. With it, any runner could get instant feedback on the effect of any particular stride manipulation. Once this tool is in widespread use, we may discover that some particular stride tweaks do immediately boost efficiency for some runners. However, I doubt we will find many.

TRAINING AS STRIDE PRACTICE

The conventional, energy-based model of running performance encourages runners to view training as a means to increase fitness—to change the physiology inside the blank vessel of body form and biomechanics. The new, stride-based model that is taking shape in the hands of the likes of Stephen McGregor suggests that training is something else entirely: It is stride practice. Every step of every run is a step in the direction of a more beautiful (that is, efficient and powerful) stride. Yes, physiology changes in the process, but such changes are not ends in themselves. They simply support the stride changes that enable a higher level of performance. For example, an increase in the muscles' capacity to burn lactate as fuel is a physiological change that enables a runner to sustain a faster speed longer before her stride loses entropy and fatigue sets in. In other words, it is a change that lifts a fatigue-inducing constraint on the stride.

MIND-BODY RUNNING

Don't waste your time trying to learn a one-size-fits-all running technique system. You have to find your own best stride by trial and error.

Practically speaking, what does it mean to approach training as stride practice? I suggest that it is rather different from compartmentalized "technique training" as it has come to be known. The best way to pursue improvement in running form is not to think about how you run but rather to simply facilitate and hasten the unconscious process that produces specific stride refinements through communication between the brain's motor centers and the muscles. There are three obvious ways to hasten this process, alluded to earlier: repetition, variation, and exposure to fatigue.

Repetition

The key difference between trained and untrained runners is, of course, that trained runners have done a lot of running and untrained runners have not. Thus, the research of Steve McGregor and others that demonstrates superior efficiency in the strides of trained runners is a rationale for high-mileage training, above all else. The more you run, the more time your brain and your muscles spend in collaborative communication about the problem of running efficiently, and the faster the fruits of this communication will accumulate. It takes years of training experience for any runner to develop the most beautiful stride she will ever have, but high-mileage training will accelerate the evolution. Likewise, a runner of any given level of experience will run most efficiently at a high training volume than at a low one.

High mileage and low mileage are relative phenomena, of course. As we have seen, not all runners benefit equally from equal amounts of running. Some runners thrive best on relatively low-volume training, either because they are injury prone, they excel with a heavy emphasis on high-intensity running (which necessarily limits volume), or there are psychological factors at work. But even low-volume runners have to run a heck of a lot more miles than zero to get their best results and will run best when training at a volume level that is close to their personal limit. Bear in mind that low volume at the elite level among marathoners is 100 miles per week, and there's a reason for that.

Many runners speak of something magical that happens to their stride when they raise their mileage above a certain threshold. I had this experience when I started running consistently more than 80 miles per week for the first time. My stride became effortless in a way it never had before. It was a great feeling.

MIND-BODY RUNNING

Be sure to run enough, because the stride is everything. The stride improves through refinements in communication between the brain and the muscles. More running equals more time with the lines of communication fully active.

Variation

The process by which the brain and muscles learn to communicate in new ways that produce a more beautiful stride is similar to the process of biological evolution. Both processes adhere to the maxim "Necessity is the mother of invention." Species living in a stable ecosystem do not evolve rapidly because there is little pressure to evolve. But a changing ecosystem creates a necessity for evolution by taking away one or more of the conditions that its species depend on for survival. And when evolution becomes necessary for survival, it happens quickly. Similarly, if you run more or less the same way every time you run, there is little need for your brain and muscles to come up with new and better ways to put your stride together. But when you vary your running by running fast some days and slow other days, flat some days and hilly other days, on roads some days and trails other days, your neuromuscular system is constantly stimulated to adapt to the new challenges imposed on your stride. Some of these adaptations will benefit your stride generally. For example, suppose you have never run uphill before, and one day you give it a try. To meet this challenge, your brain will have to fire your leg muscles with patterns it has never used before. Having practiced these new movement patterns, your brain may call on some of them again the next time you run on flat ground and discover that one or more of them enable you to run more efficiently.

There is no formula for optimal variation in training. As a general rule, I suggest that each week you do some running at paces ranging from a slow jog to a full sprint, at least one hilly run, and at least one off-road run (if you normally run on the roads).

> **MIND-BODY RUNNING**
>
> Consistently vary your running (different speeds, surfaces, gradients) to create an unstable environment for your neuromuscular system as it relates to running and thereby trigger rapid stride evolution.

Exposure to Fatigue

The most potent stimulus for improvements in running biomechanics is mostly likely running in a fatigued state. As we have seen, fatigue manifests as a deterioration of running form that can be measured as a reduction in entropy. When you become tired, you become unable to run the way you normally do. Your stride turns ugly. Resisting fatigue is largely a matter of trying to continue to run normally despite factors such as joint decoupling and muscle fuel scarcity that pull your stride apart. Through this effort to keep your form together, your neuromuscular system learns new patterns that increase your resistance to stride deterioration and increase your running efficiency in a rested state.

The idea that running in a fatigued state is something to be sought out in training for its performance benefits is unusual. The conventional, energy-based model of running performance views the work that makes you tired as beneficial. For example, exposure to VO_2max in training increases VO_2max. But what I propose is that the fatigue itself—or more particularly, the effort to resist it—is the point.

I am not suggesting that the more fatigued running you do, the better. You could very easily run tired all the time by overtraining. There is a difference between quality fatigued running and nonproductive fatigued running. Fatigued running is quality when you have some capacity to resist it. When it goes past a certain point, fatigue wrecks your stride and there is nothing you can do about it. Any running you do in this state is unproductive. So the objective is to subject yourself to judicious doses of fatigued running in training. As a general rule, to maximize the rate of stride improvement, run in a fatigued state as much as you can without accumulating fatigue from day to day and eventually week to week.

MIND-BODY RUNNING

Expose yourself to fatigued running as often as you can without accumulating fatigue; this helps stimulate rapid evolution of your stride.

There are three main ways to achieve this objective. First, your training program should include a few workouts per week that result in a high level of fatigue—typically a tempo run, a session of high-intensity intervals, and a long endurance run. Doing too few fatigue-inducing workouts will not produce sufficient fatigue exposure to maximize the neuromuscular adaptations you're seeking. However, attempting to do too many hard workouts per week will cause you to carry too much residual fatigue between workouts, hampering your performance in them.

Second, instead of trying to do more than three hard workouts per week, you can increase your exposure to fatigue in a more productive way by adding short, easy recovery workouts to your schedule. Such workouts are gentle enough so that they will not hinder your recovery from previous hard training, but because you start these runs in a prefatigued state (within 24 hours after completing a hard run), they provide extra exposure to fatigue despite their brevity and slow pace.

Third, engage in interval workouts. The recovery periods that occur between high-intensity running intervals enable you to spend more total time running at high intensity than would be possible with a single, sustained, high-intensity effort to exhaustion. With rare exceptions, anytime you train above anaerobic threshold intensity, your workout should have an interval format.

The most important pace at which to experience fatigue is race pace. As Stephen McGregor's research has shown, the stride becomes more efficient only to the degree that it has to. It will not become more efficient at paces you seldom run, and it will become only marginally more efficient at running paces at which you seldom experience fatigue. This is why McGregor's accelerometer data show that very good runners tend to be rather uneconomical at slower paces. You must run at race pace to the point of entropy—that is, to the point where some specific constraint in your stride limits your performance—to stimulate the neuro-muscular adjustments that will make you more efficient at your race pace. Therefore race-pace running needs to be a regular part of your training regimen.

MIND-BODY RUNNING

Use conscious manipulation of your stride only to correct specific problems that have caused injuries. In other words, if you're not broken, don't fix your stride.

Again, the rationale for running in a fatigued state is that it forces the neuromuscular system to confront the primary constraint that limits performance and thereby creates opportunities for the neuromuscular system to experiment with new stride patterns, one or more of which may alleviate that specific constraint. But exposure to fatigue is not the only way to stimulate this process. Runners are also limited by structural factors including muscle power, joint mobility, and leg stiffness (or the capacity to quickly tense the right motor units to the right degree in the instant before impact to maximize the bouncing effect). Research has shown that specific training to enhance these structural characteristics alters the stride in ways that boost performance.[8] Aware of these effects, many elite runners incorporate large amounts of strength training, explosive jumping exercises, mobility drills, and dynamic warm-up activities into their training. In fact, this huge commitment to cross-training for stride improvement is the greatest difference between the training of today's top runners and that of past generations. One of the best young middle-distance runners in America, Anna Pierce, who has a 1,500 m PR of 3:59.38, told me that at times she spends more time each week lifting weights, tossing medicine balls, bounding, and so forth than she does running.

A PLACE FOR CONSCIOUS CONTROL

We have seen that there is little scientific support for the practice of consciously manipulating the stride to conform to some universal ideal of good running form, and that new research evidence provides strong support for the idea that the best way to run more beautifully is to just run—and more specifically to run a lot, run with variation, and run fatigued. Nevertheless, there is other evidence, from real-world training and clinical environments, that supports limited use of conscious stride manipulation. Specifically, I encourage runners to limit themselves to making two specific types of conscious stride changes: those that reduce injury risk and those that reverse the stride distortions imposed by shoes.

Changeable aspects of running form contribute to many running injuries. It is often possible to identify these technique flaws, consciously change them, and thereby reduce the risk of future injuries. One of the college runners Stephen McGregor studied was a talented young fellow who struggled to fulfill his potential because he got injured every time he tried to ramp up his training load. Once this runner was hooked up to an accelerometer, the reason for his dilemma became clear: The young man's vertical accelerations were off the charts. He landed with a force equal to seven times his body weight at a slow pace of 12 kph (8:00/mile). Research on gait retraining in injured runners by Irene Davis, a professor of physical therapy at the University of Delaware, demonstrated that runners could, through conscious control, learn to run with less impact and thereby reduce their risk of injury.

Many running injuries are partly caused by muscle imbalances, such as those that are discussed in Chapter 10, most of which develop as consequences of excessive sitting. Stretching and strengthening exercises or alternatives such as yoga poses are required to correct these imbalances, but these activities will not automatically correct the stride. Davis's work has shown that conscious learning of new stride patterns is often necessary as well. For example, weakness in the hip musculature causes the pelvis to collapse during running and leads to knee injuries. Strengthening the hip muscles gives the runner the wherewithal to run without a collapsing pelvis, but does not in fact suffice to stop the pelvis from collapsing. Davis teaches injured runners to consciously activate their hip muscles to correct this stride flaw. After a few weeks it becomes an ingrained motor pattern, and the runners are able to maintain their new form without thinking about it.

Running shoes are known to wreak havoc on running efficiency. A 2008 study by French researchers found that running shoes decreased running economy both by adding weight to the feet and by altering biomechanics in ways that reduced the ability of the legs to capture "free energy" from ground impact forces and reuse it to propel forward motion.[9] On the biomechanical side, the core problem is that running shoes encourage runners to overstride, striking the ground heel first with the leg extended ahead of the body, instead of flat-footed with the foot underneath the hips. Overstriding exerts a strong braking effect—a pronounced heel strike even looks like pressing the brake of an automobile. No runner overstrides without shoes, because heel striking without the presence of cushioning material between the foot and the ground would be painful and injurious. Fully 80 percent of runners instantly become heel strikers when they put on a pair of shoes. It is not clear why four in five runners overstride in shoes but not in bare feet. There is some evidence that naturally gifted runners are more resistant to the stride-ruining effects of shoes, as the minority of runners that do not overstride in shoes also tend to be more efficient without shoes.

In any case, it is safe to say that overstriding is unnatural, because no runner does it in the natural, unshod state. For this reason, I believe that overstriding is one of the easier stride technique "errors" to correct. Again, though, correcting this error is best done primarily through means other than conscious control. Practicing running barefoot on grass, on sand, and/ or on an at-home treadmill will get your neuromuscular system accustomed to making ground contact with a flat foot underneath the body's center of gravity. Wearing the lightest, least-cushioned running shoes in which you are comfortable in your everyday training will help you transfer your barefoot running form over to your shod running. But you will probably need to exercise a conscious effort for a while to keep from reverting back to overstriding while wearing your shoes. I am living proof that this is one gross motor stride change that can be made fairly easily. I switched from traditional to minimalist running shoes and from a moderate heel strike to a midfoot landing to overcome a prolonged case of runner's knee, and it worked.

BORN TO RUN?

Evolutionary biologists believe that human beings are "born to run" in the sense that many of the anthropometric features that we developed after splitting from the common ancestor we share with our closest genetic relative, the chimpanzee, specifically enhanced our long-distance running capacity. These features include rigid feet, upright posture, large buttocks, and copious sweat glands. However, it is patently obvious that not all humans are equally suited to running. In fact, there are many humans who are scarcely better suited to running than the average chimpanzee. I have known many people who, even as children, could barely run a step. So while our species is generally well designed for distance running, there is far greater variation in distance-running ability throughout the total human population than there is (for example) variation in sprinting ability in the population of cheetahs, a species that is generally designed for sprinting and all of whose individual members sprint exceedingly well. I believe that this is because distance running was never more than a specialty in early hominid and human populations. It was never the job of every member of a prehistoric clan to run, so there was never sufficient natural selection pressure to force the genes that support the highest level of running ability to overtake our entire species.

Today's running technique instruction phenomenon loosely purveys the idea that each of us has the potential to run in the image, if not at the velocity, of the best of us. All that is required to realize this potential is to learn the "right" way to run and practice it. This idea is false. A clear-eyed look at reality reveals that we are not all born to run to the degree that Lukas Verzbicas and Kenenisa Bekele are. Aerobic capacity aside, such runners are gifted with body structure and innate neuromuscular coordination (research has shown that athletes who master sports skills quickly have more adaptive brain motor centers than slower learners) that enable them to run with an extremity of power and efficiency that the rest of us could never match with any amount of conscious emulation.[10]

There are many ways in which nonelite runners can emulate elite runners and benefit thereby. Beyond a very limited degree, copying their strides is not one of them. Indeed, our inability to copy the strides of the best runners is the very reason we are not as fast as they are. This is just the cold, hard fact of the matter.

That's the bad news. The good news is that runners of all natural ability levels have a tremendous capacity to improve—or beautify—their strides. And the way to do it is to copy the methods that the best runners use to develop their own, naturally superior strides. These methods are mind-body methods in the sense that they function to refine communication between the unconscious brain and the muscles in ways that enable the neuromuscular system to generate more power with less energy. The methods that work best for this purpose include running a lot, running fast, and running far. These simple, but seldom properly exploited methods help each runner find a unique solution to the problem of overcoming running performance limits imposed by the particularities of body structure and neuromuscular coordination. To paraphrase Friedrich Nietzsche, "I wish that everyone would follow my example and find his own way to run."

NINE

THE GIFT OF INJURY

> If something is there for me,
> it's going to wait for me.
>
> —Khalid Khannouchi

OF ALL THE ELITE RUNNERS I've encountered, Khalid Khannouchi has had the most extreme combination of good luck and bad luck. His one great piece of good fortune was to have been born with an ideal set of genes for distance running. Thanks to those genes, and a lot of hard work, Khannouchi was able to break the marathon world record twice, set a 20K world best, and amass five major marathon victories (four at Chicago, one at London). But he could have accomplished so much more if not for the bad luck of being exceptionally injury prone. Throughout his career Khannouchi has fought a seemingly endless battle with all manner of injures. He has suffered injuries to his feet, hamstrings, groin, low back, and his feet again. These various breakdowns have kept him out of serious training and competition for a cumulative six years, or nearly half of his total career span.

In 2007, I saw Khannouchi at the Rock 'n' Roll San Jose Half Marathon. He had recently recovered from a foot injury and had only a few weeks of healthy training in his legs. It showed. He finished 13th in 1:05:04. This performance did not bode well for his hopes of claiming an Olympic Team slot at the following month's Olympic Trials Marathon in New York City. Amazingly, though, and thanks again to those rare genes, Khannouchi improved enough over the next three weeks to come within one place of making the team, finishing 4th in 2:12:34.

Sure, Khannouchi was disappointed to have missed out on the Olympics yet again (incredibly, he has never gone), but at least he seemed to be on the comeback trail. Not so. His foot problems returned, and in the spring of 2009 he underwent a surgery that he was still recovering from when I spoke to him several months later.

As a fellow brittle runner driven to the brink of madness by recurring bodily mutiny, I asked Khannouchi how he had managed to keep his injury frustrations from driving him insane. "It is frustrating when you want to go and compete and improve, but your body doesn't allow you to," he said. "But I'm always a true believer that whatever is there for you, you will get. No panic whatsoever. If something is there for me, it's going to wait for me."

In talking to Khannouchi, I discovered that he had forged a genuine peace with his limitations and their consequences, even as he continued to strive for the most he could do within those limitations. "I love the fact that I'm a runner, that I can be my own boss," he told me. "I still want to do that if I can. But if I can't, at least I can jog and go do races at a slower pace and have fun with people."

Khalid Khannouchi is a Muslim, and in the vocabulary of his faith he came to a place of acceptance that enabled him to enjoy running despite not being able to run as he pleased. I am not a Muslim, yet my own injury woes have led me to pretty much the same place of acceptance, probably because that's the only state of mind that allows me to continue to find fulfillment in running when the spirit yearns to perform but the body is unable.

All mature religions and philosophies teach an outlook of acceptance. In Buddhism, accepting things as they are is the path to enlightenment and happiness. The Buddha taught that it is useless to try to eradicate all causes of suffering from your life or to try to numb your capacity to hurt. Suffering will always be there. Indeed, "life is suffering," he said. It is better to accept the inevitability of suffering and the truth of each specific episode of distress, because such acceptance actually takes some of the sting out of the suffering. Knee pain is bad, but knee pain that you curse or deny is twice as bad as knee pain that you accept as an occasional part of being a runner. What's more, knee pain that you accept is likely to go away faster than knee pain that you curse or deny, as the mind has a powerful influence on healing and a positive mind-set is a healing mind-set.[1]

In the preceding chapters we have considered many facets of the mind-body approach to running. In this chapter I will explain the mind-body approach to running injuries. It is simple. As manifest in the likes of Khalid Khannouchi, the mind-body approach to running injuries is to minimize the negative effects of injuries on your *enjoyment* of running and, to the degree possible, maximize the potential *positive* effects of injuries on your enjoyment of running. The justification for this mind-centered approach to dealing with problems of the body is derived from the fact that injuries are all but inevitable in the life of a runner. So which would you rather have: an injury that makes you depressed as long as it stays with you or an injury that frustrates you briefly but then ceases to bother you much even before it is fully healed?

The reason you are a runner is that you enjoy running. The objective of everything you do as a runner should be to increase or preserve your enjoyment of running. Injuries tend to spoil the fun of running. Preventing injuries is, of course, one way to limit the negative effects of injuries on your fulfillment in running and one that only a fool would not pursue. But no competitive runner is able to prevent every injury, and those runners who, like Khalid Khannouchi, are naturally injury prone can expect to experience more than their fair share of breakdowns. Therefore, learning to be at peace with injury as best you can is a more important and effectual way to minimize the negative consequences of injury on your enjoyment of running than is learning how to prevent them. As Jason Lehmkuhle, a 2:12 marathoner, said in an interview: "It has certainly been my experience that if you try to figure it out, you will just drive yourself crazy. I think that you just have to accept that you are probably going to get injured every once in a while. It's part of the sport. The way that you *deal* with the injury is probably more important than trying to do everything to prevent injuries."

What Lehmkuhle is saying implicitly here is that he prefers to look forward than to look backward or even inward when he's injured. And the reason he prefers doing so is that it makes him feel less miserable; it lets him enjoy being a runner more. When an injured runner looks backward, he says, "Why me? How could this possibly have happened to me?" These are very unpleasant and unhelpful sorts of questions to ask. When an injured runner looks inward, he says, "This sucks! I'm losing fitness! My goals are vanishing in a puff of smoke!" These are very unpleasant and unhelpful things to say. But when an injured runner looks forward, he asks, "How can I make the best of this unfortunate situation? What can it teach me about my body or myself? How might it help my running in the long term?"

These are positive and productive questions to ask, because they come from a place of hope, acceptance, and self-empowerment, whereas looking backward and inward comes from a place of helplessness and victimhood.

MIND-BODY RUNNING

Accept the reality that you will probably get injured occasionally.

From the mind-body perspective, injuries are a case of mind over matter: If you don't mind the injury, it doesn't matter. This formulation might sound glib, but any wise and oft-injured runner (like Khalid Khannouchi) will tell you that, with respect to preserving your enjoyment of running, accepting the inevitability of injury, accepting the reality of each individual injury, and looking forward instead of backward or inward when injured are worth more than active release therapy, prescription orthotics, stretching, icing, and all of the other physical measures that constitute the conventional approach to dealing with running injuries.

THE UNAVOIDABILITY OF INJURIES

When I was a younger and more naïve "running expert," I used to say that a runner could learn something from every injury. Scarred but smarter now, I can state with total certainty that it is not possible to learn something from every injury. Every fragile runner learns this truth sooner or later. "It is part of the sport," Khannouchi told me, echoing Jason Lehmkuhle. "If you push your body to the limit, you will get injured." Trying too hard to learn something from every injury—something that will ensure it never happens again—will only drive you nuts, as Jason Lehmkuhle suggests. But on a general level, the more experience I acquire with injury, the more I learn about the nature of the phenomenon. In the remainder of this chapter I will present the top ten lessons about running injuries that I have learned. Use these truths to prevent injury from spoiling the fun of running for you.

Some of these lessons can help you avoid the truly avoidable injuries and to get over unavoidable injuries faster. But most are about dealing with injuries in the sense of moving forward with them, despite them, and even through them to become a better runner because of them.

TEN LESSONS TO BE LEARNED FROM INJURY

1. Most injuries are not caused by "doing too much." A patient walks into a doctor's office and says, "Doc, it hurts when I do this." The doctor replies, "Then don't do that."

We've all laughed at this joke. What makes it funny? The doctor's utterance sounds perfectly sensible but is in fact totally absurd. Presumably, the movement that hurts the patient is required for a normal life, so not doing it to avoid pain is no solution at all. Perhaps there is no other solution, but the doctor should help the patient exhaust all other possible fixes before telling the patient to stop doing that.

Runners often become the butt of a very similar joke. They run. They get injured. What caused the injury? Running too much, they are told. How can they prevent the injury from recurring? Run less, they are told.

It sounds so reasonable. After all, if you do not run a single step, you cannot ever suffer a running injury. If you run just 100 yards a day, it is still very unlikely that your running will cause any sort of breakdown. If you run 5 miles a week, the chances of a running injury cropping up are a little greater. At 10 miles a week, the risk is greater still, and so forth. In this way of thinking, all running injuries are almost definitionally caused by running too much. But there is one major problem with this definition of running too much. A runner who gets injured when running 20 miles per week this year might not get injured when running 20 miles a week, or even 30 miles a week, next year. It happens all the time.

Injury is the primary training limiter for most competitive runners. We train as much and as hard as we can without getting injured with unacceptable frequency. As discussed in Chapter 3, learning how much and how hard you can train without breaking down all the time is a major part of the process of developing your optimal training formula. But interpreting injuries is tricky. It's never as simple as discovering that, for example, you never get injured when you run 59 miles per week or less and you always get injured when you run 60 miles per week or more. Very few competitive runners find that they get injured only when they run more than a certain amount. And limits change. I used to run 60 miles per week and got injured all the time. Later I ran 80 miles per week and got injured less often. Refusing to accept a 60-mile limit motivated me to find ways to run more without falling apart, and that quest made me more durable. Thank goodness I didn't listen to those who said I was doing too much!

Because it is difficult to define limits through injuries, and because limits can be increased, it makes more sense to use factors other than injury risk as the primary determinants of how much and how hard you train. Namely, you should try to run as much as you feel you need to run to achieve your goals and/or as much as you feel you should be able to run healthily. Table 9.1 presents normal running mileages for different categories of runners that were developed by Brad Hudson. Most runners naturally choose running mileage targets that are appropriate for their category, and most runners can hit those targets without unacceptable injury frequency. Nevertheless, there is a small chance you will never be able to healthily run as much as you want to. If you keep hitting your head against a wall, eventually you will have to read the writing on that wall and set your target lower.

However, it would be a mistake to give up too easily. Your first, second, and third injuries at a given training load should not be read as "dead end" signs but rather as "detour" signs. Take them as challenges to find another

Table 9.1 Brad Hudson's Optimal Running Volume (miles) for Five Levels of Runners at Four Race Distances

Distance	Beginner	Low-Key Competitive	Competitive	Highly Competitive	Elite
5K	20-30	25-35	40-50	50-60	90-110
10K	25-35	30-40	45-55	60-70	95-115
Half-marathon	35-40	35-45	50-60	70-80	100-120
Marathon	40-50	50-60	60-70	80-90	110-130

Source: Brad Hudson with Matt Fitzgerald, *Run Faster from the 5K to the Marathon: How to Be Your Own Best Coach* (New York: Broadway, 2008). Reprinted with permission.

way to get where you want to go, whether that's by exercising patience and slowing your march toward that target, identifying and addressing the specific susceptibilities that cause your individual injuries, switching to a softer running surface, or doing whatever else makes sense.

Refusing to take "no" for an answer from your injuries will help you become a better runner in two ways. First, the effort to find a workaround means to run as much as you want to run will lead you to discover tools that improve your running. Second, finding a healthy way to run as much as you want to will result in your running more than you would if you responded to your injuries with permanent reductions in running mileage. And again, this happens all the time. Runners routinely develop durability that enables them to run more healthily at higher mileage levels.

A good example from the elite realm is Meb Keflezighi, who first tried 130 mile weeks in his mid-20s, but quickly broke down under the burden. "My body wasn't able to take it," he told me. So he found a detour. "When you have aches and pains, you can't do the double days, so your mileage is minimized," he said. "So what I did in the past was a lot of biking and some swimming." Meb rode this self-created, low-volume, cross-training approach, peaking at just 99 miles of running in a week, to a second-place finish in the 2004 New York City Marathon. Five years later, after recovering from the worst injury of his career (a hip stress fracture suffered during the 2008 U.S. Olympic Trials Marathon), Meb took another crack at 130 mile weeks and found that his body was now durable enough to handle them. Those 130 mile weeks led him to victory in the 2009 New York City Marathon.

Elite runners rarely respond to injuries by permanently reducing their mileage targets. They know that they must run a certain amount to be competitive on their level, so instead they respond to injuries by trying new things that might enable them to run more. A typical case is that of James Carney. In his first four years of postcollegiate running, Carney struggled with injuries and performed poorly in the few races he was healthy enough to run. Eventually, he decided enough was enough and left his longtime coach, Bob Sevene (who cannot be faulted for Carney's injuries), for Brad Hudson. As he does with all of his runners, Hudson had Carney run steep hill sprints (we're talking 10 × 8 seconds at full speed) to develop overall leg strength and thereby reduce injury risk. It worked. For the first time in his professional career, Carney was able to train injury free for long stretches of time and he blossomed, lowering his 10,000 m PR from 28:27 to 27:43 in 2006 and winning the U.S. Half Marathon Championship in 2008.

Let elite runners like James Carney be your role models in this regard. Don't give up too easily on your desired running mileage because of injury. Try to identify and address the specific susceptibility that is holding you back now, whether it is lack of general strength, as in the case of Carney, or something else entirely. Be aware also that too much running today might not be too much running in the future. Consistent training increases durability and thereby increases mileage tolerance. Be patient and persistent, and do not listen to those who reflexively insist, "You're trying to do too much!"

2. Some injury causes are identifiable, whereas others are not. Jason Lehmkuhle's quote implies that trying to identify the cause of an injury is never worth the bother. That's a bit exaggerated. Sometimes the cause of an injury is easily identified, if not by the injured runner himself then by a more experienced runner, a coach, or a sports physician. Early in my return to endurance sports in my mid-20s, following an eight-year hiatus through college and beyond, I developed a crippling case of iliotibial band friction syndrome. I had never heard of the IT band at the time the injury struck. My friend and fellow *Triathlete* magazine editor T. J. Murphy, a former massage therapist, said that the injury was probably caused by tightening in my IT band and said he could very likely fix it with a little deep tissue work. Disliking the idea of another man, a friend no less, rubbing my leg with his hands, I declined the offer repeatedly, counting on the problem to resolve itself. Months later the problem still had not resolved itself, so at last I submitted to T. J.'s hands. He worked on the sore spot for five minutes and it was gone. I have performed regular self-massage with a foam roller ever since, and the injury has never returned full-blown.

Years later I returned the favor. T. J. was 34 years old when I met him and had then recently run a 2:38 marathon. By the time he reached age 46, he was a shell of his former self as a runner. He tried and tried again to make a comeback to something resembling his old form, but each time his body fell apart. His right knee gave him the most trouble. It was painful just to

watch him try to hobble along the sidewalk, knowing how swift and grace-
ful he had once been. One day T. J. and I were talking about our respective
injuries when I asked him if he had tried working to strengthen his hip
abductors and external rotators, as weakness in these muscles had come to
be considered a widespread cause of knee injuries
in runners. To my surprise, T. J. told me that he had
never heard of this connection. I showed him some
exercises to do and urged him to get after them as
though it were his job. Weeks later T. J. reported
to me that his knee pain was gone, he was up to
35 miles a week of running, and his entire right
leg was probably 25 percent stronger than it had
been a month earlier.

As these anecdotes indicate, it would be fool-
ish of the injured runner to make no effort to
identify the cause of each new injury. However,
it is often very difficult to do so, and not uncom-
monly a prolonged injury will heal on its own before the answer-seeking
runner can figure out why it happened. Indeed, T. J. had tried for years to
figure out why his knee hurt before I was able to help him. In these common
cases, when the cause of an injury is difficult to identify, the runner's des-
perately impatient scramble to find a magic bullet adds tremendous stress
to the overall injury experience. In fact, in my experience, the anxiety of
struggling vainly to solve the mystery of a particular injury often becomes
the very worst part of the injury experience.

It is better to understand and accept that some injury causes cannot be
discerned and to address each injury accordingly. By all means, make every
reasonable effort to find the cause, but do not expect to succeed in every
case. Be prepared to come up empty and to heal up and return to running
without knowing the cause of the pain that made you stop. This mind-set
will enable you to get through your injuries with less stress and anxiety.

3. Stubbornness (sometimes) makes small injuries big. When abnormal
pain emerges during or after a run, you have two options: You can ignore
the pain and continue training as normal, or you can modify your training

---

MIND-BODY RUNNING

Try to find what caused your
injury, and address it to prevent
reoccurrence. Don't assume there
is always going to be an identifiable cause. Regardless, try to
intuitively study and learn
from your injury.

(take a few days off, move your workouts to a softer surface, or whatever) until the pain goes away. Most competitive runners choose to sometimes ignore their pain. And they get away with it just often enough to keep taking chances. But sometimes they pay a heavy price for their willfulness. An incipient injury that could have resolved itself in less than a week with a little rest becomes a multiweek or even a multimonth setback.

A classic case from the elite ranks is that of Mary Cullen, the 2006 NCAA 5,000 m champion. Cullen was training for the 2008 Irish Olympic trials when she developed pain in her sacrum. She tagged it as the type of minor ache that had gone away on its own many times before and tried to train through it, but the pain grew worse and worse. Eventually, weeks after the problem first manifested, she got an MRI (magnetic resonance imaging), which revealed a stress fracture. Had Cullen responded aggressively to the pain when it emerged, she probably would have been training normally again by the time that MRI forced her to stop training and lose all hope of competing in the Beijing Olympics.

I am not faulting Cullen. For starters, I have made the same mistake, more times than I care to remember. Also, the competitive runner who is at all injury prone has to take some risks with aches and sore spots, which crop up frequently in training. If you panicked over each one of them, you would never get into any kind of groove in your training. The best you can do is use your experience to develop the ability to guess right most of the time about whether ignoring a new pain is worth chancing. This ability depends not only on experience but also on your willingness to be honest with yourself. Backing off of training is an emotionally difficult call to make, and it is all too easy to talk yourself into believing that a pain is no big deal when in your heart of hearts you know it probably is. Guard against this tendency.

Typically, competitive runners have to learn the hard way to be more cautious in dealing with incipient injuries. The older they get, the less often the gamble pays off. Eventually, they get tired of bearing the consequences of their bad risks and become less brazen. Dathan Ritzenhein suffered frequent foot stress fractures during and immediately after college. They started off as dull aches and, as he persisted in running, eventually became searing agonies that made running impossible. By 2006 he had learned his lesson. When a foot pain emerged during a spring track workout, he immediately ceased all land running and instead trained on an antigravity treadmill (more on this later in the chapter) for several weeks. The pain went away, he maintained his fitness, and his summer racing plans were salvaged.

Taking the risk of training through pain is not equally worth doing at all times in the training cycle. Generally, there is less cause for risk-taking early in the training cycle, when you have plenty of time to make up for a brief reduction of training before your important races. Training through pain is most worth the risk during the peak period of training, when you are trying to do some work that must get done if you are to achieve your race goals and time to get that work done is running short.

4. Injuries follow change. The sheer unpredictability of injuries never ceases to amaze me. I always seem to get injured when I least expect it, and I seldom get injured when I do. But there is one general pattern of injury onset that makes injuries a little more predictable, hence avoidable, and it is that injuries tend to follow change. The most common changes that precipitate injuries are increases in running mileage and running intensity, but there are others. For example, I once sailed through most of a marathon training cycle injury free, then moved from one apartment located in a flat area to another located in a very hilly area three weeks before race day. After just a few days of running in my new environment, I developed an Achilles tendon strain that was clearly related to the unaccustomed stress of uphill running.

In previous chapters I have discussed various reasons for including plenty of repetition in training. The benefits of repetition include psychological momentum and the ability to easily track progress. Another potential benefit of repetition in training is reduced injury risk. After all, if injuries tend to follow change, the less your training changes, the more your injury risk falls. Specifically, it is wise to keep your running mileage fairly high year-round, except during breaks between training cycles, and to always include at least a small amount of high-intensity running in your training, as doing so will reduce the incidence of injuries caused by increases in mileage and intensity. In my experience, injuries are much less likely to occur at times when I am running consistently high mileage than at times when I am running less but increasing mileage.

It goes without saying that too much repetition in training is as bad as too little, but among competitive runners too little repetition (especially in the form of big swings in weekly mileage and in the amount of high-intensity running) is a far more common error, whose consequences include less consistent fitness development and increased incidence of injury.

5. Impact is everything. The injury rate is much greater in running than it is in swimming and cycling. The difference between running and these other two endurance sports is impact. It is the high-impact nature of running that makes it so injurious. Thus, any reasonable measure you can take to reduce impact forces without compromising the overall quality of your training will enable you to run more with fewer injuries.

Eschewing pavement in favor of dirt is perhaps the most proven means of reducing injuries by reducing impact, at least in the real world. As they are in so many ways, East African runners are our role models in this regard. Several years ago I had an interesting conversation about the Africans' avoidance of pavement with John Connors, a podiatrist with offices in New York City and New Jersey who specializes in the treatment of runners and has developed a cottage industry in treating Kenyan runners in America, including Tegla Loroupe, Catherine Ndereba, and Joyce Chepchumba. (He's also the doctor who performed Khalid Khannouchi's foot surgery.) Connors told me: "Many African runners grow up running on dirt roads, and few of those who do can ever get used to training on pavement—so they don't. The African runners I've trained with go to extreme lengths to avoid running on pavement—for example, they might circle a soccer field for several miles—and I think they are very smart to do so." American runners tend to be lazy in seeking out softer running surfaces and will run on the roads right outside their front doors instead of driving a few miles to the nearest trail. Those Kenyans, including Catherine Ndereba, who train in America drive those few miles to reach softer surfaces, and Connors, who ought to know, believes doing so makes a big difference.

A more high-tech way to reduce impact forces is to replace some outdoor running with running on an antigravity treadmill or walking at a steep gradient on a normal treadmill. A less proven but potentially very effective way to reduce impact forces is to simply modify your stride to reduce impact. Most runners are unaware of the fact that impact profiles differ tremendously among individual runners, even when factors such as body weight and pace are held constant. It is not always easy to tell if someone is a high-impact or low-impact runner from personal running experience. Force plate measurements of impact forces often reveal surprises. Nor do biomechanics experts understand why some runners naturally land so much harder than others, even in the elite ranks.

What's important is that individual impact profiles are correlated to injury rates, and that individual runners can reduce their impact levels through stride modifications. Irene Davis, founder of the Running Injury Clinic at the University of Delaware, is one of the world's leading experts on the relationship between running biomechanics and overuse injuries and is a pioneer in the development of "gait retraining" methods to reduce injury risk. Her research has proven that high-impact runners are more susceptible to various injuries, including plantar fasciitis and tibial stress fractures.[2,3] In one study, Davis attached accelerometers to the lower legs of 10 high-impact runners. These accelerometers measured impact forces and were attached to displays that allowed the runners to see a visual representation of how much impact force they generated with each footstrike while running on a treadmill. Davis instructed the runners to try to cut their impact levels in half by feel—that is, by fiddling with the way they ran while watching the displays. Not only were all of the runners eventually able to do it, but a six-month follow-up revealed that the runners were able to make their new, lower-impact stride permanent.[4]

Davis told me that there is a simple, do-it-yourself way to get the same result. Just listen to how much noise your foot impacts make when you run and consciously try to run more quietly. You might think that this effort would lead you to run weirdly, and it's true that you could reduce the noisiness of your running in weird ways, but you will only be able to sustain noise-reducing stride changes that are efficient and unlikely to cause new problems. In fact, using visual and auditory biofeedback to make stride changes is a better way to improve your running form than trying to learn global techniques such as Chi Running, because the biofeedback method encourages you to modify your biomechanics more unconsciously (you think about the feedback, not your body itself) and organically.

Finally, there are the shoes. For decades, shoe cushioning was considered the most effective means of reducing impact forces and injury risk. But actual research has revealed a very complex and unpredictable relationship between shoe cushioning and impact forces and absolutely no effect of cushioning on injury risk.[5] Research by Benno Nigg at the University of Calgary suggested that what mattered more than the effect of a shoe on impact forces was how comfortable a shoe felt when a person ran in it. His research indicated that the degree of comfort was related to how much effort the muscles had to put into dampening the vibrations passing through the lower extremities after each footstrike. The brain prefers a certain vibration frequency of impact forces passing through the soft tissues of the lower extremities and automatically "tunes" the muscles toward that frequency. The amount of muscle activation required to tune the muscles correctly depends on the running surface and shoe cushioning characteristics, as well as the weight, speed, and biomechanics of the runner and other factors. Nigg's research also suggested that (1) the less effort the muscles had to put into dampening vibrations, the more injury risk fell; (2) running in more comfortable shoes reduced injury risk; and (3) it was impossible to predict which running shoe would be most comfortable for any given runner.[6]

Nigg told me that "there is a sort of body intelligence at work" in relation to the comfort level of running shoes. Feelings of comfort in a given shoe are your unconscious brain's way of telling you that muscle tuning is easy in that shoe and hence that injury risk is low. Therefore, every runner is well advised to run in the most comfortable shoe she or he can find. Since most runners can run comfortably in more than one shoe, and there is solid scientific evidence that heavier, higher-heeled running shoes worsen running economy, I would refine this recommendation and advise every runner to run in the lightest, lowest-heeled shoe that he or she finds comfortable.

6. Time is the only healer. The human body is a healing machine. It is programmed to automatically repair any damage it sustains. The body does not have unlimited capacity for self-healing (good luck growing back an arm lost in an industrial accident), but it is fully capable of fixing most of the common running overuse injuries. Healing unfolds in the medium of time. So when you are injured, it is only a question of how much time it will take your body to regenerate sufficiently to allow you to resume normal training.

Doctors, physical therapists, and other types of healers have come up with all kinds of ways to accelerate the natural healing process: acupuncture, massage, cold therapies, ibuprofen, the Graston technique, electrostimulation, plasma injections, iontophoresis, and more. I have used most of these measures, and the conclusion I have drawn from my aggregative experience with them is that they do not work. Even the most honest sports medicine professionals admit that their treatments are minimally effective. Scott Warden, assistant physical therapist and athletic trainer for the Colorado Avalanche hockey team, told me, "You can't do much to make injuries heal faster, because healing is based on a process that happens on its own time."

The phenomenon of self-healing even makes it more difficult for medical researchers to determine the effectiveness of any given treatment. As leading sports medicine expert and orthopedic surgeon James Garrick explained to me, researchers seldom learn much from traditional controlled experiments in which one group of injured persons receives the treatment under scrutiny and another group does not, because the members of the control group tend to heal anyway.

Countless runners believe that one or another of the commonly practiced healing techniques has helped them, and who am I to doubt these stories? Without question, cold therapies and medications effectively reduce the inflammation that attends most injuries and thereby place the body in a better position to heal itself. So I would never advise other runners against using these treatments, and in fact I am rolling a frozen can of refried beans under my recovering left heel as I write this. But I do caution runners against expecting too much from these treatments.

Accept that time is the only real healer, and embrace any small boost you get from massage therapy or whatever as "gravy." All too often runners layer extra stress and anxiety onto the injury experience by grasping at healing measures like lifelines and expecting miracles from them. I have driven myself half loony in this way. But no more. As an exceptionally injury-experienced runner, I promise you that it is better to approach the various healing treatments as measures that, at worst, can't hurt, and that, at best, may help a tiny bit, but put your real trust in time and in your body itself.

7. It helps to have an alternative to running. The most frustrating part of being injured is knowing that your hard-earned fitness is deteriorating while you take time off from training to heal. In fact, this frustration can be so great that runners are often too reluctant to take time off or are tempted into resuming training too soon. Consequently, injuries become worse or last longer than they should.

One way to prevent this sort of self-sabotage is to choose a favorite go-to cross-training activity that you can switch to whenever an injury makes running impossible or unwise. Having such a fallback option greatly reduces the temptation to run when you should not because it enables you to preserve fitness even when you cannot run. Obviously, there is no alternative to running that builds and maintains running-specific fitness as well as running itself does, but there are some alternatives that come relatively close.

The best running alternatives are those that are most similar to running itself. Activities such as swimming and rowing are not great alternatives to running because, while they stimulate the cardiovascular system, they are arm-dominant versus leg-dominant movements. So what are the best activities for "training through" running injuries?

The Alter-G antigravity treadmill is, in my opinion, the single most important running-related invention in history. It is a normal treadmill with a tentlike enclosure attached to it. The user steps through a hole at the top of the enclosure and zips herself in around the waist, creating an airtight seal. The chamber is then pressurized, and this high-pressure zone effectively reduces the force of gravity within it. The amount of pressure is adjustable, enabling the user to run at anywhere between 20 percent and 100 percent of her actual body weight.

I have had every type of running overuse injury that exists, and I have used the Alter-G treadmill several times. Based on this experience, I am able to say that runners can train through any injury—pain free and without setting back the healing process—on this machine. What's more, it is not an alternative to running; it *is* running. Therefore, it is superior to every form of cross-training in terms of building and maintaining running fitness.

Case in point: Dathan Ritzenhein trained exclusively on an Alter-G for several weeks while nursing an IT band injury. (This was after he trained through a foot issue on the Alter-G.) He was ready to return to regular outdoor running only two weeks before the 2008 USA Cross-Country Championships. Nevertheless, he won the race easily. That simply would not have been possible had he been forced to resort to pool running or bicycling.

The downside of the Alter-G antigravity treadmill is that the flagship model costs $75,000. There is also a scaled-down version that is marginally more affordable at $25,000. Only a handful of units are accessible for injured runners to use in high-end physical therapy facilities. It will be a while before antigravity treadmill running is a realistic option for most runners.

In my opinion, the next best thing to running on an antigravity treadmill is steep uphill treadmill walking. Research has shown that the human brain uses the same motor pattern to run or to walk briskly on steep gradients. In other words, when you crank the treadmill incline up to 12–15 percent, running becomes walking and walking becomes running. Therefore, walking on a steep incline is a highly specific way to maintain running fitness. But impact forces are reduced drastically compared to running, so steep uphill walking is possible with most injuries.

Many runners don't think of walking as a good alternative to running when injured because they assume they cannot match their normal intensity. Trust me: You can. Set the incline on a treadmill at 12–15 percent, increase the belt speed to 4 miles per hour or so, check your heart rate, and you'll see.

The only limitation of steep uphill walking is that, while it is a low-impact activity, it is not a nonimpact activity. Thus, it cannot be done pain free with all injuries. For example, I was unable to use steep uphill walking as an alternative to running with a recent Achilles tendon strain.

8. Injuries make you hungry for a comeback. In Chapter 5 I discussed various factors such as setting goals and gathering performance feedback that increase the ability to tolerate the suffering of hard running and thereby increase performance. Another, more peculiar factor that I did not discuss in that context is the special appreciation for running that attends a postinjury comeback. All else being equal, the runner who "wants it more" wins the race, because in wanting it more, he is willing to bear a greater affective load in chasing his goal. Perversely, having everything go your way in training can take the edge off your desire to excel. You begin to take the sport for granted, if only to a small degree. When an injury interrupts the smooth flow of training, you realize how fortunate you were to be healthy and able to run.

Upon having this blessing restored, you return to training with a stronger sense of the preciousness of healthy running. Understanding that it can be taken from you at any time, you run with a determination to make the most of however much time you may have to keep running. You gladly suffer more and thus train harder and race faster.

MIND-BODY RUNNING

When you suffer an injury, experience the frustration that normally follows a physical breakdown, but then transform that frustration into fuel, taking your running to a new level.

The comeback experience is truly one of the most wonderful experiences in the life of a competitive runner. Having had my share of injuries, I have also experienced my share of comebacks, so I know this feeling well. Even in the early days of a postinjury return to form, when your fitness level is still low, the combination of feeling steady improvement, seeing the prospect of continuing improvement ahead, and relishing every step of every run makes running more enjoyable than it is at almost any other time.

Now, I would never wish an injury upon myself just for the sake of a postinjury comeback. But I earnestly believe that in many cases a runner can race better at the end of a year that begins with an injury than she can at the end of an injury-free year, because the greater hunger of the recently injured runner more than makes up for the lost training. So powerful is the brain's influence on running performance that it is sometimes better to be hurt than complacent.

If you're skeptical concerning this point, consider the example of Shalane Flanagan. In the first phase of her running career, which began in high school and ended when she developed a foot injury in 2004, at which time she was fresh out of college, Flanagan accomplished a great deal. She won a national title in the mile while at Marblehead (Massachusetts) High School and won two NCAA cross-country titles at the University of North Carolina. She was destined to become a successful professional runner, but few could have predicted the heights of greatness she would reach after struggling for nearly a year and a half to overcome her foot injury. In her very first race after having surgery to remove an extra bone from her foot, Flanagan broke the American record for 3,000 m. She has since set American records at 5,000 m and 10,000 m and won a bronze medal at the latter distance in the 2008 Olympics.

Flanagan herself believes she was helped by the injury. In an interview for the Web site Take The Magic Step, Flanagan was asked if she had ever considered giving up during her long battle with the foot problem. "I never have thought that I was going to give up," she answered.

> If you listen to anyone who has gotten to the top, they have always had a bump in their road. I have never known anyone who went directly to the top without a small setback. I don't call them setbacks, actually. They just mold you into a tougher person. If I hadn't had that injury, I wouldn't have reevaluated my love of running. It made me reevaluate a lot of stuff—how serious I was to this sport. I asked myself: Is this the right coach? Is this the right training? I think what truly seems like a bad situation is there for a reason. My husband [Steve Edwards] sometimes says that bad things happen for a reason. I believe it happened for a reason: for me to reevaluate my goals and my commitment to the sport. I believe that the down times lead you to be a stronger person.

It is natural to experience frustration, bitterness, and even outright despair when dealing with a protracted injury. Even if you understand and accept the idea that injuries can benefit your running by making you hungrier, you will almost certainly experience such emotions the next time you are injured. But believing in the potential benefits of injury will reduce your frustration and help you pass from the woe-is-me phase to the looking-ahead phase of the injury experience more quickly. So next time you break down, remember Shalane Flanagan.

9. Injuries point the way forward. Even when injury causes cannot be identified and learned from, injuries can prompt changes in training methods and other running-related practices that not only reduce the risk of future injuries but also make a runner better. When injured, the mindful runner sometimes receives ideas or hunches about how to do things differently going forward. As the injured runner is often in a "nothing to lose" position, these ideas and hunches are generally worth trying and often pay dividends.

Among the changes runners commonly make to avoid injury recurrence that also turn out to be performance enhancing are adding strength training, power training, drills and technique work, stretching, or cross-training to their program; maintaining more consistent mileage throughout the year; including at least a small amount of high-intensity running throughout the year; switching to softer surfaces; slowing the pace of easy runs; adding easy running to their program; increasing or reducing the length of training cycles; and shifting to a lower-volume, higher-intensity training system.

By motivating the runner to try such changes, injuries can actually accelerate the process of developing a personal magic training formula. When a runner's body holds together for a long time, she may never think to experiment with new methods that would make her a better runner if she only tried them. Injuries force the runner to get creative—to find alternative roads to improvement. Not infrequently, new training methods that a runner adopts primarily to avoid future injuries also address weaknesses in her fitness profile and thereby enhance her performance.

Even when an injury seems to create an immovable barrier to training in the manner you feel is necessary for success, a creative workaround can leave you better off. In 2005, chronic Achilles tendon problems forced Haile Gebrselassie to forever swear off short intervals, a type of training he had relied on to develop his speed throughout his career. His workaround consisted of an increased commitment to weightlifting, increased training volume, and technique work specifically focused on replacing his forefoot footstrike (which put tremendous stress on his Achilles tendons) with a midfoot landing. In 2006, Gebrselassie broke the half-marathon world record, and the following year he set his first marathon world record.

Seize the opportunity that injuries present to discover new and better ways to train. Consult experts and your intuitions to identify sensible new methods to try. They may not always work, but more often than not they will lead you in a good direction.

10. You never know what might work. If you talk about injuries with other runners as much as most runners do, you are bound to hear some crazy magic solutions advocated now and again. One time I complained about a case of piriformis syndrome to a friend and athlete, and she suggested I try something called the Sacro Wedgy. This is a small, wedge-shaped piece of plastic available only through the Internet. You sit on it and supposedly it lets your piriformis muscle relax and thereby alleviates the nerve impingement that causes pain. I was highly skeptical about this product, but my friend was adamant and the thing doesn't cost much, so I bought it, sat on it, and 20 minutes later my injury was gone.

Sometimes things that should not work do. But just as often, things that should work do not. In 2004 I had knee surgery to clean up some fissured cartilage that my orthopedist assured me was the cause of my nagging knee pain. The surgery did not work. Eccentric strengthening exercises for the calf muscles and Achilles tendon are touted as a miracle cure for Achilles tendonopathy. I have done these exercises until I was blue in the face, to no avail.

The lesson in the unpredictability of injury treatments is twofold. First, try just about anything to fix your breakdowns, and never give up trying to find a solution no matter how many treatments fail you. Second, never place too much hope and expectation on any single measure. That is another sure way to drive yourself nuts. Try everything and expect nothing. This is the way to find solutions without making yourself miserable in the process.

My most recent spate of injuries included plantar fasciitis in the left foot and Achilles tendonosis in the left leg. After taking 10 weeks off from running with no abatement of pain, I decided to start running again a little, figuring that, if rest did not help, running would not hurt. The morning after I completed my first short, slow run, I was surprised to find that my Achilles and heel felt a bit better. After my next run, they felt better still, and after two more runs I was almost pain free. So an injury that was caused by running and perhaps exacerbated by rest was ultimately cured by running.

See what I mean?

TEN

ANGER, FEAR, AND SPEED

I put a dagger in that pain, and it was no more.

—Jim Spivey

THE FIRST MAJOR WESTERN THINKER to formulate a "mind-body" theory of human emotions was seventeenth-century Dutch philosopher Baruch Spinoza. In a stark departure from the Western tradition of conceiving the mind and the body as completely separate entities made of wholly different substances, Spinoza defined the emotions (or "affects") as consciously felt physical responses to influences affecting the body's well-being. He wrote in his *Ethics*, "By emotion I understand the affections [changes in state] of the body by which the body's power of activity is increased or diminished, assisted or checked, together with the ideas of these affections." In other words, according to Spinoza, the primary source of feelings is changes in the state of the body that occur in response to some influence, internal or external.

Two centuries later, the development of the theory of evolution provided conceptual tools that enabled thinkers to begin the process of transforming the study of human emotions from a philosophical endeavor into a scientific one. Charles Darwin himself wrote an entire book about human emotions. As you might guess, Darwin argued that emotions are inherited traits that have survived the process of natural selection because they are useful to the organisms that exhibit them. In Darwin's view, emotions are fundamentally the same in humans and other animals. "Negative emotions" such as anger, fear, and disgust are useful because they encourage us to avoid and defend ourselves against threats and harmful influences, while "positive emotions" encourage us to seek after healthful influences. Darwin also went a few steps further than Spinoza in specifying the changes in body state that underlie the felt aspect of emotions, such as increased heart rate, perspiration, and muscle tension in the case of anger.

In the late twentieth century, scientists developed instruments that allowed them to observe the inner workings of the brain. These advances enabled researchers to learn a great deal more about what the emotions are, where they come from, and how they work in relation to other functions of the body and the mind. One of the great pioneers in this field of research has been Antonio Damasio, a neuroscientist at the University of Southern California. Damasio's work led him to propose that emotion is fundamental to the very fabric of consciousness—that there is an emotional aspect to every single thought we think and sensation we experience. In *The Feeling of What Happens*, Damasio argued that consciousness is basically a representation of the state of an organism with respect to both its internal environment—the body—and its external environment. These representations of states are inherently evaluative. In other words, the myriad systems that make up the organism, and the organism as a whole, are represented in consciousness always as good or bad, well or unwell, threatened or fortified, to some degree. Hence, consciousness is fundamentally emotional. There is no pre-emotional or extraemotional consciousness. Consciousness exists solely to let the organism know how it's doing and to enable the organism to act for its own well-being in more sophisticated ways than it could act if it were not conscious.

Damasio described as "background feelings" the emotions we experience when we're not experiencing the strong emotions (fear, joy, anger, etc.) induced by acute positive and negative stimuli. These background feelings represent a sort of equilibrium emotional state. When the organism is well, this state is pleasant. To the degree that the organism is unwell, the background feelings are negative. Happiness must then be a background feeling or a group of positive background feelings such as "wellness," "harmony," and "balance" (Damasio himself named these) that predominate when body and brain are well. This would explain why scientists have found that exercise makes people measurably happier.

Perhaps Damasio's greatest contribution to our understanding of emotions was to demonstrate that there is no clear separation between our emotional and our reasoning faculties. Because every thought, including such things as the performance of mathematical calculations, passes through emotional channels within the brain, we cannot think effectively if our emotional faculties are compromised in any way. Solving a math problem, for example, includes an effort to overcome the stress of not knowing the answer, and this emotional dimension of the experience hastens the discovery of that answer.

Indeed, there is an emotional aspect of all learning. This truth was neatly demonstrated in studies in which subjects were exposed to a series of images, most of which were pleasant or benign, but a few of which were disturbing. Although the order of the images seemed random at first, it was not. What's interesting is that subjects began to correctly anticipate the disturbing image emotionally before they consciously recognized the pattern. Specifically, there was increased activity in brain regions associated with aversion—regions that had previously become active only after the subject had seen a disturbing image. The lesson here is that often we figure things out emotionally before we figure them out consciously, and often we figure things out consciously only because we first figured them out emotionally. This observation validates the mind-body running method of using emotions such as enjoyment and confidence to guide the course of training. These emotions are the products of subconscious intuitive learning about cause-effect patterns in training—learning that is often way ahead of conscious learning.

I used scare quotes around the phrase "negative emotions" earlier because, while such emotions are typically unpleasant to experience and are in that sense negative, they are natural, necessary, and useful and in that sense are not really negative. In this chapter I will discuss the so-called negative emotions of fear and anger. These emotions play roles in every field of endeavor, including running. Too often, traditional sports psychology treats fear and anger in sport as something to be overcome with little tools such as deep breathing and visualization exercises. But from a mind-body perspective that is informed by our current neuroscientific understanding of emotion, fear and anger are sources of valuable information about perceived threats to well-being. As knowledge is power, the best way to deal with anger or fear in your running is to identify its cause and then make a rational decision about how to use this emotion to benefit your running. As we will see, the best move is not always to quash the emotion reflexively.

WHAT WE ARE AFRAID OF

The seat of the emotional faculties is a region of the brain called the limbic system, which is one of the most primitive parts of the brain. A core structure within the limbic system is a pebble-sized thing called the amygdala, which exists in even the dumbest of animals, including fish, rodents, and reptiles. We know what the amygdala does in part because of research involving surgical lesions to the amygdalas of laboratory animals; these lesions disturbed the animals' capacity for emotional learning (that is, for recognizing stimuli associated with rewards or pain and modifying behavior accordingly).

The fear response to particular types of stimuli appears to be hardwired into the limbic system. For example, like many people, my wife experiences vertigo and tingling skin when she finds herself near the edge of a high place; this is an innate fear that need not be learned. But the limbic system is interconnected with every other part of the human brain, including those parts responsible for the most advanced conscious faculties, and these connections enable us to learn to fear all kinds of things that are much worse than high places, such as failing to achieve our goals in running events.

Basic fears like the fear of heights and intangible fears like the fear of failure in sports competition are different in ways other than their relative simplicity and concreteness. The utility of, for instance, fearing snakes is obvious: It helps us avoid being bitten by them. And inasmuch as fear is unpleasant, what we need to do to avoid experiencing the fear of snakes is obvious: We must steer clear of situations where we are likely to encounter them. (There are some great running trails near my home that some runners never visit because they are trafficked by snakes.) The benefit of some of the most common running-related fears, such as not achieving race goals, is not so obvious. After all, this specific fear often causes runners to choke—that is, the fear of failure precipitates failure. It is also not so obvious what we should do about this fear.

While the fear mechanism generally works to our benefit, like every other physical mechanism in the body, it is not perfect. Just as the immune system exists to protect us but can make us sick when it overreacts to certain physical stimuli, some fears develop as maladaptations to psychological stimuli and become much greater problems for us than those stimuli. In most cases, however, fear of failure in running races is not a maladaptation. Instead, it serves two specific purposes. First, it actually primes us physically and psychologically to perform well. The physiological changes that occur when a person sees and fears a snake enable him to escape it (or possibly fight it) more effectively. Likewise, the anxiety that a runner feels before a race makes it possible for him to run faster. While the mental component of this anxiety does create some risk of choking, that risk notwithstanding, the runner will generally race better when he is scared before the race than when he is not. Second, fear of failure in all contexts discourages us from taking unnecessary risks. It is the body's way of asking, "How important is this really?" If we understand this message and decide that the task we face is not worth the attending risk, we have an opportunity to back out. But if, understanding the message, we decide that the task is worth the risk, then we go into it with a fuller sense of its importance, which enables us to try harder and perform better than we would have done without anxiety.

Highest-performing elite athletes typically understand intuitively that the fear they feel before competition is not a symptom of something gone wrong that should be quashed with relaxation techniques but a natural way for the body to prepare the mind and body to go hard. An Olympic swimmer once said to British sports psychologist Mark Nesti during a session, "If I wasn't anxious before a big event, I would be very anxious."

High-performing elites also typically understand that the best way to cope with fear is to hear the question that fear is asking—"Are you sure you're up for this?"—and answer it definitively. In running, the greatest fear besides fear of failure is fear of the intense suffering that always attends 100 percent efforts in racing. I asked Kara Goucher how she dealt with this fear, and she said: "I think it's important to be honest about it. Denial sets you up to fail. It's unrealistic to think, 'Oh, well, I'm in such good shape and I've tapered; it's going to feel awesome.' No, it's not. It's going to hurt. You have to accept that the pain is going to come. Then you're more prepared. You have to make a choice: Is it worth it? I think it's worth it."

CHOOSING FEAR

The pattern of directly confronting fear that so many elite athletes fall into naturally is rather existential—or existentialist, I should say. Developed by nineteenth-century Danish philosopher Søren Kierkegaard and further developed by the likes of French philosopher Jean-Paul Sartre, existentialism prizes the "authentic life" above all other individual goals. In the existentialist perspective, the purpose of life is to become your true self, which you do step-by-step by bravely confronting life's challenges with open eyes, recognizing the choices that these challenges present, and decisively choosing the path that is most consistent with the person you desire to be. (It's all very grown-up.) Anxiety, or fear, has an important place in existentialism because anxiety is a way of feeling a difficult choice coming. Where there is anxiety, there is almost always an important decision lying underneath.

To me, the language of existentialist philosophy makes better sense of sports than the language of sports psychology. I am not alone in this belief. Mark Nesti has written a couple of books on the application of existentialism to sports. A few years back he explained the gist of it to me in a very expensive international phone call.

"The general psychological view," he said, "is that anxiety before competition is not a good thing, because it's unpleasant and it causes the athlete to waste nervous energy, lose focus, and have fear of failure. The conventional view in sports psychology is that if you have an athlete who is shaking, sweating, and miserable before a competition, you need to give them interventions to stop it. The existential view is that anxiety often is a sign that you are challenging yourself. That anxiety is about you pushing yourself into a challenging situation."

Existentialism calls upon the athlete to muster courage and work through the source of anxiety instead of taking the easy way out and trying to make it just go away. "It's about facing up to the discomfort that is associated with the sport experience, whether it's the pain of racing, the grind of training, or the entire lifestyle sacrifice," Nesti told me. Why? "The existential view is that the encounter with anxiety that comes with facing up to challenges—repeatedly facing up to those challenges and going through them—strengthens the core of who you are," Nesti continued. "Every time there's a chance to step up—every time there's an opportunity to move beyond where you are now—and the recognition dawns on you that that choice is yours—if you repeatedly say 'no' to these opportunities—if you make 'no' your typical response—that undermines your personality and character and makes you less of an authentic person. You become less of the real you."

MIND-BODY RUNNING

Fear is a natural part of the competitive running experience. Like all emotions, fear gives information. You are better off discerning the information encoded in your running-related fears than trying to eliminate them.

Think of how Kara Goucher asks herself whether the racing pain that she fears is worth it and then decides that it is—this is a great example of successful self-recognition. Goucher's natural distaste for suffering and her desire to be the best runner she can be are both parts of her, but they are mutually incompatible to a degree. So there are times when she must choose one or the other, and as these choices are repeated, the balance determines who she really is: whether she is a cowardly good runner or a brave great runner.

"The idea is to become more and more authentic, which involves you fully engaging the question of why you should step forward," Nesti told me. "The more you do that, the more authentic you become, because you've gone through this process of wrestling with your own values and thought processes to make a decision. Often what happens is that people make a decision without making a decision." Indeed, when you don't think about the choices that underlie your fear, you are all but bound to make a decision without making a decision.

Existential counseling sessions with athletes are somewhat different from traditional counseling sessions. To begin with, they are not called counseling sessions but "encounters." They dispense with all psychobabble and focus squarely on rational, clear-eyed problem-solving. The client describes current sports-related anxieties or anxieties affecting her sport. The counselor then challenges the athlete to discern the decision underlying the fear, consider which course of action is truest to the person she wants to be, and make a full commitment to that course of action.

You can be your own existential sports psychologist, as many elite runners are. All you have to do is gradually train yourself to become aware of your anxieties, catch them early, and think about them instead of just feeling them. Ask yourself, "What am I afraid of?" Consider all of the possible options you have for addressing the source of that fear, from fleeing it to charging straight at it. Picture yourself taking each option, and then ask yourself, "Which version of me am I most proud of?" Finally, go out and become the you who makes you proud.

More than other forms of therapy, existential sports counseling demands courage of the client, and I think that is appropriate, because alongside talent and hard work, success in running demands courage above all else. Distance running is among the most painful and scariest sports we have come up with, and a runner must be brave in the purest sense to succeed in it. Steve Prefontaine famously said, "I run to see who has the most guts." He was wise to do so, because by making a consistent, overt effort to be brave as a runner, he could run to the best of his ability.

Winning easily is not even satisfying. When I asked Alberto Salazar to rate his overlooked victory in the 56 mile 1994 Comrades Marathon among his career accomplishments, he told me that it was among the two or three most treasured moments in his life as a runner precisely because it was the hardest thing he had ever done in running. All runners are the same in this regard. The very thing that hooks most of us on the sport is the experience of making it to the finish line of a race after having resisted intense temptations to slow down or stop in the preceding miles. There's just something uniquely soul satisfying about proving our courage to ourselves.

It's good to remind yourself why you got hooked on running in those inevitable moments when you are tempted to be cowardly. You love running in large part because it proves your guts. That gutsy person is the authentic you. Always choose to be that person.

Just be sure to not lose sight of what is truly courageous and what is really cowardly. Sometimes quitting is the brave thing to do. For example, in football there is tremendous team social pressure to "play hurt." Players who hit the field and try hard despite the pain of injuries are celebrated; those who sit out with anything less than a blown knee are shamed. And sometimes the praise and the criticism are fair. Other times, however, it is simply stupid to play hurt. In that case, players risk their long-term health and really only hurt the team. But because of that tremendous social pressure, it actually takes more courage to sit out and bear teammates' contempt than to bear the mere physical discomfort of playing with an injury.

Similar situations occur in running. Once I ran a 10K race in hopes of setting a PR at a time when I was very fit but showing signs of being overtrained. I ran the first mile on my 5:16 goal pace but knew already that I was in trouble. At mile 4 I was 25 seconds off my goal pace and slowing, I was in agony, and moments later I dropped out. Now if I dropped out of any race simply because I was in agony, I would never forgive myself. But in this case I knew that I was overcooked and that I would only jeopardize my chances of performing well in the peak race ahead of me if I foolishly persisted under the misguided belief that quitting is always cowardly. Yes, I was embarrassed to be seen walking by the side of my road, but I knew that caring too much about what others think, rather than living to fight another day, is the cowardly thing. Always remember that oftentimes discretion really is the better part of valor.

ANGER ISSUES

Of the more than 100 million animal species on earth, only two are known to actively hunt and kill members of their own species. One of them is, of course, *Homo sapiens*: us. The other is the chimpanzee, our closest genetic relative in the animal kingdom. Human beings—particularly male humans—are exceptionally violent creatures by nature, and it appears we inherited our savagery directly from the common ancestor we share with our cousins the chimpanzees.

Chimpanzee wars look very much like modern human urban gang turf wars. The males of a chimpanzee clan gather and march into the territory occupied by another clan, where they kill as many rival males as possible in a surprise raid. Anthropologists believe that these wars serve to expand chimpanzee clans' area of control, giving them access to more food resources and more female breeders. You see, it's all quite practical.

It is not, however, cold blooded. There is a definite emotional state that supports the violent behaviors of chimps and humans alike, and that state is anger. Both species have a tremendous capacity for anger that is hardwired into their brains and is especially sensitive to activation by other members of their own kind.

The neurobiology of anger overlaps extensively with that of fear. Like fear, anger is rooted in the primitive limbic system, particularly the amygdala, which essentially decides whether a particular stimulus routed to it through the perceptual faculties is something to get angry about. And like fear, anger is a whole-body emotion, and it reaches the whole body through some of the same mechanisms as fear, including the hormone epinephrine (adrenaline). With so much biological overlap, it's easy to see why there is fluidity between the emotions of fear and anger. The latter often manifests secondarily to the former: Some threat frightens a person, and the fear quickly transforms into anger to enable the person to fight back against the threat.

One key difference between humans and chimpanzees with respect to anger is that humans have a greater capacity to control and redirect anger. As with fear, the brain regions that generate feelings of anger have two-way connections to every other part of the brain, including our highest conscious faculties. These connections allow anger to filter into our most sophisticated thoughts and expressions (consider the anger that infuses many of history's greatest philosophers' disagreements with one another) and also allow us to consciously suppress anger—at least to a certain degree, sometimes. Neuroscientists have identified the ventral prefrontal cortex as a brain area responsible for such suppression. Activity in this area is lower than normal in persons who are prone to anger attacks.[1]

The human capacity to sublimate anger has been critical to our ability to develop large, stable, and complex social systems. Mighty modern nations could not survive, let alone have come into existence in the first place, if every surge of anger led to a killing. But the powerful anger instincts that fuel the rampant violence seen in chimpanzee cultures and that are believed to have existed in early human cultures have not exactly gone away. They are expressed in different ways. Much of our anger is channeled into our behavior behind the wheels of automobiles. I daresay most of us drive in a state of simmering hatred directed against every other driver on the road—a hatred that, at the least provocation, comes gushing forth in the form of outright threats of violence: curses, extended middle fingers, horn honks, and aggressive maneuvers. Even little ladies who are as meek as church mice outside of their cars become bloodthirsty savages in them. (You know I'm telling the truth.) But perhaps the best place to see just how ready we humans are to hate each other is on Internet chat forums. I don't care what the subject of the forum is; scarcely ever does a message thread extend beyond a dozen comments before it degenerates into a sequence of back-and-forth, vitriolic, ad hominem attacks. Runners are hardly above this kind of behavior. Anyone who has ever spent time on letsrun.com's "world famous message boards" knows what I mean.

RUNNING ANGRY

Perhaps the most positive way in which our violent tendencies are sublimated in modern society is through sports competition. Sports do not exist entirely as a productive means of channeling our desires to bash one another's brains in, but they surely would not exist if these instincts did not also exist. Simply put, sports are, to some extent, a substitute for fighting (except, of course, in the cases of combat sports such as boxing, which are at least substitutes for fighting to the death—usually). Now, one of the functions of anger is to enable a person to fight effectively when fighting is necessary. Thus, inasmuch as sports are substitutes for fighting, anger ought to help athletes perform better. Could this really be true? I think so.

I will not go so far as to say that anger always enhances athletic performance or that athletes always perform better when angry than when not angry. But I believe that some athletes do perform better when angry and that every athlete can productively channel anger into competition.

MIND-BODY RUNNING

Anger is a natural part of the running experience. A strong response to fear, it is more performance enhancing for runners than not. Do not let someone tell you not to run angry.

Like fear, anger is widely considered a negative emotion that should be prevented and, if not prevented, annihilated in all contexts. This idea becomes absurd when we consider the science of anger, which reveals anger as natural, ineradicable, and useful. Therefore, as runners, we are well advised to accept the inevitability of anger and be open to using it for the benefit of running performance.

Traditional sports psychology is dominated by the notion that anger is bad and can only harm performance, but actual research on this subject has proven otherwise. In a 2008 study psychologists from Boston College and Stanford University tested whether anger would help students perform better in a violent video game.[2] The study had two parts. In the first part, subjects were asked to identify activities they would prefer to engage in before playing each of two video games: a violent combat video game and a nonconfrontational video game in which the player acts the role of a waitress trying to serve customers as fast as possible. The subjects identified very different lists of preferred activities with respect to the two games, naming activities likely to generate anger, such as listening to loud music, as preferable before playing the combat game but not the nonconfrontational game. In the second part of the study, the subjects were exposed to the anger-inducing activities they had named and then randomly assigned to play either of the two games. Their performance was compared to their performance when playing the same game on a different occasion without anger-inducing preparatory activities. The researchers found that the subjects performed significantly better in the combat game, but not in the nonconfrontational game, when angry.

So is running a confrontational sport or not? I think it can be either, depending on how a person looks at it, and I think those who tend to look at running as a confrontational sport are likely to run better when angry, whereas those who view running nonconfrontationally will not benefit from anger. Still, though, I think every runner can run better with anger at least in some circumstances.

There are certainly many noteworthy examples of runners whom no one would consider to be especially angry people and yet have clearly benefited from anger in races. One such example is Catherine Ndereba, without question the most accomplished female marathon runner in history, whose nickname is Catherine the Great not only because of her great running achievements but also because of her consistently demonstrated generosity and big-heartedness. In 1996, in her first year of international competition, the young Kenyan won 13 races and reached the number two spot in USA Track & Field's World Road Running Rankings. Ndereba seemed on her way toward greatness, but she had her own priorities and took the entire year of 1997 off to give birth to her first child. She returned to competition in 1998 and picked up right where she had left off. Yet the notoriously draconian Kenyan Athletics Federation, in an apparent move to punish her for taking the previous year off to have a child, left Ndereba off its roster for the 1999 World Cross-Country Championships.

This made Ndereba very angry. "I was so mad, I didn't know what to do," she said. She ultimately decided to enter the Boston Marathon (which took place a few weeks after the cross-country championship she was excluded from), her first crack at the 26.2 mile distance. Although she wisely set a conservative goal of running 2:30, her anger lifted her performance above expectations, and she ran 2:28:27 on a tough day for sixth place. "At the finish I felt like I was the winner," she said. This performance convinced Ndereba that she was born for the marathon and became the springboard for all that followed, including four subsequent victories in the Boston Marathon.

Ndereba is a woman. While women are much less prone to violence than men, they are no less prone to anger and no less competitive. In chimpanzee culture, females always occupy definite positions on a rigid hierarchy of dominance, just as males do. Various forms of competition are used to determine the pecking order, and there is no question that anger infuses those competitions. We all know how competitive human females can be among one another, and there is also no question that social competition among women gives rise to much anger. These instincts are brought to bear in sports. So female runners are no less competitive, and no less likely to benefit from anger, than their male counterparts.

Another noteworthy example of a runner benefiting from anger in competition is Jim Spivey, one of the best American milers of the 1980s and early 1990s, who recorded a career-best time of 3:49.80. The night before the final of the 1992 Olympic Trials 1,500 m, Spivey's coach, Mike Durkin, told Spivey to visualize his chief rivals—Steve Scott, Joe Falcon, and Terrence Herrington—breaking into his home as he ran the last lap of the race. Understanding the benefits of racing angry, Durkin wanted Spivey to manufacture anger when he could most benefit from it. As silly as this tactic sounds, it worked. With 200 m to go, and in a dead heat with his rivals, "I literally saw people breaking into my home," said Spivey in an interview for the Tennessee Running Web site. "I was ready for a fistfight." He pulled away from the others and won the race handily.

The first time I raced angry was when I was 15, about to turn 16. My best friend and teammate and nearest running rival, Mike, and I moved down from our normal distances to form a 4 × 800 m relay team with a couple of other teammates. Neither of us had ever run a competitive 800 before nor had any idea how fast we could run the distance. But we both knew one thing: We had to beat our best friend.

It was totally out in the open, of course, our being best friends. We talked straight trash, competing to come up with the funnier put-down. I hope I came up with the funniest put-down, because Mike handed my ass to me in the relay. I ran a 2:12. Mike blasted a 2:04. When, smiling like the Cheshire cat, Mike told me his split after the race, I was devastated. I remember sulking like an overgrown baby all the way home in the backseat of my parents' car.

I made sure to run the 800 again in the very next meet a few days later. Mike gave me the pleasure of a rematch. But I really wasn't interested in beating him any longer. I accepted that he had just moved out of my league and congratulated him on it. I just wanted to get closer. But what little I wanted, I wanted with a vengeance. I continued to burn with the humiliation I had suffered in the relay. So I ran angry, and I ran 2:07. Boom. Five days, 5-second improvement. Anger.

Since then I have raced angry many times. Sometimes I race angry to stick it to people who tell me I cannot achieve my race goals. Doubters are a classic motivator for many athletes. Michael Jordan's entire legendary basketball career was an act of angry revenge against the coach who cut him from a junior varsity team. Lance Armstrong always went out of his way to make people doubt him, because, he said, "the surest way to get me to do something is to tell me I can't." Other times I race to vent the frustration of recent setbacks, usually injuries. This is also quite typical. Indeed, the anger that fueled Jim Spivey's victory in the 1992 Olympic Trials 1,500 m was itself fueled by the frustration of his having failed to qualify for the 1988 Olympics. "I put a dagger in that pain, and it was no more," he said of his 1992 Trials victory.

When I race angry, I feel that I can tolerate more pain, and that is why I am able to run faster. There is scientific evidence that supports this perception. Some of it comes from another videogame study—this one conducted by Bryan Raudenbush at Wheeling Jesuit University in 2005. In it, subjects played a variety of different videogames prior to receiving a pain stimulus in the form of intense cold exposure. The researchers found that all of the games reduced pain perception compared to when the pain stimulus was not preceded by any type of distraction, but that pain was reduced most after subjects had played those games that generated the most anger.[3] A 2009 study, out of Britain's Keele University, found that uttering profanity—a common expression of anger—reduced pain sensitivity.[4] Other research has shown that acute anger triggers the release of chemicals known as endogenous opioids within the brain to dull pain.[5] It stands to reason that anger would increase pain tolerance. Since anger often precedes fighting, where pain is sure to occur, the effect of reduced pain perception helps a person fight better and reduces the chances of being killed.

Anger is a double-edged sword, of course. Anger-prone individuals tend to be less healthy and less happy than others and tend to die younger. But letting out a normal amount of anger is actually healthier than not expressing anger at all; one study found that men who routinely bottled up their anger were more prone to heart attack.[6]

A person who is incapable of feeling anger is as vulnerable as someone who cannot feel physical pain. Normal anger reactions are healthiest.

Runners whose anger responses are within the normal range are likely to find themselves naturally channeling anger into racing on occasion. Don't stand in the way of this phenomenon under the misguided notion that all anger is bad.

ELEVEN

MUSCLE TALK

A leg extension isn't teaching me
to relax in a painful moment.

—Tera Moody

TIM DEBOOM, A TWO-TIME WINNER of the Hawaii Ironman World Championship, jokes that his longtime massage therapist, Kris, knows his body better than his wife does. Because of his work with Kris, he knows his own body better than he ever would have known it without her, and this self-awareness has been a boon to his training and racing. One story that De-Boom has told suggests that it would be difficult to exaggerate how much information the body can provide through massage. DeBoom was receiving his last treatment before flying to Hawaii to compete in the 2001 World Championship. Midway through the session, Kris said, "You're ready to win." She had never said anything like this before. DeBoom had competed in Hawaii several times already and had never won. This time he won.

Many amateur runners and most elite runners receive regular massage therapy treatments. Although the main purported benefits of massage—recovery enhancement and injury prevention—have not been validated by research (a 2008 meta-analysis provided little support for these benefits but did find evidence of other, "moderate" benefits),[1] my hunch is that the effects of massage therapy are various and subtle and in some cases almost intangible. These effects may well hold the potential to make a worth-the-money difference in helping athletes recover faster, train harder, and avoid injury.

One thing is certain: Massage does something. No physical influence that causes such powerful sensations could possibly do so without changing the body in measurable ways. One benefit of massage that is often overlooked, and may be its chief benefit regardless of whatever else it does, is that it teaches athletes about their bodies. The muscles talk in unique ways through bodywork. As the therapist's hands (and sometimes elbows— ouch!) work over your body, you feel things that you do not feel at any other times: hidden painful spots, areas of tightness, trigger points, and the like. In each session you will feel different things—changes from the last treatment. Over time these changes will reveal useful information. Newly discovered sore spots will warn of impending injuries. An increased ability, say, to relax a piriformis trigger point under the therapist's thumb will correlate to a breakthrough in opening up your stride. You will learn new dimensions of how your body feels when it is rested, when it is fatigued, when it is fit.

LISTENING WITHIN

A good massage therapist is, in other words, a potentially valuable biofeedback tool. Biofeedback is any source of objective information about physiological processes that aids the individual in becoming aware (or more aware) of those processes. In the specific case of sports massage, biofeedback is essentially a kind of "muscle talk" that informs the athlete about the state of his or her muscles and connective tissues.

One of the early pioneers in the field of biofeedback was a Canadian scientist named John Basmajian, who made his name in the early 1960s by performing some of the first studies of human muscle function involving electromyography (EMG). This technology uses sensors placed on the surface of the body to measure the amount of electrical activity in the underlying muscles. In one study, Basmajian rigged up an EMG sensor to measure electricity in a single motor unit in the thumbs of volunteers in such a way that, when the motor unit was activated, a click was issued from a loudspeaker.[2] Several of the subjects were able to use this novel form of biofeedback to practice an exquisitely high degree of control over that single motor unit, tapping out Morse code, creating musical rhythms, and so forth. Now a motor unit is a bundle of muscle fibers that is connected to a single brain cell through a nerve snaking up the spinal cord. So this study showed that at least some people are able to intentionally activate one brain cell—one—out of the roughly 100 billion neurons that form the human brain. When Basmajian asked his volunteers how they were able to make the loudspeaker click in any pattern they chose, they answered that they did not know. They just did it by feel.

As weird as this study is, it is actually a fair representation of how we learn to do everything we do with our muscles—including run. Humans are born with relatively little control over their muscles. The infrastructure that enables the brain to communicate with the muscles is only half completed at birth. We have a few hardwired muscular reflexes such as the suckling reflex, but almost everything else has to be learned, and most of it is learned through a process of biofeedback that is not all that dissimilar from Basmajian's study. For example, a newborn infant does not know that his hand is his hand and cannot visually distinguish it from other objects in the environment. But the baby can *feel* his hand, whereas he cannot feel those other objects. Over time, through random, uncontrolled flailing and interaction with adults, the baby gradually discovers that his hand is his hand and by roughly four months of age has learned how to reach for and grab small objects (and usually put them in his mouth!). From this time forward the child is able to expand his repertoire of motor skills very quickly, because the basic connection between the brain and the muscles already exists; it's just a matter of learning how to control the brain-muscle communications that occur through this connection.

But there is a slower aspect of the learning process. Unlike telecommunications between phones and computers in which a latent link is activated and deactivated without causing any change to the link itself, communications between the brain and muscles change the very physical link that makes their communication possible, especially early in life when the brain-muscle communication infrastructure is only half built. For example, if a motor unit is to effectively contract on the brain's command, a neurotransmitter delivering the command must reach the right motor unit and then find the right receptor to receive that particular neurotransmitter at the neuromuscular junction. A neurotransmitter is like a key, and a receptor is like a lock;

when the key turns the lock, the motor unit contracts. In infants, the dominant neurotransmitters used to activate motor units have not been selected from a pool of candidates and receptors have yet to aggregate at neuromuscular junctions to the degree needed for efficient and forceful muscle contractions. As the child repeats learned motor skills, the repeated activation of specific neuron-motor unit links triggers the selection of neurotransmitters and the aggregation of receptors, so that muscle contractions become increasingly efficient and forceful.

Also, the myelin sheaths that surround nerves are thin and incomplete in newborns. Repeated activation of particular nerves triggers further myelination of these same nerves—an even slower process that likewise serves to make movement patterns more efficient and forceful.

Brain-muscle communication continues to change the physical communication lines throughout life. The greatest changes occur in the linkages that are most often activated. In runners, the linkages undergo major transformations. As discussed in Chapter 8, the running stride improves by becoming more powerful and more efficient. Both of these changes entail neuromuscular adaptations. For example, the firing rate of motor units increases with training, enabling the running muscles to develop peak torque more quickly. This improves stride power by giving the runner the capacity to apply force to the ground more quickly, which results in the runner's body receiving a bigger return push from the ground, which in turn increases the distance the runner flies forward before the opposite foot comes down. As for efficiency, training increases this in part by reducing wasteful muscular co-contraction. In other words, training teaches the muscles that oppose the working muscles to relax more, which reduces the internal resistance the working muscles must overcome to do their job.

CROSSED SIGNALS

Overall, running does a marvelous job of evolving brain-muscle communications in ways that facilitate faster running. But sometimes this process is limited by problems in the linkages between the brain and particular muscles. The brain forgets how to fully relax certain muscles. These muscles constantly hold tension and become functionally shortened, and thus the efficiency of the running stride is reduced and injury risk is increased. The brain forgets how to fully activate other muscles. These muscles become functionally weakened, and their weakness compromises their performance of whatever role they might have in the running stride.

How does the brain forget how to relax a muscle? It can happen in a couple of ways. If a person spends too much time in a position where a muscle is shortened, actively or otherwise, and does too little to counterbalance the effects of this pattern, the muscle may essentially become stuck in a shortened position. Muscle tissue readily adapts to the specific demands placed upon it—even the demands of lack of use. Thus, when a muscle repeatedly finds itself subjected to prolonged shortening, the fibers of that muscle will lose some of their elasticity. Thereafter, inasmuch as this muscle is used, the brain will recognize its reduced elasticity from information received from the muscle through afferent feedback channels—specifically, through sensory receptors within the muscle called spindles, which convey information about the degree of stretch in the muscle. Simply put, the muscle will tell the brain, in effect, "Careful now, I'm not used to relaxing and stretching." The brain will respond to this information by maintaining extra tension in the muscle—that is, not allowing it to fully relax or stretch—to protect it from injury caused by overstretching, as the less elastic a muscle becomes, the more prone it is to being overstretched.

MIND-BODY RUNNING

Regularly do some form of strength and mobility training to improve communication between your brain and muscles in ways that help you run with greater joint stability, more power, and more ease.

The brain sometimes also holds tension (that is, creates tightness) in muscles, not to protect those muscles themselves, but to protect the muscles that oppose them on the opposite side of a joint. Consider the example of the quadriceps muscle group, which extends the knee joint, and the opposing hamstrings muscle group, which flexes the knee. In order for the quadriceps to effectively extend the knee, the hamstrings must relax and stretch. But if for some reason the brain thinks it best not to allow the quadriceps to fully contract, it may tighten the hamstrings and thereby inhibit full contraction of the quadriceps.

Why would the brain want to protect a muscle in this way? One reason is injury or pain. A 2007 study by Danish researchers looked at the effect of experimentally induced quadriceps muscle pain on control of the knee joint during walking.[3] Not surprisingly, when subjects walked with pain created by a saline injection in the vastus medialis muscle (a quadriceps muscle that plays a crucial role in stabilizing the knee during walking), EMG sensors revealed that brain activation of the vastus medialis and the vastus lateralis (another quadriceps muscle that works in coordination with the vastus medialis) was reduced compared to normal pain-free walking. Clearly, this unconscious change in muscle activation patterns was a protective adjustment to minimize pain. But the researchers also discovered that brain activation of these two muscles remained reduced afterward, despite the disappearance of pain. Once the usual connection between the brain and these muscles had been disturbed, it was difficult to reestablish.

It is not always injury that causes the brain to lose the ability to properly activate muscles. Lack of use may have the same effect. Most of the muscle imbalances that plague runners are caused by prolonged sitting. In the seated position, the hip flexors, hamstrings, and calf muscles are held in a shortened position. For the reasons just explained, this pattern causes these muscles to become chronically tight. In nonrunners, excessive sitting also causes these muscles to become weak, but the hip flexors, hamstrings, and calves are among the hardest-working muscles during running, so they are typically not abnormally weak in runners. Other muscles, however—namely the abs, quads, hips, and glutes—are relaxed during sitting, so they tend not to become abnormally tight, but they do become weak. And because these muscles (with the exception of the gluteus maximus) are not prime movers during running, they remain weak even in runners. The weakening effect of lack of use in muscles is caused by a combination of structural changes, such as diminishment of contractile proteins and reduced neural drive, but the latter factor is believed to be more important because reduced neural drive may trigger many of the structural changes. It's a vicious circle: When you do not use a muscle, your brain gets out of the habit of talking to it. The less the brain talks to the muscle, the weaker its signals to the muscle become when they are issued. As the muscle is neglected, it shrinks, and its shrinking further weakens the communication link between it and the brain.

Research has shown that the weakness of muscles that are neglected during sitting causes postural abnormalities, joint instabilities, and bio-mechanical inefficiencies during running. For example, the first muscles that must contract before a person moves any limb are the deep abdominal muscles, whose tightening creates a more stable platform to support limb movements. These muscles are almost totally inactive during sitting, and consequently the brain of the average desk worker is virtually unable to even "find" these muscles. The inability to properly engage the deep abs during running causes energy waste. Running with loose abs is like firing a cannon from a canoe on a river.

RESTORING COMMUNICATION

To run most powerfully, efficiently, and healthfully, runners must restore proper communication between their brains and their muscles. This can be done by performing any of a number of different types of movements that demand communication between the brain and the targeted muscles. I have long been a proponent of using functional strengthening exercises such as barbell split squats and mobility exercises such as giant walking lunges for the purpose of restoring structural balance in the body through improved brain-muscle communication. Descriptions of effective strength and mo-bility sessions can be found in some of my previous books. In the present context I would like to advocate a different means to achieve the same end that may have a unique advantage with respect to the others: yoga.

The difference between yoga and other forms of strength and mobility training is that it not only develops strength and mobility, but it also trains body awareness better than most, if not all, other forms of exercise. Body awareness is conscious sensitivity to afferent feedback of any form, be it the level of tension in a muscle or the degree of fullness of the stomach. It is well established that some people are less sensitive to their bodies' signals than others, and that body awareness is trainable, and there is evidence that yoga is an especially effective tool to develop general body awareness.

Have you ever noticed that regular yoga exercisers are never fat? Sci-entists may have discovered a reason for that. A study conducted at the

Fred Hutchinson Cancer Research Center provides evidence that regular yoga participants eat more mindfully than the average person does.[4] Mindful eating has to do with paying attention to hunger and satiety levels and choosing food portions accordingly.

In the study, more than 300 individuals who exercised regularly in a variety of modalities filled out a questionnaire designed to quantify the mindfulness of their eating habits. Subjects also provided information about the types and amounts of exercise they did. The researchers found that regular yoga participants achieved higher-than-average scores for mindful eating while those who participated in other types of exercise did not. They also found a significant negative correlation between mindful eating and body weight; in other words, the most mindful eaters tended to weigh the least. Because mindful eating was related to the type of exercise, not the amount, the authors of the study speculated that yoga develops body awareness in a way that transfers to eating habits.

I mention this example merely to show how generalized is the increased body awareness that comes from practicing yoga. All forms of exercise increase body awareness in relation to that specific activity, but yoga seems to increase body awareness in ways that reach far beyond the practice of yoga itself. Most relevant to your interests as a runner are benefits such as increased awareness and control of muscle tension and increased sensitivity to the effects of training on your fitness, fatigue, confidence, comfort, and enjoyment levels, which enable you to customize your training to better suit your needs.

Yoga is the only widely practiced form of exercise that involves almost no movement. The relatively static nature of yoga may account for its unique ability to generally enhance body awareness. The more complex an exercise movement is and the faster that movement is performed, the more difficult it is for conscious awareness to fully capture that movement. A yoga pose is as simple and slow as an exercise movement could possibly be, so it is easy for conscious awareness to capture. It presents the mind with less to think about than running, weight lifting, and other forms of exercise. Of course, standing still, sitting in a chair, and lying on a bed are also static postures, but the difference between these everyday postures and yoga poses is that the latter are unnatural and challenging positions that force conscious awareness to focus on them. You can easily sit for hours in a chair working on a computer with very little awareness of your body, but when you assume a yoga pose, you have no choice but to root your attention on your body: on your form, your breath, the stretch in some muscles, the burn in others, and so forth. Yoga is essentially meditation in difficult positions. Meditation is well known for enhancing mindfulness. The difficult positions that yoga entails ensure that mindfulness increases specifically in relation to the feeling of the body.

LESS STRESS, MORE POWER

Lots of elite runners have discovered the beneficial effects of yoga on "muscle talk"; these benefits include enhanced body awareness as well as increased capacity to activate stabilizing muscles and to relax nonworking muscles. Yoga is a core component of the training done by the ZAP Fitness elite running group in North Carolina, which is coached by Zika and Pete Rea. Tera Moody also swears by yoga. The fifth-place finisher in the 2008 U.S. Olympic Trials Marathon, Moody took up yoga for reasons that had nothing to do with running while she was a student at the University of Colorado. "I used to get really stressed out about grades, and running, and pretty much everything else," she told me. Yoga was recommended to her as a good way to combat anxiety by increasing awareness of anxiety and its causes and cultivating the ability to relax. Moody discovered that yoga worked. The peace that she experienced in clearing all the crap out of her head and concentrating her full attention on her heartbeat, breathing, and muscles during yoga sessions spread to the rest of her life and reduced her anxiety. But she also discovered that it made her a better runner.

"It made me stronger and more powerful," she said. Moody could feel the effects of her yoga training in every stride of every run. A propensity to suffer hip injuries disappeared as the yoga strengthened her core and made her lumbo-pelvic and hip joints more stable. That's not all, though. Whereas any form of strength and mobility training will make a runner feel stronger and more powerful, yoga helped Moody run more relaxed. She was able to keep her muscles from tensing up as fatigue encroached, which boosted her efficiency. She had better control of her breathing, which reduced the suffering (or affective load) of running hard and thus allowed her to run harder before reaching her tolerable suffering limit. All competitive runners who make a serious commitment to yoga report these effects, which other forms of strength and mobility training do not offer. "A leg extension isn't teaching me to relax in a painful moment," said Moody, who relied on yoga entirely for supplemental strength and mobility development, except for a little extra core work.

Most beginners perform very poorly in yoga lessons. Those who stick with it typically experience drastic improvements in their ability to hold poses correctly and to hold advanced poses that were impossible for them initially. The poor performance of beginners—including highly trained runners who are yoga novices—indicates that other types of exercise do little to develop isometric muscle strength and endurance, condition stabilizing muscles, increase functional joint range of motion, increase balance and postural stability, or increase neuromuscular efficiency specific to prolonged static muscle contractions. The drastic improvements seen in those who commit to yoga comes through improvement in each of these characteristics.

Experienced yoga students note that above all they feel more relaxed in the various poses, as though their muscles do not have to work nearly as hard to hold them. In fact, improvement in the performance of any type of exercise or sports movement entails reduced muscle activation input relative to performance output. Improvements in running performance are largely a matter of running in a more and more relaxed way.

The question is whether the increased ability to relax in yoga poses transfers over to running and helps runners run even more relaxed than they can through run training alone. Runners who practice yoga insist that it does. While the fitness benefits stimulated by any form of exercise are highly specific to that form of exercise, the chief benefits do transfer to other activities. The huge boost in endurance capacity that running provides undoubtedly enables yoga students who also run to resist fatigue better in their poses. If endurance is the signature fitness benefit of running, then the capacity to relax under muscular strain is the signature benefit of yoga and is sure to transfer over to running.

YOGA FOR RUNNERS

Yoga is not for everyone. Men and women exploring the mind-body connection are more likely than others to be attracted to it and, having tried it, are more likely to enjoy and stick with it. Also, more women than men dig yoga. Every runner who wants to fully realize her innate running potential must do some form of strength and mobility training. It does not have to be yoga, however. The same principle of enjoyment that I encouraged you to use to guide your training in Chapter 2 should be applied to your cross-training activities. There are many effective ways to develop the extra strength and mobility needed to run better. You will get the most out of your cross-training if you choose that form or those forms you most enjoy. And even after having found the type(s) of cross-training you like best, you will benefit further from going about it in the way you like best. There are many ways to incorporate yoga or any other form of cross-training into your training. Tera Moody likes to do two hard, 90-minute power yoga sessions per week. Sage Rountree prefers to do shorter, less intense yoga sessions more frequently.

> **MIND-BODY RUNNING**
>
> Consider practicing yoga instead of, or in addition to, more commonly used types of cross-training. Yoga not only increases strength and mobility but also increases body awareness better than other forms of exercise.

Rountree is a runner and triathlete who wrote the book on using yoga to enhance sports performance (*The Athlete's Guide to Yoga*). According to Rountree, the mistake that many runners make when they first try it is to do too much. They expect that they must engage in challenging yoga "workouts" to get any benefit from yoga. But this is all wrong. "Yoga for athletes is not athletic yoga," Rountree said. Runners subject their muscles to enough strain and fatigue in their runs. They don't need yoga to do more of the same. Instead, runners should do yoga in a way that complements their running. They should perform gentler routines that are focused on increasing mobility, balance, stability, and, of course, body awareness. Hard-core power yoga is fine for those who want to take it to the next level, but it is not the place to start and need not be attempted at all.

The best time to do more intense, strength-focused yoga sessions is during the off-season, when you are less concerned about the effects of fatigue and soreness caused by these sessions on your running. As you get into focused race preparation, phase out the strength stuff and phase in the gentler kind of yoga. Consider three half-hour sessions per week a minimum for noticeable benefits.

It is impossible to learn yoga entirely from a book or video. Every beginner does the poses wrong, and you will get little out of doing poses with bad form. You need to get yourself into some classes where a qualified instructor can watch you and correct your mistakes. This is a form of biofeedback in which you learn to connect the subjective feeling of doing a pose a certain way with the objective feedback of an instructor saying, "Okay, now you're doing it right." Once you have made that connection, you can do the pose right on your own by re-creating that feeling. Eventually, you can graduate to doing most of your yoga sessions on your own, if that's more convenient. But just as Olympic swimmers continue to receive technique instruction from their coaches, even the most advanced yoga students exhibit little form flaws that only another, expert pair of eyes can catch. Therefore, Rountree recommends that even runners who are advanced yoga students attend at least one yoga class per week.

Rountree classifies yoga sessions performed as cross-training for endurance athletes by 10 types: balance, breath, cool, core, flow, focus, gentle, power, restore, and warm. The runners she coaches emphasize power sessions (flowing workouts made up of briefly held strength-building poses) and core sessions (made up of poses that strengthen the abdominals and of backbends that undo the fetal curl that excessive sitting creates) in the base-building phase. In the racing phase her students do mostly flow sessions (similar to power sessions but less intense), balance sessions (made up of poses that strengthen the stabilizing muscles of the legs and core), and warm sessions (flowing sessions designed to activate the running muscles before speed work and races).

YOGA AT HOME

Here is an example of a balance session for getting started in using yoga to enhance muscle talk for better running performance.

PLANK

Start by kneeling on all fours with your hands positioned directly underneath your shoulders. Now move into a push-up position with your legs fully extended behind you and only the toes of your feet on the floor. Your body now forms a straight line from the ankles through the crown of the head. Your eyes are on the floor. Avoid lifting your hips out of alignment with the rest of your body or allowing your hips to sag. These two common errors are ways of taking stress off weak abdominal and low back muscles. Also avoid rounding or sinking into your shoulders, instead holding your shoulder blades in a neutral position.

Experienced yoga students are able to hold this pose efficiently by maintaining consistent, moderate tension in the upper back and abs and relaxing everything else.

SIDE PLANK

Start in the plank position. Rotate 90 degrees to the right, extend your right arm straight overhead, and lift your right foot and stack it on top of the left. Rotate your head to the right also, so that you are looking at your right hand. Beginners tend to allow the upward extended arm to tilt forward and their hips to sink toward the floor as they fatigue in this position. Concentrate on keeping your hips high and your arms in a perfectly straight line. After completing your hold, reverse your position and hold the side plank with your left arm extended overhead for an equal amount of time.

REVERSE TABLE

From the side plank position with your left arm extended overhead, rotate 90 degrees to the left, and drop your left hand to the floor underneath you. Your two hands are now positioned palms down directly underneath your shoulders with the fingers pointing toward your feet, and your belly is open to the ceiling. Bend your knees 90 degrees, and position your feet flat on the floor directly underneath your knees. Draw your hips upward so that your body forms a straight line parallel to the floor from the knees to the shoulders. Hold your head in the position that is most comfortable. Concentrate on keeping your hips high as you hold this position.

BOAT

From the reverse table position, drop your butt to the floor, extend your arms straight in front of you, and lift your feet off the floor so that you are balanced on your butt only. Try to extend your legs fully so that your body forms a "V" shape with your straight legs forming one side of the V at a 45-degree angle to the floor and your torso and head forming the other side of the V. If you lack the core strength and/or hamstrings flexibility to hold this pose, keep your knees slightly bent. If this position is still difficult, bend your elbows and place your palms under your lower hamstrings for support. As you gain mastery of this pose, gradually work toward being able

to hold the full boat pose with arms and legs fully extended. Once you have reached this level, continue to improve by challenging yourself to hold the pose more and more "quietly" (without any of the shaking that comes with the strain of trying to maintain balance in this challenging position).

BOW

From the boat position, flip over so that you are lying on your stomach. Bend your knees fully, reach behind your body with both arms, and grab hold of a foot with each hand. Relax as much as you can in this position, and keep your head in alignment with your torso. Also concentrate on keeping

your knees close together. If you have tight quads, your knees will tend to splay to the sides.

CHILD'S POSE

From the bow position, draw your knees underneath your chest and sit on your heels. Lay your forehead on the floor, and extend your arms in front of you with the palms on the floor. Relax as completely as you can in this position.

I know what you're asking: "How long should I hold each pose?" Typical runner! Ignore the clock when performing this session. Just hold each position long enough so that it gives you a good challenge but not so long that your form breaks down or the pose becomes painful. Work toward holding the poses longer as you gain mastery of them, but always prioritize form over duration.

TAKING THE NEXT STEP

IN RUNNING, EVERY END IS ALSO A BEGINNING. No sooner have you crossed one finish line than you look ahead to the next with loftier goals in mind. We have reached the end of this guide to mind-body running, and now it is time to begin to apply what you have learned. Perhaps you are not sure how to start this process. Traditional running books that tell you exactly what to do are easier to apply; all you have to do is choose a prefabricated training plan and follow the workouts. This book is different. Instead of feeding you fish, as it were, it teaches you how to fish on your own.

I think you will find your first step in the practice of mind-body running to be less daunting, more fruitful, and more capable of building momentum in your training if you focus on the details instead of the big picture. Mind-body running is a coherent approach to running based on the simple idea that your perceptions tell you everything you really need to know to succeed in the sport. Each of the specific methods presented in this book is consistent with that overarching philosophy. I recognize that many of these individual methods contradict conventional practices and are otherwise unfamiliar. Thus, you might find it challenging to abruptly incorporate every method into your running life all at once.

Instead, I suggest that you identify one or more specific methods that make sense to you and seem to offer you the greatest potential for immediate improvement, then practice only these methods initially. As you master them, I think you will begin to find that some of the other unfamiliar methods make a lot more sense to you. Implementing those first techniques will initiate increased self-awareness and help you better understand certain ways of running by feel that at first may have seemed strange or counterintuitive. When this happens, take advantage of your increasing momentum as a mind-body runner and add those other methods to the mix. Before long you will be practicing all of the methods presented here and will clearly see how they fit together to form a coherent whole.

To help you begin this journey, I have summarized the specific mind-body running methods below. Review them and make note of those that you feel most comfortable incorporating into your running life now. There are no wrong choices. As your journey progresses, refer back to this epilogue for next steps, and steps to follow those, until you have fully implemented the mind-body running methodology—never forgetting that there is no real end to the process.

LEARNING TO LISTEN

When you start listening to your body with the same mindfulness that you give to your performance feedback, you will begin to run by feel. Along the way you might have to let go of some unhealthy habits or stop comparing yourself to other runners. Only you can hear the feedback your body has for you.

Cultivate confidence in your training. Throughout training, ask yourself, "What sorts of training experiences will give me the most confidence that I will be able to achieve my race goal?" Then be prepared to go out and do whatever intuition tells you in answer to this question, even if it is unusual. Make it your primary objective in training to develop confidence in your ability to achieve your specific race goals.

Trust your intuition. Your experience as a runner decides the extent to which you should trust intuition: The more experienced you are, the better your intuitions about what you should do next in training will be. Thus, as a beginner, rely almost entirely on established principles and methods to guide your training. As you become more experienced, rely less on what others do and increasingly on your own hunches.

If you are an experienced runner, you can rely on intuition to:

- Choose peak workout formats (the most challenging race-specific workouts you do at the end of a training cycle, just before you taper for a peak race).
- Identify specific training practices that work and that do not work.
- Make day-to-day adjustments to workout plans based on how you feel.
- Address weaknesses identified and specific problems encountered in training.

Reality check: *Bear in mind that intuition is not always right and that it is not always easy to distinguish the voice of wise intuition from other, less reliable voices, such as those of insecurity and habit. Don't follow your hunches blindly. Evaluate each, and look before you leap.*

Make your training more enjoyable. Pay close attention to how much you enjoy training, and do more of what you enjoy most and less of what you enjoy least. Also, try new methods that you have a hunch you would enjoy. The feeling of enjoyment is your body's way of telling you that your training is working.

Rearrange your training to make improvement more obvious. Because improvement naturally makes running more enjoyable, and enjoyment stimulates improvement in running, feel free to arrange your training in whichever way makes your improvement most evident to you. This will require that you include some repetition in your training so that you can make apples-to-apples comparisons, and some variation so that you can stimulate improvement. You will also need to collect performance feedback such as distance, pace, and heart rate to measure improvement.

Evaluate which training methods work well for you. Pay attention to two types of feedback: performance feedback (workout split times, race times, etc.) and affective feedback (fluctuations in your training enjoyment and confidence levels). Rate your enjoyment level for each run. A "1" indicates that, on balance, you did not enjoy it; a "2" indicates that you neither enjoyed it nor hated it; and a "3" indicates that, on balance, the run was enjoyable. In addition to tracking your daily run enjoyment scores, keep weekly and 28-day averages. Look for cause-effect relationships between your enjoyment level and your running performance, and use your observations to modify your training in ways that make it more fun and effective.

Define your optimal training formula. There are countless causal factors in training that are worth paying attention to, but the three most important factors are

1. Training volume: What is your optimal average weekly running mileage?
2. High-intensity training: What is the best use of high-intensity training for you?
3. Periodization method: Do you prefer a traditional (Lydiard) or nonlinear approach to periodizing your training?

If you can answer these questions, you will have gone a long way toward defining your optimal training formula. Each runner is genetically unique and responds to training uniquely. Through mindful, ongoing experimentation you can refine your training to better fit your genetic makeup and personality.

MASTERING THE PRACTICE OF MIND-BODY RUNNING

When you embrace mind-body running, your training objectives shift. Things that used to be less important become more important. Specifically, elements of training that enable you to fully harness the power of your brain to improve your running move from the shadows to the forefront.

Allow more repetition and routine in your training. Consider including more week-to-week repetition in your training than many runners do. The physiological benefits of repeating optimal training methods from week to week over extended periods of time are underappreciated. Repeating a trusted training formula—as elite runners such as Moses Tanui and Constantina Dita-Tomescu have done—also promotes the mental benefit of psychological momentum.

Do everything you can to create a comfortable personal environment and lifestyle to support your training, as doing so will facilitate psychological momentum, or a feeling that things are going your way and will continue to go your way in training.

Increase your capacity to suffer over the course of each training cycle. This reduces the amount of reserve muscle capacity your brain protects in races and will thereby enhance your racing performance. Try some of these strategies:

- Make it personal. Find ways to make your individual key workouts, the overall training process, and your important races as personally meaningful as possible, as the more personally meaningful a given running effort is, the closer your brain will allow your body to come to its true physiological limits and the better you will perform.
- Set goals for both races and key workouts. Goals provide anchor points for your brain's subconscious mechanism that allow it to make better and more aggressive calculations of what your body can really do. You will almost always run better when you try to beat specific marks than when you merely try to run as fast as you feel you can.
- Constantly monitor pace and time information in pursuit of workout goals. This will enable your brain to tolerate a greater affective load in pursuit of workout goals, enabling you to run faster and derive greater benefit from the run.
- Grade your "mental toughness" in key workouts and races. That is, after each, ask yourself whether you held back unnecessarily at any point to spare yourself from suffering. Be satisfied if you did not; be dissatisfied if you did, and vow to do better next time. You will.

- Seek out competition and accountability. Take advantage of the scientifically proven fact that, thanks to hardwired social instincts, you can run faster when people are watching you and when you are competing against others than you can alone. For example, train with a well-matched partner instead of solo, and sign up for big marathons with lots of spectators and hoopla instead of small ones with few onlookers.

Reality check: *Don't ever train so hard that running is no longer fun. Give yourself enough easy days to balance out the hard ones. Doing whatever is necessary to keep your training enjoyable will generally make the suffering you experience in hard workouts more tolerable and will thus increase your work capacity and your capacity to suffer.*

Be comfortable with winging it. Never train in strict obedience to a pre-fabricated training plan. If you use such plans, consider every scheduled workout tentative, and be ready to change or substitute it based on what your body tells you it needs day to day.

If you are an experienced runner, consider training improvisationally. This approach to training will be most successful if you establish three basic parameters within which to improvise: a standard weekly workout schedule, a handful of peak workouts and a peak training week, and a training cycle duration.

Know your personal records and try to break them. Pursue personal records as single-mindedly as great runners pursue world records. When you go after a personal record, you essentially set up a race against yourself—specifically, against your former best self. Such a goal awakens those ancient survival instincts that enable you to run faster in pursuit or flight than you can without a specific purpose. Chasing personal bests encourages your mind and body to conspire to allow you to run faster than you ever have before.

Make your key workout progressions effective. Follow these six guidelines:

1. Make them repetitive.
2. Ease into them.
3. Build them gradually.
4. Do them frequently, but not too frequently.
5. Do not overextend them (you can keep bettering yourself only for so long).
6. Use target times (such as Greg McMillan's Running Calculator).

THE FINER POINTS OF THE MIND-BODY METHOD

There is more to the successful practice of running by feel than doing workouts. The mind-body approach encompasses every factor that is relevant to performance. To refine your running, you will need to channel setbacks and negative emotions to positively effect your training and motivation. Over time, running and crosstraining will improve communication between the brain and the body, which will extend your potential.

Find your own best stride. Don't waste your time trying to learn a one-size-fits-all running technique system. You have to find your own best stride by trial and error. Reflect on your running habits to determine which of these strategies you need to incorporate:

- Be sure to run enough, because the stride is everything, and the stride improves through refinements in communication between the brain and the muscles. More running equals more time with the lines of communication fully active.
- Consistently vary your running (different speeds, surfaces, gradients) to create an unstable environment for your neuromuscular system as it relates to running and thereby trigger rapid stride evolution.
- Expose yourself to fatigued running as often as you can without accumulating fatigue, which helps stimulate rapid evolution of your stride.
- Limit your use of conscious stride manipulation to specific technique changes that are likely to prevent the recurrence of specific injuries. In other words, if you're not broken, don't fix your stride.

Accept injury. When you suffer an injury, try to figure out why your injury occurred, and if there is a clear cause, address it to prevent the injury from recurring. But don't assume there is always going to be an identifiable cause. Let your intuition feed you hunches about what to do differently in your future training. In doing so, you may find that your injury steers your running in a new and better direction even if you never figure out what caused it.

Go ahead and experience the frustration that normally attends a physical breakdown, but then transform that frustration into renewed hunger for the sport. Use that hunger to fuel a comeback that takes your running to a new level.

Harness fear and anger as motivation. Fear is a natural part of the competitive running experience. Like all emotions, fear gives information. As a runner, you are better off discerning the information encoded in your running-related fears than trying to eliminate those fears. For example, by acknowledging to yourself that you are afraid of the suffering that you are likely to experience in an upcoming race, you earn an opportunity to decide whether the pain is worth it. If you determine that the goal is worth the pain, you will start the race with an assurance that is greater than the fear.

Anger is also a natural part of the running experience. Anger is a strong response to fear, and as such, it is more performance-enhancing for runners than not. Don't let anyone tell you that you should not run angry. In fact, if anyone tells you that you can't do anything as a runner, that ought to make you angry—and then motivated to demonstrate what you can do in your next race.

Find time to do regular strength and mobility training. This improves communication between your brain and muscles in ways that help you run with greater joint stability, with more power, and with more ease. Consider practicing yoga instead of, or in addition to, more commonly used types of crosstraining. Yoga not only increases strength and mobility but also increases body awareness better than other forms of exercise.

None of this is easy. But it's not supposed to be easy. We like running because it is hard to improve, yet always possible. Beware those who suggest that there are simple answers to the questions of how to train most effectively, race most successfully, develop most consistently, stay healthy, become mentally stronger, and so forth—answers that you can readily learn and apply to enjoy a mistake-free running life. The true answers to these questions must be learned individually through experience. The best that any expert, coach, mentor, or guide can do is show you how to search for your personal answers most efficiently through a mindful approach to the sport, and I hope I have done that much for you.

WORKOUTS

Listening to your body will teach you everything you need to know about running except how to do the most effective basic types of workouts. The standard workout formats that all competitive runners use (with their own individual wrinkles) are the fruit of decades of worldwide collective trial and error. You could re-create them on your own by feel through individual trial and error, but that would take several lifetimes. Thus, every serious runner needs to learn and gather experience with these standard workout formats. Through your own individual trial-and-error process, you will learn how to customize these workouts to fit your individual needs, how to arrange them to most reliably build your fitness, and how to choose just the right workout to do on any given day. Following is a brief overview of classic run workouts, which are generally arranged in order of increasing intensity.

RECOVERY RUN

A recovery run is a relatively short, relatively slow run performed at a steady, comfortable pace. Recovery runs serve to add a little mileage to the runner's training without taking away from performance in the harder, more important workouts that precede and follow them. Recovery runs are best done as the next run after a hard run. They are most needed during peak periods of training when the typical competitive runner is running three hard workouts every week.

Smart runners are willing to go as slowly as necessary to feel relatively comfortable in their recovery runs despite lingering fatigue from their previous run. "Short" is a relative term, of course. While 20 minutes of easy jogging might be sufficient for some runners in some circumstances, an elite runner may go for 60 minutes without impeding her recovery.

Example   4 miles of easy jogging

BASE RUN

A base run is a relatively short to moderate-length run undertaken at a runner's natural pace. While individual base runs are not meant to be challenging, they are meant to be done frequently, and in the aggregate they stimulate big improvements in aerobic capacity, endurance, and running economy. Base runs are most useful during the base period of training, when the runner is focused on increasing his overall mileage and is not doing a lot of hard workouts that demand recovery runs afterward.

Example   6 miles at natural pace

LONG RUN

Generally, a long run is simply a base run that lasts long enough to leave a runner moderately to severely fatigued. The function of a long run is to increase raw endurance. The distance or duration required to achieve this effect depends, of course, on the runner's current level of endurance. As a general rule, the longest run should be long enough to give the runner confidence that raw endurance will not limit her in races. Long runs are often done on hillier routes to enhance the durability-boosting effect of the workout.

Example   15 miles at natural pace

PROGRESSION RUN

A progression run is a run that begins at a runner's natural pace and ends with a faster segment at anywhere from marathon to 10K pace. They are generally intended to be moderately challenging—harder than base runs but easier than most threshold and interval runs.

Progression runs can be employed for various purposes. They can be used to add a little intensity to the week during the base period of training, before the runner moves on to harder tempo/threshold runs. They can be used later in the training cycle to add a small, judicious dose of high-intensity running to the week on top of the faster running done in separate tempo/threshold and interval runs. Some runners also like to add progressions to the end of long runs to make them a little more race specific.

Example   5 miles at natural pace
1 mile at half-marathon pace

MARATHON-PACE RUN

A marathon-pace run is just that: a prolonged run at marathon pace. It's a good workout to perform at a very challenging level in the final weeks of preparation for a marathon, after a runner has established adequate raw endurance with long runs and longer progression runs featuring smaller amounts of marathon-pace running.

Example   2 miles at natural pace
13.1 miles at marathon pace

FARTLEK RUN

A fartlek run is a base run sprinkled with short, fast intervals. A fartlek run can be thought of as a gentle lactate interval or speed interval session. It's a good way to begin the process of developing efficiency and fatigue resistance at faster speeds in the early phases of the training cycle or to get a moderate dose of fast running later in the training cycle in addition to the larger doses provided by tempo/threshold and interval workouts.

Example   6 miles at natural pace
6 × 30 seconds at 5K race pace scattered throughout

HILL REPETITIONS

Hill repetitions are repeated, short or relatively short segments of hard, up-hill running. They increase aerobic power, high-intensity fatigue resistance, pain tolerance, and run-specific strength. The ideal hill on which to run hill repetitions features a steady, moderate gradient (4–6 percent). They provide much the same benefits as lactate and speed intervals while also building run-specific strength. Hill repetitions are typically done at the end of the base-building period as a relatively safe way to introduce harder high-intensity training into the program.

Example   2 miles of easy jogging (warm-up)

10 × 1 minute uphill at roughly 1,500 m race effort with 2.5-minute jogging recoveries

2 miles of easy jogging (cooldown)

TEMPO/THRESHOLD RUN

A tempo or threshold run is a workout that features one or two sustained efforts somewhere in the range of lactate threshold intensity, which is the fastest pace that can be sustained for 60 minutes in highly fit runners and the fastest pace that can be sustained for 20 minutes in less fit runners. Tempo/threshold runs serve to increase the speed a runner can sustain for a prolonged period of time and to increase the time she can sustain a relatively fast pace. Competitive runners typically use them throughout the second half of a training cycle, making them increasingly challenging and race specific (i.e., closer to race pace and duration) as the cycle progresses.

Example   1 mile of easy jogging (warm-up)

4 miles at lactate threshold pace

1 mile of easy jogging (cooldown)

LACTATE INTERVALS

Lactate intervals take the form of relatively short to moderately long intervals (600–1,200 m) run in the range of 5K race pace with easy jogging recoveries between them. They're an excellent means of progressively developing efficiency and fatigue resistance at fast running speeds. The more challenging versions of these workouts are very stressful and yield results quickly, so competitive runners typically focus on them for a relatively short period of time in the heart of the training cycle. Shorter-distance racers usually place this period toward the end of the training cycle because it builds race-specific fitness, whereas longer-distance racers usually focus on lactate intervals a little earlier in the training cycle because they are less race specific.

Example   1 mile of easy jogging (warm-up)

5 × 1 km at 5K race pace with 400 m jogging recoveries

1 mile of easy jogging (cooldown)

SPEED INTERVALS

Speed intervals are short or relatively short intervals (100–400 m) run at roughly 1,500 m race pace or faster. They boost speed, running economy, fatigue resistance at fast speeds, and pain tolerance. Distance runners typically use shorter, faster intervals earlier in the training cycle to increase their pure speed and then move to slightly longer, slower (but still very fast) speed intervals to add fatigue resistance to their speed.

Example   1 mile of easy jogging (warm-up)

10 × 300 m at 800 m race pace with 400 m jogging recoveries

1 mile of easy jogging (cooldown)

MIXED INTERVALS

Mixed intervals, as the name suggests, are intervals of various distances run at different pace levels. Mixed-interval runs are an excellent means of including a variety of training stimuli within a single workout. They can be used earlier in a training cycle as the primary high-intensity training stimulus of the week or late in the training cycle as a stimulus that is secondary to another high-intensity workout that is focused on a single, race-specific intensity.

Example   1 mile of easy jogging (warm-up)

400 m at 1,500 m race pace, 400 m easy

800 m at 3,000 m race pace, 400 m easy

1,200 m at 5K race pace, 400 m easy

1,600 m at 10K race pace, 400 m easy

1,200 m at 5K race pace, 400 m easy

800 m at 3,000 m race pace, 400 m easy

400 m at 1,500 m race pace

1 mile of easy jogging (cooldown)

NOTES

Introduction: Running by Feel

1. T. D. Noakes, Rating of Perceived Exertion as a Predictor of the Duration of Exercise That Remains Until Exhaustion, *British Journal of Sports Medicine* 42(7) (July 2008):623–624.

2. R. K. Dishman, R. W. Motl, R. Saunders, G. Felton, D. S. Ward, M. Dowda, and R. R. Pate, Enjoyment Mediates Effects of a School-Based Physical-Activity Intervention, *Medicine and Science in Sports and Exercise* 37(3) (March 2005):478–487.

3. A. R. Mauger, A. M. Jones, and C. A. Williams, Influence of Feedback and Prior Experience on Pacing During a 4-km Cycle Time Trial, *European Journal of Applied Physiology* 41(2) (February 2009):451–458.

4. A. Mündermann, D. J. Stefanyshyn, and B. M. Nigg, Relationship Between Footwear Comfort of Shoe Inserts and Anthropometric and Sensory Factors, *Medicine and Science in Sports and Exercise* 3(11) (November 2001):193–195.

5. I. Rollo, M. Cole, R. Miller, and C. Williams, The Influence of Mouth-Rinsing a Carbohydrate Solution on 1-Hour Running Performance, *Medicine and Science in Sports and Exercise* (November 2009).

6. S. C. Glass and A. M. Chivala, Preferred Exertion Across Three Common Modes of Exercise Training, *Journal of Strength and Conditioning Research* 15(4) (November 2001):474–479.

Chapter 1: Physical Confidence

1. D. Micklewright, E. Papadopoulou, J. Swart, and T. D. Noakes, Previous Experience Influences Pacing During 20-km Time Trial Cycling, *British Journal of Sports Medicine* (April 2009).

2. M. D. Lieberman, Intuition: A Social Cognitive Neuroscience Approach, *Psychological Bulletin* 126(1) (January 2000):109–137.

Chapter 2: Run Happy

1. L. E. Armstrong and J. L. VanHeest, The Unknown Mechanism of the Overtraining Syndrome: Clues from Depression and Psychoneuroimmunology, *Sports Medicine* 32(3) (2002):185–209.

2. D. M. Williams, S. Dunsiger, J. T. Ciccolo, B. A. Lewis, A. E. Albrecht, and B. H. Marcus, Acute Affective Response to a Moderate-Intensity Exercise Stimulus Predicts Physical Activity Participation 6 and 12 Months Later, *Psychology of Sport and Exercise* 9(3) (May 2008):231–245.

3. A. Quinn, C. Doody, and D. O'Shea, The Effect of a Physical Activity Education Programme on Physical Activity, Fitness, Quality of Life, and Attitudes to Exercise in Obese Females, *Journal of Science and Medicine in Sport* 11(5) (September 2008):469–472.

4. R. K. Dishman, R. W. Motl, R. Saunders, G. Felton, D. S. Ward, M. Dowda, and R. R. Pate, Enjoyment Mediates Effects of a School-Based Physical-Activity Intervention, *Medicine and Science in Sports and Exercise* 37(3) (March 2005):478–487.

5. L. Hu, R. W. Motl, E. McAuley, and J. F. Konopack, Effects of Self-Efficacy on Physical Activity Enjoyment in College-Aged Women, *International Journal of Behavioral Medicine* 14(2) (2007):92–96.

6. D. A. Baden, T. L. McLean, R. Tucker, T. D. Noakes, and A. St. Clair Gibson, Effect of Anticipation During Unknown or Unexpected Exercise Duration on Rating of Perceived Exertion, Affect, and Physiological Function, *British Journal of Sports Medicine* 39(10) (October 2005):742–746.

Chapter 3: Finding a Magic Formula

1. F. E. Orkunoglu-Suer, H. Gordish-Dressman, P. M. Clarkson, P. D. Thompson, T. J. Angelopoulos, P. M. Gordon, N. M. Moyna, L. S. Pescatello, P. S. Visich, R. F. Zoeller, B. Harmon, R. L. Seip, E. P. Hoffman, and J. M. Devaney, INSIG2 Gene Polymorphism Is Associated with Increased Subcutaneous Fat in Women and Poor Response to Resistance Training in Men, *BMC Medical Genetics* 9 (December 2008):117.

2. P. An, L. Pérusse, T. Rankinen, I. B. Borecki, J. Gagnon, A. S. Leon, J. S. Skinner, J. H. Wilmore, C. Bouchard, and D. C. Rao, Familial Aggregation of Exercise

Heart Rate and Blood Pressure in Response to 20 Weeks of Endurance Training: The HERITAGE Family Study, *International Journal of Sports Medicine* 24(1) (January 2003):57–62.

3. B. Friedmann, F. Frese, E. Menold, F. Kauper, J. Jost, and P. Bärtsch, Individual Variation in the Erythropoietic Response to Altitude Training in Elite Junior Swimmers, *British Journal of Sports Medicine* 39(3) (March 2005):148–153.

4. J. M. Devaney, E. P. Hoffman, H. Gordish-Dressman, A. Kearns, E. Zambraski, and P. M. Clarkson, IGF-II Gene Region Polymorphisms Related to Exertional Muscle Damage, *Journal of Applied Physiology* 102(5) (May 2007): 1815–1823.

5. N. D. Barwell, D. Malkova, M. Leggate, and J. M. Gill, Individual Responsiveness to Exercise-Induced Fat Loss Is Associated with Change in Resting Substrate Utilization, *Metabolism* 58(9) (September 2009):1320–1328.

6. D. M. Williams, Exercise, Affect, and Adherence: An Integrated Model and a Case for Self-Paced Exercise, *Journal of Sport and Exercise Psychology* 30(5) (October 2008):471–496.

7. P. Ekkekakis, Let Them Roam Free?: Physiological and Psychological Evidence for the Potential of Self-Selected Exercise Intensity in Public Health, *Sports Medicine* 39(10) (2009):857–888.

Chapter 4: Comfort Zones

1. L. Crusti and M. A. Nesti, Review of Psychological Momentum in Sports: Why Qualitative Research Is Needed, *Athletic Insight* 8(1) (March 2006).

2. S. Perreault, R. J. Vallerand, D. Montgomery, and P. Provencher, Coming from Behind: On the Effect of Psychological Momentum on Sport Performance, *Journal of Sport and Exercise Psychology* 20 (1998):421–436.

Chapter 5: Trying Harder

1. C. Foster, K. J. Hendrickson, K. Peyer, B. Reiner, J. J. deKoning, A. Lucia, R. A. Battista, F. J. Hettinga, J. P. Porcari, and G. Wright, Pattern of Developing the Performance Template, *British Journal of Sports Medicine* 43(10) (October 2009):765–769.

2. B. Baron, F. Moullan, F. Deruelle, and T. D. Noakes, The Role of Emotions on Pacing Strategies and Performance in Middle and Long Duration Sport Events, *British Journal of Sports Medicine* (2009).

3. Here, of course, I use the phrase "comfort zone" differently from how I used it in Chapter 4. There are good and bad comfort zones!

4. P. Ord and K. Gijsbers, Pain Thresholds and Tolerances of Competitive Rowers and Their Use of Spontaneous Self-Generated Pain-Coping Strategies, *Perceptual and Motor Skills* 97(3 Pt 2) (December 2003):1219–1222.

5. M. R. Rhea, D. M. Landers, B. A. Alvar, and S. M. Arent, The Effects of Competition and the Presence of an Audience on Weight Lifting Performance, *Journal of Strength and Conditioning Research* 17(2) (May 2003):303–306.

6. E. E. Cohen, R. Ejsmond-Frey, N. Knight, and R. I. Dunbar, Rowers' High: Behavioural Synchrony Is Correlated with Elevated Pain Thresholds, *Biology Letters* 6(1) (September 2009):106–108.

7. H. Foo and P. Mason, Analgesia Accompanying Food Consumption Requires Ingestion of Hedonic Foods, *Journal of Neuroscience* 29(41) (October 2009):13053–13062.

Chapter 6: Winging It

1. M. Glaister, C. Witmer, D. W. Clarke, J. J. Guers, J. L. Heller, and G. L. Moir, Familiarization, Reliability, and Evaluation of a Multiple Sprint Running Test Using Self-Selected Recovery Periods, *Journal of Strength and Conditioning Research* 41 (December 2009).

Chapter 7: How Records Are Broken

1. I. I. Ahmetov, A. G. Williams, D. V. Popov, E. V. Lyubaeva, A. M. Hakimullina, O. N. Fedotovskaya, I. A. Mozhayskaya, O. L. Vinogradova, I. V. Astratenkova, H. E. Montgomery, and V. A. Rogozkin, The Combined Impact of Metabolic Gene Polymorphisms on Elite Endurance Athlete Status and Related Phenotypes, *Human Genetics* (August 2009).

2. J. M. García-Manso, J. M. Martín-González, N. Dávila, and E. Arriaza, Middle and Long Distance Athletics Races Viewed from the Perspective of Complexity, *Journal of Theoretical Biology* 233(2) (March 2005):191–198.

3. P. Zamparo, R. Perini, C. Peano, and P.E. di Prampero, The Self-Selected Speed of Running in Recreational Long Distance Runners, *International Journal of Sports Medicine* 22(8) (November 2001):598–604.

4. S. C. Glass and A. M. Chivala, Preferred Exertion Across Three Common

Modes of Exercise Training, *Journal of Strength and Conditioning Research* 15(4) (November 2001):474–479.

Chapter 8: Run Beautifully

1. S. J. McGregor, M. A. Busa, J. A. Yaggie, and E. M. Bollt, High Resolution MEMS Accelerometers to Estimate VO_2 and Compare Running Mechanics Between Highly Trained Inter-Collegiate and Untrained Runners, *PLoS ONE* 4(10) (2009): e7355, doi:10.1371/journal.pone.0007355.

2. S. J. McGregor, M. A. Busa, J. Skufca, J. A. Yaggie, and E. M. Bollt, Control Entropy Identifies Differential Changes in Complexity of Walking and Running Gait Patterns with Increasing Speed in Highly Trained Runners, *Chaos* 19(2) (June 2009):026109.

3. P. R. Hayes, S. J. Bowen, and E. J. Davies, The Relationships Between Local Muscular Endurance and Kinematic Changes During a Run to Exhaustion at vVO_2max, *Journal of Strength and Conditioning Research* 18(4) (November 2004):898–903.

4. Incidentally, in conversation McDougall insisted to me that his book was not meant to advocate barefoot running, as is generally believed, but rather to advocate what he calls "natural running," or technically correct running.

5. G. M. Dallam, R. L. Wilber, K. Jadelis, G. Fletcher, and N. Romanov, Effect of a Global Alteration of Running Technique on Kinematics and Economy, *Journal of Sports Sciences* 23(7) (July 2005):757–764.

6. L. Schucker, N. Hagemann, B. Strauss, and K. Volker, The Effect of Attentional Focus on Running Economy, *Journal of Sports Sciences* 27(12) (September 2009):1241–1248.

7. P. R. Cavanaugh and K. R. Williams, The Effect of Stride Length Variation on Oxygen Uptake During Distance Running, *Medicine and Science in Sports and Exercise* 14(1) (1982):30–35.

8. P. U. Saunders, R. D. Telford, D. B. Pyne, E. M. Peltola, R. B. Cunningham, C. J. Gore, and J. A. Hawley, Short-Term Plyometric Training Improves Running Economy in Highly Trained Middle and Long Distance Runners, *Journal of Strength and Conditioning Research* 20(4) (November 2006):947–954.

9. C. Divert, G. Mornieux, P. Freychat, L. Baly, F. Mayer, and A. Belli, Barefoot-Shod Running Differences: Shoe or Mass Effect? *International Journal of Sports Medicine* 29(6) (June 2008):512–518.

10. J. B. Nielsen and L. G. Cohen, The Olympic Brain: Does Corticospinal Plasticity Play a Role in Acquisition of Skills Required for High-Performance Sports? *European Journal of Applied Physiology* 104(4) (November 2008):625–631.

Chapter 9: The Gift of Injury

1. L. Ievleva and T. Orlick, Mental Links to Enhance Healing, *Sport Psychologist* 5(1) (1991):25–40.

2. C. E. Milner, R. Ferber, C. D. Pollard, J. Hamill, and I. S. Davis, Biomechanical Factors Associated with Tibial Stress Fracture in Female Runners, *Medicine and Science in Sports and Exercise* 38(2) (February 2006):323–328.

3. M. B. Pohl, J. Hamill, and I. S. Davis, Biomechanical and Anatomic Factors Associated with a History of Plantar Fasciitis in Female Runners, *Clinical Journal of Sport Medicine* 19(5) (September 2009):372–376.

4. I. S. Davis, H. P. Crowell, R. E. Fellin, and A. R. Altman, Reduced Impact Loading Following Gait Retraining over a 6-Month Period, *Gait and Posture* 30 (October 2009):S4–S5.

5. B. M. Nigg, Impact Forces in Running, *Current Opinion in Orthopedics* 8(6) (December 1997):43–47.

6. A. Mündermann, D. J. Stefanyshyn, and B. M. Nigg, Relationship Between Footwear Comfort of Shoe Inserts and Anthropometric and Sensory Factors, *Medicine and Science in Sports and Exercise* 33(11) (November 2001):1939–1945.

Chapter 10: Anger, Fear, and Speed

1. M. Best, J. M. Williams, and E. F. Coccaro, Evidence for a Dysfunctional Prefrontal Circuit in Patients with an Impulsive Aggressive Disorder, *Proceedings of the National Academy of Sciences* 99(12) (June 2002):8448–8453.

2. M. Tamir, C. Mitchell, and J. J. Gross, Hedonic and Instrumental Motives in Anger Regulation, *Psychological Science* 19(4) (April 2008):324–328.

3. B. Raudenbush, J. Koon, T. Cessna, and K. McCombs, Effects of Playing Video Games on Pain Response During a Cold Pressor Task, *Perceptual and Motor Skills* 108(2) (April 2009):439–448.

4. R. Stephens, J. Atkins, and A. Kingston, Swearing as a Response to Pain, *Neuro Report* 20(12) (August 2009):1056–1060, doi:10.1097/WNR.0b013e32832e64b1.

5. J. W. Burns, S. Bruehl, O. Y. Chung, E. Magid, M. Chont, J. K. Goodlad, W. Gilliam, J. Matsuura, and K. Somar, Endogenous Opioids May Buffer Effects of Anger Arousal on Sensitivity to Subsequent Pain, *Pain* 146(3) (December 2009): 276–282.

6. C. Leineweber, H. Westerlund, T. Theorell, M. Kivimäki, P. Westerholm, and L. Alfredsson, Covert Coping with Unfair Treatment at Work and Risk of Incident Myocardial Infarction and Cardiac Death Among Men: Prospective Cohort Study, *Journal of Epidemiology and Community Health* (November 2009).

Chapter 11: Muscle Talk

1. T. M. Best, R. Hunter, A. Wilcox, and F. Haq, Effectiveness of Sports Massage for Recovery of Skeletal Muscle from Strenuous Exercise, *Clinical Journal of Sport Medicine* 18(5) (September 2008):446–460.

2. V. J. Basmajian, Control and Training of Individual Motor Units, *Science* 141(3579) (August 1963):440–441.

3. M. Henriksen, T. Alkjær, H. Lund, E. B. Simonsen, T. Graven-Nielsen, B. Danneskiold-Samsøe, and H. Bliddal, Experimental Quadriceps Muscle Pain Impairs Knee Joint Control During Walking, *Journal of Applied Physiology* 103(1) (July 2007):132–139.

4. C. Framson, A. R. Kristal, J. M. Schenk, A. J. Littman, S. Zeliadt, and D. Benitez, Development and Validation of the Mindful Eating Questionnaire, *Journal of the American Dietetic Association* 109(8) (August 2009):1439–1444.

ABOUT THE AUTHOR

Matt Fitzgerald took up writing when he was 9 years old. He became a runner two years later after running the last mile of the 1983 Boston Marathon with his father (who, of course, ran the whole thing). More than a quarter century later, Matt is still running and writing—mostly about running. He has authored or coauthored more than 17 books and written for numerous national publications and Web sites, including *Outside* and *Runner's World*. Currently he serves as a senior editor for *Triathlete* magazine and senior producer for the Competitor Running Web site (Running.Competitor .com). He has run more than 15 marathons and recorded a personal best time of 2:41 at age 37. Matt lives in San Diego with his wife, Nataki.